# TORN ALLEGIANCES

# TORN ALLEGIANCES

## The Story of a Gay Cadet

JIM HOLOBAUGH
with
KEITH HALE

Boston ♦ Alyson Publications, Inc.

Typeset and printed in the United States of America.

This is a paperback original from Alyson Publications, Inc.,
40 Plympton St., Boston, Mass. 02118.
Distributed in England by GMP Publishers,
P.O. Box 247, London N17 9QR, England.

This book is printed on acid-free, recycled paper.

First edition, first printing: March 1993

5  4  3  2  1

ISBN 1-55583-216-4

Library of Congress catalog card number 92-56166

With the onset of media coverage surrounding my removal from the ROTC, I was approached about writing a book on the experience. Because of other priorities and commitments, a lack of desire to put in the effort required to produce such a work, and the feeling that I had already opened my personal life to too many people, I declined. However, as time passed, I began to regret that I had not kept a journal recording my experiences, thoughts, and fears at the time. Many of the young gay men and lesbians I met while speaking on university campuses led me to believe that putting my experiences in writing might be beneficial to others as well. Therefore, when Keith Hale approached me about writing this book, I agreed to do it. I must, however, give most of the credit to Keith. I simply consented to interviews. He expended the vast majority of time and effort in writing this book.

Brent and I thank Bill Rubenstein, Marc Wolinsky, Barry Skovgaard, John Dallas, and Gerry Studds for their assistance, generosity, and friendship.

All of our share of profits from this work will go to the American Civil Liberties Union Lesbian and Gay Rights Project.

*Jim Holobaugh*
*December 1992*

Many thanks to: Carolyn, Steve, James, and Björn Hale; Chuck Harvey; Stuart Stelzer; Raymond-Jean Frontain; Bill Bolden; Wendy Flory; Rick Eli; Alan Douglas and the Arkansas Gay and Lesbian Task Force; Wordsworth Books of Little Rock; Lt. Daniel Berger; Miriam Ben-Shalom and the Gay, Lesbian, and Bisexual Veterans of America; Kurt Krickler and Homosexual Initiative Vienna; Denmark; Wendy Pelton of BI-GALA (Rolla, Missouri); Steffen Jensen and Landsforeningen for bøsser og lesbiske/Forbundet af 1948 (Denmark); George Sved and the Swedish Federation for Gay and Lesbian Rights; Casimir Elsen and the International Lesbian and Gay Association Information Pool on Gays and Lesbians and the Military; Steven Desmet and Homo-en Lesbienne Jongeren Koepel (Antwerp, Belgium); Klaas Soesbeek and the University of Utrecht Interfaculty Homostudies Workgroup (the Netherlands); Mette Sorensen and Det Norske Forbundet Av 1948 (Oslo), and the Campaign for Homosexual Equality (United Kingdom). Thanks, too, to Jim, Brent, Mr. Holobaugh, and all of Jim's friends who good-naturedly agreed to contribute their recollections.

*Keith Hale*

# CONTENTS

# Introduction

## by U.S. CONGRESSMAN GERRY E. STUDDS

As I write these words, it is just six weeks before President-elect Bill Clinton will take office. Washington is filled with a level of hope and excitement not seen since John Kennedy was inaugurated three decades ago.

Among gay people, that hope runs particularly high. For the first time in our history, as gay men and lesbians, we have a president who not only does not hate us, but truly welcomes us as American citizens; a president who does not wish we'd go away, but who genuinely respects the contributions we have made, and will continue to make.

As the clearest sign of that respect, Bill Clinton has pledged to end the nearly fifty-year-old policy that bans gay people from the military. By ensuring that the country's largest employer does not discriminate on the basis of sexual orientation, President Clinton will take us one critical step closer to a world in which such discrimination is found only in history books.

This change, however, has not come without a price. It comes only because a handful of courageous individuals put their reputations and careers on the line. People like Leonard Matlovich, Miriam Ben-Shalom, Perry Watkins, and Jim Holobaugh challenged the military policy with no expectation of reward or even of justice. They simply did what they knew was right. They acted honorably and told the truth, which is exactly what they swore they would do when they entered military service.

Soon after Jim Holobaugh realized that he was gay, he informed his ROTC commander. He came out not to make trouble, or to avoid service, or as a political act; he did it simply because to do otherwise would have been dishonest. Instead of welcoming his honesty and courage, ROTC immediately expelled him. Further, the Army claimed that because he could not fulfill his military obligation now that they had expelled him, Jim had to repay his full $35,000 scholarship.*

Jim Holobaugh was not the first ROTC cadet to face this gross injustice, but he was the first to publicly challenge it. He asked for my help. As he put it to me then: "I am not breaking my contract with ROTC; I am ready, able, and willing to serve. ROTC is breaking its contract with me by not allowing me to do so."

His case started an avalanche, the likes of which the military had never seen. He gave vital hope to other cadets who were being expelled for being gay, some of whom followed his lead and refused to go quietly. Jim's case also focused a bright media spotlight on the fact that schools with nondiscrimination policies were making an embarrassing exception to those policies by allowing the blatantly antigay ROTC on campus. Literally thousands of college students challenged their schools on this issue, and campus demonstrations erupted nationwide.

Because of the extensive — and highly critical — media attention that Jim's case generated, the Pentagon quickly abandoned its effort to make Jim and others repay their scholarships. Unfortunately, however, the ROTC policy did not change. In fact, it got worse: The Navy now requires all potential ROTC midshipmen to sign an affidavit acknowledging that they can be expelled and forced to repay their scholarship if they are discovered, at any point in their ROTC career, to be gay.

Jim Holobaugh's case highlights the absurdity of the military's archaic policy more forcefully than any commission or study could possibly do. Since we first met in 1989, I've had the

---

* The *New York Times*, based on Jim's first estimates, stated in a story that he was being asked to repay $25,000, and that figure has been widely circulated. However, when we later added up everything he was being asked to repay, we found that the total came to approximately $35,000.

privilege of getting to know Jim and his partner, Brent, and regard them as close personal friends. It is impossible for me to conceive of anyone who could better represent our country in the armed forces. For Jim to be barred from such service, merely because of his sexual orientation, is bigotry. But for a country to deprive itself of the chance to be served by a man of Jim Holobaugh's character is sheer insanity. It squanders both tax dollars and talent, both of which we can ill afford to waste.

By coming forward with their stories, people like Jim Holobaugh have driven this point home for millions of Americans. These individuals are responsible for the change in public understanding that led to Bill Clinton's pledge. They deserve our respect and deepest gratitude.

The old-guard generals have lost this battle, even if they refuse to do so gracefully. The military of tomorrow will be open to all qualified citizens, gay or nongay. Tomorrow's army will break down — rather than reinforce — the barriers that divide our nation. And I, for one, will rest much easier knowing that our country is being served by men and women like Jim Holobaugh.

# "I'm asking *you,* Cadet Holobaugh"

December in Saint Louis. Outside it's freezing, but it's warm inside the Reserve Officer Training Corps building on the campus of Washington University, where I am about to undergo an "informal investigation."

Most of the university campus is attractive enough, centered around Brookings, the administration building — an ivy-draped, gothic-castle-like structure of Missouri red granite and limestone that's visible for about two miles down Lindell Avenue. The Academy Building housing ROTC, on the other hand, across Millbrook Boulevard from campus, is not so attractive. Below a crest, the door to Army ROTC leads up drab stairwells to equally drab offices and classrooms. Air Force ROTC is housed in the bottom level. During the sixties, ROTC was headquartered in two buildings north of Francis Field House, but on February 23, 1970, the Army ROTC building was fire-bombed and gutted. That was actually the fourth attempt to blow up the buildings during the turmoil of the Vietnam years.

Although the university's board of trustees voted to repair the ROTC building immediately, the structure turned out to be unrestorable and a contract was signed with Saint Louis University for a joint Army ROTC building on Forest Park Boulevard. Meanwhile, following the disruption of eleven ROTC classes by student protesters and a midnight occupation of Brookings Hall in which the building was damaged and one student was seriously injured while resisting arrest, the Air Force deactivated its ROTC program at Washington University and transferred it to Saint Louis University.

Although ROTC's current headquarters at Washington University is off-campus, the university does provide the Academy Building space for ROTC free of charge. Inside the building is a photograph of the firebombed Army ROTC building, along with the words "Lest We Forget."

The "informal investigation" on this sixth day of December, 1989, will take place in the office of Lieutenant Colonel Bates, who is not present. The bleak room, with its dull paneled walls and worn brown carpet, is furnished with chairs and a couch that might have come from a garage sale. Headed for these unimposing surroundings, I decided not to wear my ROTC uniform, and dressed instead in what I considered *my* standard uniform — jeans and a bulky sweater. Nor is my attorney, Arlene Zarembka, a dark-haired woman in her late forties, done up in lawyerly power gear. She looks, in fact, as if she has already gone home and changed clothes to relax. She apparently took the authorities at their word that the investigation would be *informal*.

Military officials, however, frequently don't mean what they say. The investigation may be officially "informal," but it is anything but casual to them or to me.

Entering the room, I see three officers in "Class B" uniforms — dress shirt, tie, green slacks, and black shoes ("Class A" is identical, but with a jacket). Also present is "Hansen," the ROTC secretary, listed in various transcripts as Mrs. Toni Hansen and Mrs. Mary C. Hansen. Once seated, I find myself surrounded on all sides.

In front of me is Captain Jon Boyle, a short, stocky, balding man. To my left is Hansen, a woman in her fifties with short, light-colored hair, who is serving as recorder. To my immediate right is Arlene. Next to her is Major Richard Thevel, who looks to be nearing retirement. Behind me, seated at Colonel Bates's

[14]

desk, is Staff Sergeant Ralph Ritchey, a baby-faced, bespectacled man of about thirty. Surrounded by these people, I feel as if I am on trial. As it turned out, I might as well have been.

As soon as I sit down, Captain Boyle starts the proceedings.

"I'm Captain Jon Boyle. I will be serving as the informal investigating officer in this case. With me is Major Richard Thevel, who will be serving as my witness for the informal board—"

This is a jolt. Although I *feel* on trial, I am not supposed to be — not yet, at least. This is the first time I've heard that this is to be a "board" of any kind. All of a sudden, my legs are shaking.

"—and Mrs. Toni Hansen, who will take notes for me and serve as my recorder. Also, Staff Sergeant Ritchey is here to assist me in an administrative capacity."

Arlene interrupts. "I didn't know this was going to be a board."

"An informal investigation and informal board are the same thing," Boyle says.

"What do you mean when you say it is an informal board?"

"I have a witness—"

"If you should decide there will be a formal board later, we will be advised?"

"Yes."

That's all the explanation we receive. Arlene and I are thinking this is an early, preliminary step, and the main event will come later. Little did we know that this would be my only chance to appear before the military to state my case. This was unfortunate not only because I was not prepared, but because, as the hearing progressed, it became obvious that none of us was. Nobody — neither Boyle, nor Arlene, nor myself — appeared to know exactly what we were doing. None of us had ever been through a proceeding like this before. Captain Boyle said he knew what he was doing, and he obviously had more of an idea than Arlene and I did since he called the meeting and was calling the shots. But part of the problem with Captain Boyle was his convoluted English. I often found it difficult to determine exactly what he was trying to say.

So, here I sit with people all around me, including a secretary transcribing stuff, two guys sitting in front of me and a guy sitting behind me, and I suddenly know beyond a doubt that all of this is really just meant to intimidate me. And I *am* intimidated. I'm nervous, I'm stuttering, my palms are cold and wet, and I'm rocking my chair. I keep thinking that if I keep moving then Sergeant Ritchey, sitting behind me, can't tell that my legs are shaking. I absolutely do not know what is going to happen and I feel like everybody is judging me. But my biggest fear is that I will say the wrong thing.

Captain Boyle continues:

"I am conducting this informal board to gather facts and to make a determination as to whether or not I feel that you willfully evaded your contract. After we have completed this board I will make my recommendations to the ROTC battalion commander. If I find that you have not willfully evaded your contract, the commander will make a final recommendation, from my letter to him, and he will forward his recommendation to higher headquarters for determination. You will be provided a copy of his recommendation and given the opportunity for rebuttal. If I determine that you willfully evaded your contract, you will be requested to appear before a formal board, at a later date."

So that's it. There won't be a formal board unless Boyle determines that I willfully evaded my contract with the military.

They hand me a waiver of rights form, then Boyle goes on:

"If you determine that you did not receive proper information as to this being an informal board and do not want to continue, let me know."

Boyle turns to Arlene and says, "He was asked to read this waiver of rights as to the announcement of this informal board." Then, turning back to me: "Since you are present for this informal board, will you please sign it? That's based on our phone call of last week. I figured that I made it clear enough to you to go through the informal process. That's up to you."

Yes, the phone conversation. I remember it well...

On April 12, 1989, I told my commanding officers I was gay. Then for an entire semester nothing happened. They had almost a whole year to take care of the matter, but they waited until now, December, when they call me and want me to show up the following week. I had told them well in advance that I

[16]

was moving to Connecticut for the next semester, and they call finals week — two weeks before my move. It looked as if they just wanted to screw up my life.

They had even tried to get me to come without an attorney. They said, "It's just an informal investigation. We'll merely be asking a few questions regarding procedures, so you don't really need her." Well, I'm glad I had her. Boyle had not made it clear in our phone conversation what this hearing involved. He hadn't given me any clue he would be asking the sort of questions he asked. If I hadn't brought Arlene with me, then I'd have had to ask them to postpone the whole thing until I could bring an attorney.

Arlene asks to see me in private before I sign any papers. I'm thinking that she's really slowing things down. My experience with the Army was that they had a form for everything, and even though this one was called a "waiver of rights," I didn't think I was actually giving up any rights by signing it. Arlene, being an attorney and not accustomed to dealing with the military, just wants to be careful. We discuss the matter and when we return, I sign.

Gradually, though, it becomes clear that Boyle's agenda is not what Arlene and I thought it would be. He asks if I have any letters of reference or documents that I want to submit, and I tell him that I don't at this time.

Arlene says, "What we want to do today is find out what is going on and what information you may need, and then we might supply some information later."

Boyle says, "Right. Do you want some time to obtain any documents?"

"Oh yeah, we may need some time," Arlene replies. "But I think once we get through this process today we can figure out what we might need or not need to do."

Boyle asks if I'm ready to answer questions. Arlene indicates that I am, but reserves our right to object to certain questions.

Boyle then starts the questioning:

"First question. Are you fully aware of the United States government policy toward homosexuals in the armed forces?"

Before I can answer, Arlene interrupts.

[17]

"Let me ask you — are all of your questions pertaining to homosexuality?"

"No."

"I have advised Mr. Holobaugh not to make any further statements with regard to the issue of homosexuality."

"Cadet Holobaugh, is that your wish? Do you wish to answer that question or don't you wish to answer that question?"

Boyle's tone is abrupt, loud, and intimidating. I realize that he's trying to get me to answer right away, without thinking, so I play it safe and look at Arlene for guidance, stammering, "I, I can't—"

Boyle presses the point. "Are you fully aware of the policy? That's all I'm asking. If you are not, I have a policy written up here for you to read, and you may read it now and then tell me whether yes or no, you are fully aware or you're not fully aware of the policy."

I look at the piece of paper. It's only a couple of paragraphs. Since I had thought the Department of Defense had several regulations on homosexuality, I ask if that is the entire Army policy.

"That's the Army policy for — DoD policy toward homosexuals in ROTC and Department of Defense. You can read that and answer the question for me whether you are aware of the policy."

Arlene and I read the policy. Boyle explains that he's asking the question because of the letter I wrote on April 12. He does not mention that I later rescinded this letter because I had written it under bad advice from an ROTC instructor. It had read, "I now feel that it is in my best interests to speak up and not accept a commission rather than to take the risk of the military finding out at a later time." A second letter had made it clear that I wanted my commission, but more on that later. The point is, I had rescinded this letter and Boyle is referring to it regardless, saying he wants to clarify what I meant by the "risk." Arlene advises me not to answer the question, feeling my subsequent letters already had explained this issue.

Boyle ignores Arlene and with his scrambled syntax attempts to get me to answer. "That's up to Cadet Holobaugh today, though, as an informal investigation. This is not, you know, we're not in court or anything so, we're not doing anything like that. This is up to you." I swear, the man must have taken speech lessons from President Bush.

"Right," says Arlene. "But, I mean, you are recording these statements—"

Boyle again turns to me, suddenly getting rather formal if no less murky. "As in reference with your attorney, you make the decision on whether you want to answer yes or no or say I wish not to answer at that time."

"I wish not to answer at this time."

To my left, Hansen silently shakes her head.

It's clear that Boyle does not like Arlene. First, he didn't want me to bring her. Then, she shows up not really looking like a lawyer. Actually, I was a little embarrassed by the way she was dressed because I was afraid they wouldn't take her seriously. I think Boyle saw her as a liberal lawyer, maybe a lesbian, and he simply didn't like her. The antipathy was no doubt mutual.

Boyle returns to his first question, the matter of whether or not I am aware of DoD policy.

Having just read the policy, it seems to me a stupid question. "If this is the Army's policy," I answer, "obviously, I'm aware."

"No," Boyle says, "At the time."

"At what time?" Arlene asks.

Boyle says he means on April 12, when I wrote the letter. Again, Arlene advises me not to answer, and I do not. Boyle turns his attention to when I realized I was gay, and I tell him he already has that information in the letter. But he wants something more specific than "this past year," which is what I said in the letter.

"Well, I would never be able to specify—"

"A date," says Boyle, finishing my sentence for me.

Arlene again objects to the line of questioning, and Ritchey makes an attempt to translate Boyle into English. "I think what he's trying to get at," says Ritchey, apparently not quite sure himself, "is that if it's determined willful evasion—"

"Right," says Boyle, which must have reassured Ritchey.

"—willful evasion is usually deemed either pay back or someone's asked to be—"

"Right," says Boyle.

"—an enlisted—"

"Right," says Boyle. Ritchey glances at him and continues:

"—an enlisted soldier; therefore, the Army would want to tie down a date or—"

Boyle says, "Right," and gets another glance from Ritchey.

"—at least a time frame—"

"That's right." Boyle again.

"—a general idea, so they would, if they wanted to — him to pay back, they would go back to that time frame."

"We have to have, yeah, we have to have some kind of an idea," says Boyle.

"Legally," Ritchey continues, "they wouldn't, or I wouldn't think that they'd be able, to make him pay back for anything earlier than that date."

"Right. Right," says Boyle. "But, that, you know, that's up to Cadet Holobaugh and, you know, if you want to, you don't think you can pin down or want to pin down the date at this time—"

There's a pause as they look at me. I say, "At this point I have to do what my attorney is telling me to do."

This seems to make Boyle angry. "You don't *have* to do what your attorney tells you," he snaps. "That's up to you."

I wonder, briefly, if he doesn't like the idea of a man not making his own decisions. But I decide that he's just angry because he is not succeeding in intimidating me into talking. I try to counter his anger by being calm, although I'm not. I look him in the eye and manage to say, "I choose to do what my attorney is telling me to do."

Zarembka 2, Boyle 0.

To my left, Hansen shakes her head again.

Next question.

"After you accepted the fact that you were gay in 1988, all right, without pinning down the date, I, I need to know why you waited until 12 April 1989 after you had used more scholarship benefits, to notify the ROTC department."

Someone please notify the Department of Defense: In the real world, one does not wake up one day and declare, "My God! I'm gay! Better call the ROTC and tell them! They'll want to be kicking me out."

Arlene knows what I'm thinking. She says, "And again, I am advising Mr. Holobaugh not to make any further statements on these matters."

So, when did I realize I was gay? Inquiring minds want to know. Although Captain Boyle had asked for something more specific, narrowing it down to 1988 was the best I could do. For many gays — maybe even most — the realization is so gradual that one could say "thirteen" or "twenty-three" with equal truthfulness. It's especially hard to pinpoint for the multitude of men and women who enjoyed childhood sex with friends and relatives, as I did.

I honestly cannot remember the first time I had sex with another male. As a child, I messed around with cousins and friends like a lot of kids do. My earliest memories of sex with another guy are taking baths with my cousin, but that was all very innocent — just playing with each other. I couldn't have been more than five when this started; he was two or three years older. I remember one time we fooled around in my grandmother's car at the K-Mart parking lot in Springfield, Missouri. She'd gone inside to buy some things, and my cousin said, "Put my penis in your mouth." I said, "No, you put mine in yours" — and he did. A few minutes later I saw my grandmother coming to the car, and I was world-wise enough to know that she shouldn't be seeing this. He pulled off me. It seems funny now — in my grandmother's car at K-Mart.

My childhood sexual partners soon went beyond cousins to include friends. Ironically, the first friend I experimented with was a guy who ended up going into the military. But I messed around with so many cousins and friends, so many times, that there is no way to remember all the occasions. I was from a big family — I have thirty-five first cousins — and I had a lot of friends. Many times when I stayed all night with one of them, or they stayed with me, we messed around. There was neither forethought nor afterthought; we just did it. It was enjoyable and no one felt guilty about it. That's one reason it took me so long to come to terms with my being gay. I knew all my friends were doing it when we were kids, and it just felt normal. The image I had of a gay person did not match my image of myself or my friends. The people I thought of as gay did not seem happy. Because I had no other role models, there was no reason to see myself as being gay.

Next question.

"On 4 May 1989, Captain Erickson and Sergeant Ritchey explained the specifics and possible outcomes of your initial request. When did you first consult your attorney?"

"I certainly would object to that as invasion of attorney-client privilege," says Arlene.

"Okay," says Boyle, trying a different approach. "What occurred between 12 April and 19 May to make you decide that your homosexuality was not an obstacle to being commissioned in the United States Army?"

Arlene doesn't like this either. "Again, I believe that we have already answered those questions in the letter that I sent."

Indeed, we had. And the next question as well:

"Would you be willing to serve on active duty in order to fulfill your scholarship obligation?"

By this time, I'm wondering if the captain can read. Annoyed, I reply, "You have that information in the letter — in the second letter."

Boyle does not like being told what he has and doesn't have. He barks, "I'm asking *you:* Would you be willing to serve on active duty as a way to fulfill your scholarship obligation?"

"Yes."

There is a pause as Boyle stares at me, pondering his next question.

"Okay. What do you feel you have to gain as a commissioned officer in the United States Army?"

This query seems a bit too broad to answer in a few sentences. I hesitate, then turn to Arlene.

"Arlene—"

"I'm asking *you,* Cadet Holobaugh."

"I know," I reply, wishing the guy would quit badgering me. "I need to talk to my attorney."

Arlene tells me I can answer the question if I want to answer it. This puts me on the spot, because I really can't comprehend how to begin answering such an all-encompassing question. At a loss, I say stupidly, "Why anyone wants to become an officer."

This doesn't cut it with Boyle. "Why do *you* want to become an officer is what I'm trying to get at. I know anybody can go in for different reasons. I need to know why *you* specifically feel you're going to gain something as an officer in the U.S. Army."

The emphases above are from the transcript of the informal board, as transcribed by Hansen. She recorded my answer this way:

"Well, if you can read any of your (let's [*sic*] out a chuckle) recruiting brochures — I mean, it's for the experience, it's — I mean"

A chuckle? I would like to ask Mrs. Toni Hansen how she decided it was a chuckle, and not an all-out laugh, or perhaps a giggle, or cackle, or chortle, or maybe a titter, or even a guffaw. But of course, no military personnel will comment on any detail of any case even remotely concerning homosexuality. They refer anyone who asks to DoD policy.

In any case, what Hansen called a "chuckle" would be better described as a nervous laugh. I wasn't laughing at Boyle's question, or the recruiting brochures, or the reasons I would join the military. I was laughing because I was nervous as hell and couldn't think of an intelligent answer to his question.

To add to the confusion, Hansen's tape recorder kept messing up throughout the hearing. When it finally died, she used shorthand.

Next, I try to answer the question of my becoming a commissioned officer by noting that my acceptance of an ROTC scholarship meant I was obligated to the military. Boyle asks if there are other reasons, and I reply — apparently without chuckling — that I could write an essay.

"It's just like going into a career. Why does anyone want to become a civil engineer or why does anyone want to become—"

"I'm sure there are reasons why they want to become a civil engineer," says the captain. "I want to know why you want to become an officer."

"I don't think it's the sort of thing that he can answer in thirty seconds," Arlene observes.

"I'm not telling him to answer it in thirty seconds."

Arlene brings up the essay idea again, although the captain has not, so far, demonstrated that he likes to read. He ignores the essay suggestion.

"Would you like to answer the question to me about why you want to become an officer?" Boyle asks. "I don't know you very well, Cadet Holobaugh. I want to know what you're thinking about becoming an officer in the United States Army."

The question wasn't complicated, but I answered it poorly. I kicked myself afterwards for just stuttering through it. I felt surrounded, though, and I was nervous. And that type of question is really hard to answer. Why did I want to be an officer? Why did I want to be an engineer? You have reasons, but it's not that easy to put them into words — at least it isn't for me. I was scared of Boyle, and angry — but mostly scared. All of these thoughts raced through my mind. I was hesitant to say anything without talking to Arlene first. I didn't trust my ability to articulate what I was thinking. I was afraid my answers just wouldn't be good enough — that they weren't what Boyle was looking for.

I took another stab at it: "I mean, when I filled out the—"

The application. ROTC scholarship. Ava, Missouri, 1983. Why did I seek an ROTC scholarship? To answer a question like that, you have to provide some background. I knew Boyle did not want to hear my life story. But if I had spent the next three hours filling the captain in on my background, my family, and the forces in my life that had motivated me to seek an ROTC scholarship, I would have had to begin with Ava...

# Ava

My father, Jimmy Moore Holobaugh, was born in 1937; my mother, Katherine Eugenia Hill, in 1939; and my sister, Melanie Kay, in 1961. I was born in West Plains, Missouri, on December 23, 1965. To avoid confusion, the family called me by my middle name, Morris. They still do, as does everyone in Ava, Missouri, which soon would become my hometown. I hate being called Morris. I always did.

*Jim's father, sitting in his office — the principal's office of Ava Middle School — is dressed exactly as one would expect a principal with conventional good taste to dress. He is a good-looking man, and there's a noticeable resemblance between father and son. Before the tape recorder is turned on, Mr. Holobaugh explains that he is not comfortable talking about the events surrounding his son because they are fresh and he may see it all differently later.*

*"Morris was our second child," he begins. "He has an older sister, and we lost one child in between — a miscarriage. He was five and his sister was ten when his mother died of cancer. She lived less than two years after they discovered breast cancer. She had been a business teacher. She and I went to a small high school in north Arkansas together, and went the last two years of college together in southeast Arkansas. We weren't high school*

*sweethearts. I was in college and she was still in high school when we got interested in each other."*

*The Hill family moved to Arkansas from Tennessee. Jim's great-grandfather on the Hill side was a Mormon. Some members of the sizable family settled in northeast Arkansas and the rest went on to Salt Lake City. The Mormon belief didn't stick with the group that stayed in Arkansas.*

*The Holobaugh family traces its roots back to Germany. Jim's grandparents live in a nursing home in Walnut Ridge, Arkansas. His grandfather was a carpenter. The grandparents had six children.*

*"When my kids lost their mother, they were well thought of and looked after by the rest of a large family," says Mr. Holobaugh.*

*When Jim was born, the family lived near West Plains in the Bakersfield community, on the Missouri side of Norfork Lake.*

*"We moved from the West Plains area to Ava because Jim's mother was having to travel to Springfield for radiation treatments, and we thought if we could locate closer to Springfield it would make it easier on her," Mr. Holobaugh explains. "One year here is what we had in mind, but we liked it here and people treated us nicely, so one year has turned into twenty-one. I plan to retire here.*

*"I didn't see any impact on Morris when his mother died. Of course, he was only five years old, and those things may not always be possible to see."*

I don't know how my mother's death affected me subconsciously, or what effect it might have had on my personality. You just don't know those things. But I've always thought that there's no reason a child must have both a mother and a father. I think if they can have both, that's great, but it's not absolutely necessary.

Sadly, I don't remember my mother very well, and I don't know if most of the memories I have are truly memories or if they're things people told me in the years after her death. But there are a few things that I know are memories: watching her at the kitchen counter, lying in her lap. But I can't remember what her voice sounds like. When you're four years old you don't know much about your mother except that she's Mom. My relatives have told me that she was a very sweet person who would never do anyone harm. She was religious. When I was younger, people told me I looked exactly like her. The family was really torn up when she died. Of all the family members, she was the last person anyone would have wanted to die from cancer at a young age.

I was not old enough to grieve, or to understand. My dad took Melanie and me to the funeral home and explained to us that she had died. Melanie was upset, but I just couldn't comprehend what that meant. The night he told us was the night of the body viewing. I still think that whole concept is kind of weird. I remember my dad picking me up and holding me over her, and I kissed her good-bye. But I still didn't realize she would never come back. The next day at the funeral my dad told Melanie and me not to cry, which seems kind of silly to me now. My Aunt Barbara was crying and Melanie was crying, and I remember saying to my dad, "Melanie's crying," like I thought she should be getting in trouble. After the service my aunt and uncle took Melanie and me to get milk shakes. I remember laughing and fighting and not understanding why my aunt and uncle were so solemn.

When we moved to Ava, we moved into a neighborhood with some older people, the Talleys, who became almost like grandparents to me. Mrs. Talley was a sweet old lady with dyed hair. I stayed with her a lot after my mother died. She was a big help to me, and I think I helped her, too. Years later I heard her husband tell family members that she had suffered a nervous breakdown, and taking care of me helped bring her out of that. Having a sense of purpose can work wonders in a person's life, and for Mrs. Talley, all of a sudden there was this little boy in her life who had just lost his mother.

It was Mrs. Talley and her store of Lincoln Logs and erector sets that spurred my interest in engineering. I loved playing with those things, and I started building complicated structures at an early age. Mrs. Talley told me about her brother, who'd gone to the University of Missouri at Rolla and was an engineer. She called the university by its other name, the School of Mines. The idea caught my fancy, even if I didn't quite understand what she was saying. For the longest time I thought she was saying, "School of Minds." It took a long time for me to realize that she meant mines as in coal mines. Then I thought the name was kind of hokey, and I never called it that. I still wanted to be an engineer, but I never told anyone that I wanted to attend the Missouri "School of Mines."

We lived next door to the Talleys from 1970 until 1981, then began a series of moves. Altogether, we lived in five different houses in the Ava area. In town, we had cats and dogs. When we moved outside of town by the country club, we had horses, too, but I didn't ride them. I've never been a horse person — they never fascinated me the way they do some kids. Living in the country, you tend to take all the animals for granted. When I took my nephew to the Saint Louis Zoo, the only animals he really got excited about were the monkeys, because they were exotic. The other animals were just animals; he sees animals all the time.

Besides building things, my childhood passion was fire. My stepbrother and I burned down a wall of our fort. We also had this curious, cruel habit of burning live animals such as minnows and snakes and turtles. We'd catch them, pour gas on them, and light a match. I don't know what to make of that now. It's spooky. We set army men on fire, and models — the war stuff such as planes and ships. After I assembled the models I took them outside and set them on fire. I suppose I could have set hot rod car models on fire, too, but for some reason that idea never caught my fancy — just the military stuff.

*While Jim remembers times he burned live snakes and turtles as part of his obsession with fire, his father will tell you of his compassion — not only for people, but even for inanimate objects:*

*"I took him to buy a winter coat when he was seven or eight, and he narrowed the selection down to two coats. One of them I liked a lot better than the other. It was obviously a more suitable coat. Well, he chose the other one. When we got home I said, 'Morris, tell me why you picked this coat over the other one.' He said, 'Well, I felt sorry for this coat because the other one's a better coat and I thought no one else would buy this one.' That*

[28]

*sounds crazy, but that's the kind of compassion that was in Morris.*

*"I've never seen anyone that Morris didn't get along with. His first year or two he was a cranky baby, but after that he was never much of a problem. He was well liked by anyone who ever dealt with him — a child anyone would want to claim as a son. I don't think you'd ever find anyone who had a problem with Morris. He was adored by everyone who knew him."*

*Mr. Holobaugh raised Melanie and Jim by himself for almost three years.*

*"You look back and you wonder how you did it. But when you're in those situations, it just works out. Then I married a woman with two kids. We put them all together and tried to make a go of it. That marriage lasted eight years."*

Mine was a normal childhood — football in the front yard, hide-and-seek with cousins and friends. My best friend from kindergarten through sixth grade was Chris Parker, a tall, skinny boy who lived in the country. We didn't see each other much in the summer. Chris was a nice kid, though somewhat spoiled. I'd spend the night with him on his farm sometimes. We'd build forts and play in the barn. His grandparents lived with him, and his grandmother often made chocolate brownies for me. It's easy to bribe me with food — give me chocolate and I'm yours. I noticed a striking difference between the pampered way Chris was treated at his house and the stricter atmosphere of mine. But I had siblings, whereas Chris was an only child.

Between sixth and seventh grade, I met a new kid, John Taylor, at the swimming pool. Unlike Chris, John lived in town, and that made it much easier for me to hang out with him. We would go to the swimming pool every day and have fun, so by the end of the summer John replaced Chris as my best friend. I've always been geared to having one best friend, and I've never in my life been without one best friend.

*John Taylor: "I moved to Ava in 1978. Booger County — that's the nickname for Douglas County — is very rural, and there are a lot of 'good-old-boys' living there. There are also a lot of*

*paramilitary groups and closet Klansmen. No blacks. It's a rough
part of the country.*

*"Jim was my best friend all through junior high and high
school. We spent about 90 percent of our waking hours together.
We'd go swimming, or take our dogs for a run — he had a Lab
and I had a bird dog. We played football together and ran track.
I liked his dad a lot, but I never really liked his stepmom too
much. She always tried to be rich in a small town."*

In a lot of ways, Ava was a nice place to grow up. It's situated
in a beautiful part of the Ozarks, one of the most scenic areas in
the United States. It's a place where you can climb the nearest
mountain and see nothing but wilderness for miles around. As
a child I would sometimes climb a tree and look with amaze-
ment over the expanse of beauty surrounding me. Besides the
thousands of acres of wooded, rolling hills in the Mark Twain
National Forest, there are a number of rivers perfect for canoeing, and a wealth of pristine lakes. Buffalo National River is a
canoe enthusiast's dream in the early spring. Bull Shoals, Table
Rock, Norfork, Taneycomo, and Beaver Lakes are mammoth
Corps of Engineers projects large enough to host thousands of
people fishing and water-skiing in the summer and still seem
uncrowded.

Our family was always camping out. My dad and I would
go to the lake, but we only had one boat — I'd want to ski and
he'd want to fish. So, there was always an argument — it's hard
to do both at the same time.

Tourist areas abound — especially Branson, Missouri,
which CBS's "Sixty Minutes" recently called the "country and
western capital of the universe." It has more country and western venues than anywhere on earth, and if CBS says the universe, I won't argue. Branson is also home to Silver Dollar City
amusement park, Whitewater Aquapark, and Shepherd of the
Hills Farm, named after the popular novel. Never heard of it?
Go to Branson. You will. I always had a season pass to Whitewater Aquapark. John Taylor and I went there a lot.

More unusual types of entertainment can also be found in
the smaller towns of the Ozarks, as is evident from this item
from the *Baxter County Bulletin:* "The annual Baxter County

[30]

Chain Saw Race will be held at the fairgrounds on Saturday, Sept. 13, at 4 p.m. in the show arena. Chain saws will be divided into six classes by their cubic inch displacement. Each contestant will start his saw and make three cuts, one down, one up, and one down; shut his saw off and return to the starting point." Sound like fun?

John is right: culturally and politically, Ava is in a rough part of the country. The Missouri Ozarks have a long history of voting conservative, usually Republican. I can't remember the last time Douglas County elected a Democrat.

There are pockets of liberalism nearby. Eureka Springs, Arkansas, has attracted a considerable number of gay couples who've moved there and opened small shops. Called "the little Switzerland of the Ozarks," the town, which is built onto a hillside, is a pleasant enough place to live with a lover and good friends. But a huge, white monolith, the Christ of the Ozarks statue (unappreciative locals call it the "Milk Carton of the Ozarks"), looks over the town from atop the next hill, and each summer thousands of tourists flock to see a mammoth, nightly reenactment of the Passion Play on the hillside below the statue. All of that can be a lot to put up with.

For the most part, this is an area of independent conservatism where people like to be left alone. On the Arkansas-Missouri border you can find the remains of the militant right-wing enclave, "The Covenant, The Sword and The Arm of the Lord" (catchy name). Several other reactionary groups can be found in the area too. On the other hand, there's an all-male social nudism group, the Arkansas Bare Society, located at Mountain Home, and at least four lesbian land collectives. One is located on a sprawling 241-acre tract and is home to twenty women, each owning a large house on five acres, with the other 141 acres owned collectively. As you might guess, though, members of these communities keep so quiet that virtually no one in the area knows of their existence. If you can blend into the surroundings, you're usually okay. Blacks — who cannot — do not live here, unless they're on an athletic scholarship at Southwest Missouri State or the University of Arkansas.

A look at the telephone directory serving Ava gives you a fairly accurate portrait of southern Missouri values and lifestyles. The first thing you notice is that there just aren't many people living here. The phone book for Ava carries listings for forty-six towns in its seventy-two white pages. In the yellow pages, the two headings with the most listings are beauty salons and churches. There are sixty-three churches listed for the area, thirty-nine of them Baptist and at least a dozen more some variety of Holy Roller. Some, if not most, of these are churches that in the middle of the sweltering summer will change the black letters on their signs out front to read, "If you think this is hot, just wait." It's an area not known for its subtlety.

But there are more beauty salons than churches. You can choose from Darlene's, Doris's, Gigi's, Jessie Marie's, Nadine's, Pat's, Rose Zella's, Sonny and Cher's, Vivian's, Wanda's, or sixty-one others.

The phone book also lists twelve auctioneers. This year there are ducks on the cover. Inside are ads for KTRI "Alternative Radio" and Buena Vista's Exotic Animal Paradise. You're probably thinking, "Alternative radio?" The station apparently explains this label to its own satisfaction by noting that it provides agriculture reports at 6:30 a.m. and 12:45 and 2:50 p.m.

The phone book also lists three boat and canoe rental outlets and two herb shops. In addition, there's a national anti-cocaine ad featuring a young woman with a pistol stuck in her left nostril.

In this part of the world, normal beer cannot be sold on Sundays. Instead, some stores sell 3.2 beer (beer with a legal alcohol content of 3.2 percent) from separate coolers, outside, with clerks making change from a money bag. It's peculiar, it's a hassle, it's southern Missouri.

Most of the people in and around Ava make their living by farming. There are a couple of factories: Emerson Electric and Rawlings Sporting Goods. The latter makes football equipment in Ava. Naturally, there's a Wal-Mart. After all, Sam Walton himself lived nearby. And the latest big news is that Ava now has a McDonald's.

The closest gay communities of any size other than the secretive lesbian collectives are in Springfield, Missouri, and Eureka Springs and Fayetteville, Arkansas. Only the Fayetteville group is particularly active, and they have had to put up

[32]

with a lot of grief. But the student group at the University of Arkansas has made enough noise to win official recognition and have the university add "sexual orientation" to its anti-discrimination policy (which, as we'll see, is important where ROTC is concerned). For most of the area, however, homosexuality is something people would rather not think about or hear about. Out of sight, out of mind.

When I was growing up, the local news never had anything regarding gays. Occasionally, I might see something in the Associated Press stories in the Springfield paper or on the national TV newscasts. There is, however, a gay couple, two real estate agents, living in Ava. So far, they haven't been attacked. But they are laughingstocks, and they did come under fire once when they advertised in a national gay publication trying to get gays to move to the Ozarks. I was in the eighth grade at the time, and I remember my sister's boyfriend talking about it. He said, "There's nothing I hate more than a queer." I've always wondered how the people in Ava found out about the ad.

You can get a pretty good idea of the mentality of the area from the following incident:

On May 21, 1991, a crowd attended a board meeting of the Rogers-Hough Memorial Library in Rogers, Arkansas, to debate whether the library should remove a book on homosexuality from its shelves. *A* book, mind you. *One.* The crowd seemed evenly split on the issue, which — for those familiar with the area — is encouraging. Indeed, ten people spoke in favor of keeping the book, and only six spoke in opposition.

Ken Perry of Rogers asked the crowd if it would be acceptable for the library to keep books on how to grow marijuana or how to commit incest.

Fortunately, Charles Reed of Springdale had an answer: "I was reading a book just the other day that was full of incest, rape and killings. That book was the King James Bible. If this book is banned, will the Bible be next? This is not Iran and you are not the Ayatollah Khoumeini."

But Greg Bledsoe of Teens United for Freedom (that's TUFF) asked, "Once we open our doors to this type of material, where do we stop? We cannot allow such people to bully society into bowing to their wishes."

[33]

Dennis Lewis, representing Fathers for Decency in the Natural State (I am not making this up), provided a good example of the misinformation that's spread when books are banned by libraries. Lewis claimed that the vast majority of cases involving sexual abuse of children are committed by homosexuals.

Larry Rudiger, who identified himself as a member of the University of Arkansas's Gay and Lesbian Student Association and "by the grace of God a gay man," set Lewis straight, adding that "people are not made gay or lesbian, straight or gay, by reading something."

For the record, Arkansas's nickname is "the Natural State," but detractors nevertheless feel free to refer to Mr. Lewis's organization as "Fathers for Decency in the Buff."

David Yates of Rogers told the board his lack of knowledge about gay relationships kept him "confused" for much of his life.

Still, argued Hank Wehmeyer of Rogers, the book goes against Christian teachings.

Patricia Simmons of Rogers replied, "I'd like to remind Mr. Wehmeyer that it's not a requirement in this city to be a Christian. It's just *not* a requirement."

When the board voted five to one to keep the book, Wehmeyer sounded this dire warning: "We're headed down the road to another San Francisco community. There's no such thing as a third sex. It's the most degrading thing a person can do to another person. If Rogers wants sodomy, sodomy they will have."

Despite the narrowness and conservatism, I think it's a nice place to grow up. I don't regret my years in southern Missouri, although I never want to move back there. It simply doesn't offer anything for me now. I don't fit in with the typical person in Ava. If I sat down with most people in Ava, there really wouldn't be a lot to talk about.

I remember when my dad remarried and suddenly I had a stepmother. I was thinking, "This is neat. I'm going to have the experience of having a stepmother and stepbrothers and stepsisters." I really liked Kay, and I've often wondered about the things I would never have learned if my dad hadn't married her. Kay was "hip." She dressed modern, she was active, she liked going to movies. And she was loud — almost *too* loud, but I liked how outgoing Kay was. Her kids were the same. I called her "Mom," but when she and my dad got divorced, I was glad in a way. I was a freshman in high school, and I suppose I just wanted more space. Melanie was in college, and I liked the idea of just my dad and me at home. But I did miss Kay.

Leslie, my stepsister, is outgoing — and loud like her mother. Lance, my stepbrother, is about five-foot-nine, with brownish red hair, a handsome face, and a good personality. He's a lot of fun. I guess *hyper* is a good word for Lance. We had a pretty normal relationship. I was pleased with having a brother, because it was so much fun to have a companion to play with. I have to admit, though, that I was often mean to him. I was older and used that psychological advantage to get my way. I'd say stuff like, "If you don't do this for me, I won't play with you." I haven't seen him in six years. After the divorce we went our separate ways. But I do want to get together with him sometime.

After a while Lance moved in with his dad and lived with him for a couple of years. We started fighting more when we were together, and there were times when I thought Kay showed some favoritism because he was her real son. Once we got in a fight and she called me a son of a bitch. I said, "No, I'm the stepson of a bitch," which landed me a good slap. But it was worth it at the time.

I always did well in school. Part of the reason, I think, was that my teachers expected it. Melanie was very smart, and when I came along the teachers treated me as if I would naturally be smart, too. It was a self-fulfilling thing, a matter of living up to their expectations — which I did.

Once in the sixth grade, in my dad's building, I got into a fight with this guy named Tate, who later went to the Naval Academy. Tate was a good student, too, but for some reason he and I got into a fistfight. In the middle of it the teacher walked in, grabbed us, took us out into the hall, and said to me, "I'm shocked. Your dad is the principal. What are we going to do? I won't send you to the principal because I know what your dad would do to you if I did." That experience made an impression.

Afterwards, I felt like I had to be very well behaved. In elementary school I talked to my friends a lot during class — although I never really got into trouble — but in junior high I got quiet. Some people thought I was shy, but I wasn't. I was simply quiet, and I stayed that way all through high school.

**Jim's father:** *"I always told people I would never work in a school where my kids went because it's unfair to them and to you. Morris was a very modest boy. We used to think that he didn't excel because he didn't want to stand out as being the top student. That's still a problem with the school system — you don't want to show up your peers because they'll criticize you on the playground. That changed a little as Morris got further in school, but I don't think he ever tried to be number one.*

*"He wasn't a great athlete, but he is pretty physical, keeps his body in good shape, and watches the foods he eats. But he wasn't too much on sports. He liked to run. I was very athletic and played all sports in school, but I'm not a person who would pressure him. As soon as I saw that he wasn't very athletic as far as basketball, football, baseball — the sports we see here — I didn't press him at all. There were never any confrontations or statements made about you ought to do this, or play this — that just wasn't there. Too often we think of sports as football, basketball, and baseball, but there are other things that are just as athletic and more beneficial. It's too bad the team sports get all the glory in this country.*

*"Jim did play football. It was the thing to do in a small high school. Although he was strong and fast, he wasn't well coordinated for football, so he didn't make the main team. Of course, if you don't, your interest fades."*

In junior high, boys my age began getting interested in girls. I did, too, but it wasn't a strong attraction; it was just the thing to do. I began going steady with girls in junior high school, about the same time my friends and I stopped messing around. I guess we realized that, hey, guys aren't supposed to do this. But one friend and I were reluctant to give it up. We used to take a sheet and put it over a fan. The fan would blow the sheet up like a bubble, and we would say that the air inside this bubble was a special air that made you gay. So when we were in the bubble it was okay to be gay. I guess we knew what the word *gay* meant, and we knew that it wasn't cool to be gay. In order to have sex we connived this little loophole that took away all the guilt on our part. After all, when we were inside the bubble we couldn't control it.

But there was a time before that, maybe fifth or sixth grade, when I spent the night with this same friend and he asked me to "be gay" with him. I asked what he meant, and he said, "Hug me and kiss me and lie here with me." I wouldn't do it. Being "gay" with him wasn't part of my agenda. Having sex with him was. Now, I keep wondering if all these guys I used to fool around with really quit having those feelings as they grew older, or if at least some of them are just suppressing them.

I never ventured out of my age group when fooling around. I remember seeing grown men on television and thinking they were attractive, but the oldest guy I had sex with was one of my cousins, and the last time I remember doing anything with him was when I was in sixth grade and he was in high school.

Sexual experiences between children are common, but the frequency of these experiences vary greatly from child to child. With me, there were more times than I can recall. Brent, my lover, thinks this is weird because he never experienced anything like this as a child. But I consider it very natural because everyone I knew did it. I think it's very common.

**Brent:** *"Maybe in Missouri."*

[37]

# Reagan youth

Ironically, sex with cousins and friends ended for me shortly after the onset of puberty. It's fairly common for males, both gay and straight, to have homosexual experiences in junior high and high school. But I guess my straight friends had got that out of their systems before high school. In any case, *my* high school years were exclusively heterosexual. My attraction to guys never went away, but since my friends stopped messing around, I did not have sex with other boys.

Instead, I turned to the usual substitute — masturbation. I remember that my sexual fantasies throughout junior high and high school involved both males and females, but a lot of the female fantasies were forced, and the male fantasies often left me with a keen sense of guilt. The objects of desire in these fantasies included classmates, people who'd pass me on the street — all kinds of people.

As for the opposite sex, I hardly dated at all in the ninth and tenth grades, and only infrequently as a high school junior and senior. It didn't interest me. I'd take a girl out a couple of times, then I'd back off to avoid getting serious. I didn't want a relationship. I enjoyed the dates, but it wasn't because I was with someone with breasts.

Although I wasn't especially attracted to the opposite sex, I didn't worry that I was gay. I just didn't think about it, because

[38]

it didn't occur to me that other guys had a stronger attraction to girls than I did. I thought dating girls was just something you were supposed to do, so I went through the motions. Which is exactly what I did later on when it came to sex.

It was the summer between my junior and senior years of high school when I first had sex with a girl. People talk about movies having an effect on teenagers, and I would have to agree. When I was in high school, all the movies seemed to be about losing one's virginity. The message was loud and clear: To be a virgin was not cool. So, I decided that I didn't want to be a virgin anymore, and that problem was easily taken care of. But solving the "problem" was really the only thing that mattered; after the first time, I was excited and happy, not because sex with a female was anything great, but because I was no longer a virgin.

*Jim's father: "Morris had a lot of friends in high school, some of them best friends. He had, like most people, one best friend he ran around with a lot. He wasn't into dating a lot. He dated some girls his senior year. I don't know if he took a girl to his junior-senior prom or not."*

I did — Michelle Lee. As a senior, I graduated in the top 10 percent of my class, and was voted "Best Dressed" and "Most Shy." I had not actively sought these distinctions — I thought I was just dressing normally, and I took offense at the "Most Shy" label. I think it was the girls who bestowed that honor on me because I wouldn't go after them. I was just quiet. I thought it was rude to disrupt class, so I didn't, and I wasn't aggressive with girls. Of course, anyone who knows me now knows I'm not shy.

I began working at Town and Country Supermarket the summer between my sophomore and junior years. It wasn't easy for a teenager to find a job in Ava, but as early as junior high I somehow knew that in high school I'd work in a supermarket. There were certain guys who worked at service stations, there were guys who worked on farms, and there were guys who worked in supermarkets before they went to college. I saw myself as belonging to this latter group. I remember one time my sister asked, "Well, how do you know you're going to get that job? They're not going to just give it to you because you ask." I was like, "I'm *going* to work there, all right?" When I turned sixteen, I went to Larry Smith, the manager, and applied. Nothing happened, so I went back and said, "I'd really like to work here." Again, nothing happened. I went back a third time and said, "Larry, I really want to work here." I got the job.

*Jim's father: "It was an excellent job. A lot of times he had to work until ten or eleven o'clock in the store and then come home and do schoolwork. His senior year, sometimes he was up until two in the morning. That was pretty tough on me as a parent, to let a child do that. But it taught him some study skills and I think it's paid off for him. I hope I'm not just saying that to pardon myself."*

I worked thirty-five hours each week. The job took all my spare time, forcing me to quit track after my sophomore year (I had dropped out of football earlier). Any time I wasn't working, I was studying. But I enjoyed the money more than I liked the sports. Also, the job was a good excuse — not conscious — to avoid dating girls. It's not that I felt I had to make excuses; I just knew I'd rather be working than dating girls and playing all those stupid high school games. And to me they *were* games and they *were* stupid, since I really wasn't interested.

In my mind, high school was like a training ground. I was always looking to the future, looking to college. I knew that high school was necessary, but to me it was only a step. It seemed that to most people my age, high school was this huge deal — they were so afraid of graduating and leaving all their friends. I didn't feel that way at all. High school life just didn't much interest me. It seemed silly. Everything I did in high school was geared to the future. I didn't spend the money I made from working because I was saving it for college. But I have to admit I put too much value on money and planning a future built around money. Now, that's not part of my agenda at all.

Although I didn't have sex with guys in high school, I was interested in a few. There was a guy at Town and Country a

[40]

year older than me whom I had a big crush on. The nights he didn't work, I'd miss him. I would get jealous when he was around a girl or another guy. We started to become friends, and one night he asked if I wanted to start working out with him when we got off work. It's hard to describe how that made me feel. I was so happy that he had asked me, but at the same time my heart just sank because I knew there was no way I could do it. I had to have that time after work to study. It broke my heart to have to tell him no, especially since he had no way of knowing how much I wanted to say yes.

The subject of homosexuality did not come up much in Ava. There were, of course, fag jokes. There was also biology class. We used to talk about sex all the time in that class, and one day the teacher just started going off on homosexuals. It didn't even faze me at the time, but looking back on it, I can't believe how irresponsible this teacher was. This was an authority figure whom kids were supposed to look up to, and he was denigrating homosexuals and criticizing psychologists for teaching gays to accept themselves rather than trying to "cure" them.

My father and Kay divorced when I was a freshman. I felt bad for my father. I think in some ways he blamed my sister and me for the divorce — particularly Melanie. I got along great with Kay, but Melanie and Kay had some problems. Still, it was hardly Melanie's fault that they got divorced. I don't know today what the real reasons were. All I remember my dad saying was that Kay was emotionally unstable, and I never heard Kay give a reason except that she "just couldn't take it anymore," whatever that meant. Less than a year later, Kay married a man with four kids, and that lasted about three days. Later, Leslie told me she had told Kay, "Mom, if you can't stay married, just don't get married." Kay hasn't married since. Leslie stayed with my father and me a while after the divorce in order to graduate.

*Jim's father: "Those are two of the most stressful things that can happen to an adult — divorce and the death of a spouse. You tie that with my job as a school principal and you wonder how I ever reached this age without having a heart attack or something.*

*Being inside the situation, it's sometimes hard to see — but I think if you asked the people of this community, they'd tell you that, with a lot of help, I did a decent job of raising my kids. They were both honor students and both well behaved."*

My father married his present wife when I was a junior in high school. Connie has two daughters: Kim, one year older than me, and Lana, one year younger. Connie is quiet, short, and pretty. She's not outgoing at all, totally the opposite of Kay. She's the county assessor, but I don't know how she gets elected to public office being such a homebody.

She's also a clean freak. Certain furniture in our house is off limits — you can't sit on it. If you're sitting on the forbidden furniture, she'll fix you with this stare. Also, you can't wear shoes in the house. It's like living in Japan. It drove me nuts. The way I feel, if you can't afford to use something, you can't afford to have it. Why have something that makes you live in fear of ruining it? Especially in Ava. I mean, who's going to see it who knows anything about it? One time I wore shoes in the house — an incredible sin — and she threw them away. They were brand-new shoes. She threw them out and the garbage man hauled them away. I was so pissed off. It was just ridiculous.

I made it a point to wear shoes in the house when Connie wasn't there. Ludicrous rules invite rebellion. Even if I hadn't, I think she would have suspected that I did, because she never trusted me. Once when Connie and my dad came back from vacation, she accused me of sleeping with my girlfriend, Allison — who went to Evangel College — in their bed. Why would I want to sleep in their bed with her? She said the bed was made up like I make mine. This bit of paranoia was all because they had put in new carpet once, and when they moved my bed Connie found a couple of used condoms from when I'd had sex with Erin. I guess she thought that when they were gone it was just a fuck frenzy.

I think Connie has the same syndrome Kay had: comparing her kids to Melanie and me. Her girls were wild and never did too well in school. They both got married at an early age, divorced, and remarried. I have no problems with them, but we

[42]

weren't very close. Kim never lived with us. Lana did, but I was out of the house after a couple of years.

*For his part, Jim's father doesn't have many problems with the relationship between his son and his present wife:*

*"We've been married about eight or nine years now. There can never be a mother-child relationship with a stepparent the same as with blood. There are cases that may approach that, but I can tell you from being a school principal that when you start in with a divorce, that's something you need to think about. There is no substitute for the real parent. I have no problems with the relationship between the two at all. In my job I see a lot of problems with that. One is that when a child gets in trouble and is disciplined by a stepparent, it shouldn't be any different from being disciplined by their real parent. But if they don't have the real parent there, they assume it wouldn't have been that way. There's really no way to overcome that. I wouldn't try to paint a picture of his relationship with his stepmother as a rosy thing at all, but it satisfies me that both of them tried."*

During this period of my life, I began to adopt some scary values. It was partially peer pressure, but I have to accept much of the blame myself: I was a young Reaganite.

Something that I am now especially ashamed of happened at the supermarket. One of my co-workers had a serious problem with people on welfare. When people used food stamps, she'd say, "Okay, Jim, here we go. It's a food stamp order." This was a signal to me to mash their groceries. Stuff that should go on top, like bread, I'd put at the bottom of the sack. It was an awful thing to do. My favorite prank at the time was crushing their candy bars. It seemed like poor people always bought a lot of candy.

I was just a little bigot for a while. I developed an affection for the South and for old Southern traditions, because I believed that was where a lot of the right-wing conservative views I'd taken up had originated. I even had a Confederate flag in my bedroom. I remember once when I was younger someone told me to call this new girl at school a "hog-nosed Catholic" and I did. In that environment you do these ignorant things; then

[43]

later, if you're lucky enough to start thinking clearly, you realize how awful you were.

I was even worse during my first years in college, where I was openly racist. When I first moved to Saint Louis, I lived in a working-class neighborhood near Saint Louis University. Cars were constantly getting broken into, and I developed this ferocious anger. Like many Americans, I focused my feelings of hate on the fact that the car vandals were black, without stopping to think of the tough circumstances in which they lived and had grown up.

My boss at the Corps of Engineers in Saint Louis, Cherrie Clausen, was black, and I'd tell her about these people breaking into cars and how fed up I was. Fortunately for me, she didn't mind talking about it. Listening to her made me think about things differently. I have to give her credit for transforming my thinking about inner-city blacks; I looked at the situation from their point of view for a change. Where I grew up there weren't any blacks. Douglas County had zero. But, thanks to Cherrie and — I think — thanks to being gay, I've come to hate that type of thinking. I've got a friend who's always saying he didn't get this or that job because he's not a black female. I'm sick of these excuses. I hate it when people blame their problems on minorities. People seem to need scapegoats, but if they'd stop to think, it's utterly ridiculous for them to be blaming minorities for their problems. Minorities are not in power; they didn't create the system; they don't make the rules.

But I was just another Reaganite zombie for much of my youth. And these were the attitudes I was developing during my junior year in high school when I looked into ROTC and the service academies, more or less on my own. I know I didn't discuss it with my dad. I'd first heard of ROTC scholarships in junior high when a recruiting officer came to the school and talked to some of the students with better grade point averages. Although I didn't finally decide then, the idea was planted in my brain. Again, I think the fact that I was a product of the Reagan era had a significant impact on my later decision to apply. It was "in" to serve your country — the whole Reagan "America-is-great" idea, which I really bought into — or was sold.

The military was not exactly a family tradition. I had two uncles who were in the military, but my dad never was. I certainly was never pushed toward the military. No one was more surprised at my decision to join ROTC than my father. He was shocked that I was even interested. What intrigued me about ROTC was the experience I would gain as an officer, the leadership ability I would acquire, and the certainty of those things helping my career. Except briefly as a young child, I had never been fascinated by war or with military equipment. But ROTC fit in very well with an engineering education. Also, if I could get a scholarship it would help pay for school. I'd done very well on my ACT, so I applied for, and received, an ROTC scholarship my senior year in high school. The scholarship paid for my college tuition and books — everything but housing. It was a good deal. In return, I would have to serve either four years active duty or eight years in the reserves. I planned on the reserves.

I don't remember exactly when I decided to apply for an ROTC scholarship. I remember my counselor discussing it with me in terms of paying for college, but I'd already sent off the application. Being an Army officer appealed to me, just from seeing it in movies. It was a life that got you respect, and it was active and often took you outdoors, which I'd always liked.

But as a junior at Ava High School, I was not counting on homosexuality being a part of my life. At the time I mailed in the ROTC application, being gay just didn't fit in my life's plans. At that point, as Mr. Looking-to-the-Future, if it didn't fit into my plans, it wasn't going to happen. I wouldn't say that the idea of suppressing my homosexuality through macho activities like ROTC didn't enter into the picture; it may have. But if it did, I wasn't conscious of it. I do know this for certain: The idea of entering the military as a means of having sex with guys never entered my mind. It was a career move and a means of financing my education.

I believed, too, in what ROTC stood for. Being a Reagan baby, I believed world communism was evil and we had to stand up and fight the communists with the best military possible. Like many others, I saw what happened with the Iran crisis and the failure of our military. So I bought into the idea that we had to pump billions of dollars into the Pentagon to keep the Russkies at bay. Once in a speech class at Rolla, I was in a group assigned to do a report on world communism. With my leadership skills, I took over — really asserted myself and dominated the group. My paper ignored the history and the pros and cons of communism. I simply wrote an essay on what we should do to stop communism. It was far from objective. My professor said, "I can't believe this. You're not even discussing communism. You don't even define it. You just automatically assume it's something evil." That's the frame of mind I had about the military. I believed in it, mindlessly, passionately. Robo, my roommate at Rolla, could certainly attest to that.

**Robo:** *"When we were in school, James was completely right-wing Republican. I mean, he was almost* extreme *right. I was Republican, but being around him really enforced it. He'd get me riled up. He was pro-Army, pro-government, pro-military spending — everything that Republicans seem to stand for today."*

I know now that there were some aspects of the military I was ashamed of, because to some people who asked why I wanted to go into ROTC, I talked up the financial benefits, and to other people I talked up the career benefits. For my parents, I played up the financial side, even though the scholarship was not necessary for me to go to college. I definitely could have gone to school without it. I would have been able to get enough scholarships, grants, and loans on my own. Later, I realized it would have been even easier than I thought. But I don't regret going into ROTC — even now.

The ROTC cadets at Missouri-Rolla and at Washington U were of high caliber. Rolla is 80 percent engineering students, which the military goes after in a heartbeat. Washington is simply a good school. The Reagan era improved the quality of cadets in all schools because, as I've said, it was "in" to be in ROTC. A lot of people who never contracted with the military took ROTC classes simply because it was the thing to do and they got to wear the uniform. It's amazing how things change from one generation to the next. As for me, I never thought of the military as my long-term future. I saw it as a way to help my career as an engineer.

One of the things I changed my mind about before signing the ROTC application was the question, "Could you ever kill someone?" I remember telling a clerk at Town and Country Supermarket that I would gladly serve my country, and gladly risk my life on the battlefield doing humanitarian things, but I would have to be a conscientious objector because I didn't think I could kill another human being — at least not for goals as vague as those in Vietnam. Somewhere along the way, I changed. It happened pretty quickly, for I started working at Town and Country when I was a sophomore, and I was seriously thinking about ROTC as a junior.

Of course, no one viewed war as a strong possibility. The Persian Gulf conflict came as a shock to me and to a lot of my fellow cadets who ended up there. We would go watch movies like *Platoon* and think, "God, this is horrible," but it's not going to happen again, and it's not going to happen to us. I never seriously thought I would use the military tactics I learned. The armed forces advertisements don't emphasize that possibility. They don't even mention it.

When I came to the question asking me if I could shoot or kill someone, I checked the box marked "yes." When I came to the question on homosexuality, it was automatic for me to check "no." I checked it and went on. In fact, it was so automatic that I don't even remember checking the box. In no way did I consider myself gay at that point.

The ROTC accepted my application, offering me one of the few four-year scholarships they award each year.

These were some of the things I was thinking about at my "informal board," along with the long process of coming out of the closet, falling in love, and deciding to tell my commanding officers that I am gay.

But how could I explain to Captain Boyle why I wanted to be an officer? If I could have told him the truth, I would have told him I wanted to be an officer because I knew I'd make a damn good one, and the idea of being one of the first openly gay officers to serve in the United States Army strongly appealed to me. But I knew that was not the answer the captain wanted to hear.

I shrug helplessly and say, "I mean, I could go on forever—"
   According to Hansen's transcript, Boyle says, "Umm hunh."
   "—saying positives or negatives about being an officer in the United States Army."
   "So you don't wish to specify?"
   "Exactly."
   "Okay."
   "I don't wish to specify."
   Next question.
   "What do you feel you have to lose by not receiving a commission in the United States Army?"
   Arlene steps in: "It seems to me the military has an obligation to give him a commission as long as he fulfills all of his course work, unless I misunderstand the ROTC program."
   This doesn't sit well with Boyle. "We have no obligation to commission this young man at all. I want to know why — you know, what it is that you would lose if you do not get commissioned? Do you think it's — I mean, if it's not a priority or an important thing in your life, then what the, you know — I mean, does it really matter with you being here? Does it? What do you feel you would lose if we did not commission you?"
   I say that I would lose being an officer in the military, adding, "I would not like for that to happen."
   Boyle's interpretation of my answer:
   "You don't know?"
   I take another stab at it, getting flustered.
   "Well, I mean, it's just like the pre-pre-pre-preceding question. I mean I could go on — I mean, 'cause I can give you reasons why I want to become an officer — reasons, benefits of being an officer in the United States Army, and I could give you bad things about being in the Army, just like anything else."
   "But there's nothing close to your heart that you feel that you would lose?"
   "By not being commissioned?"
   "By not being commissioned."

"I would — I would not be commissioned as an officer in the United States Army. I would lose the privilege of being an officer."

"Okay. Privilege of being an officer. You think that that is a privilege?"

"Yes."

"Okay. That's a good answer. That's all I'm looking for. I want to know why, you know, what you feel you would lose and what you feel you would gain as an officer. That's all I want. Okay? Is that all?"

"Yes, sir."

It's interesting that Boyle told me that "privilege" was a good answer, the answer he was looking for. In a matter of weeks Boyle would interpret this answer in his "findings" as demonstrating I didn't have a clue as to what being an officer in the U.S. military is all about. "Has not internalized any of the values which are necessary to perform as an Army officer," is the way Boyle would put it. "He only considers it a 'privilege.'" In hindsight, I had every reason to be nervous about my answers. If Boyle thought "privilege" was a "good answer," and if that was "all" he was "looking for," Boyle must have been looking for the rope with which to hang me.

What does the ROTC have to say about the benefits of being an officer? In recruitment brochure RPI667 (December 1987), under the section titled "The Benefits of Being an Army Officer," these reasons are listed: "You'll earn the respect of family and friends, and gain the satisfaction of serving your country as a leader. You'll receive valuable executive and management training, assume important responsibilities, and gain the kind of practical experience you need to help you succeed as an Army officer, and later in your civilian career." So, says the ROTC, one of the benefits to being an Army officer is that you will gain the experience you need to succeed as an officer. It sounds a lot like their goofy explanation that the policy barring gays is based on the policy barring gays (see Appendix).

As unsatisfied as I am with my answer, it doesn't seem so bad in comparison. ROTC brochure RPI664 (December 1988) is more to the point: "ROTC graduates enjoy a lifestyle with its own unique advantages. There are living quarters on nearly all

[49]

Army posts. There are numerous recreational facilities, and the officer's [*sic*] club is always available for on-post social functions, dining, or just plain relaxation. Medical care and hospitalization are covered by the Army." You can imagine the captain's response if I had said I wanted to be an officer so I could use the Army's indoor swimming pools and hang out at the officers' club.

Next question.

"Have you ever received counseling as to your homosexuality?"

Arlene objects, saying again that she has instructed me not to answer any questions about homosexuality. Boyle now presents a statement titled "Denial of Release of Records to ROTC" and suggests that I either sign it or don't sign it. Arlene wants to know the significance of either action. It is explained, sort of, that upon entering ROTC I signed a release of my records, but signing this document would deny the ROTC further access.

"Is there any reason for you to deny us accessing further access?" Boyle asks.

Since she doesn't know what records may or may not exist, Arlene isn't sure, and is inclined to err on the side of caution.

Ritchey explains that not signing the denial means that Boyle "can request any record that pertains to Mr. Holobaugh from Washington University's health care system, or Barnes Hospital, whatever."

Thinking back on it, I was probably more comforted by Sergeant Ritchey than I was by Arlene. In the sense that she was on my side, Arlene was more comforting. But she wasn't familiar with military bureaucracy and Sergeant Ritchey was. I got the feeling that he was at least neutral, and possibly sympathetic to my situation. He explained things in a way that I could understand. I felt he was genuinely trying to help me understand what was happening and what could happen later. Boyle, I think, was irritated with Ritchey for butting in and explaining things to me and making me feel comfortable.

The last explanation by Ritchey, actually, is interrupted by two "right's" and one "yeah" from Boyle, who then adds at the end: "Or anywhere. Right. And — but if there's something that, you know, if you don't want me to have any records for my investigation, then I won't, you know, then I won't bother."

This sounds a little pathetic. "It's not that," says Arlene.

"If you don't have anything, then don't sign the denial," says Boyle.

Arlene asks to see me outside the room. We talk it over and decide to play it safe. Back in the room, I tell Boyle that I'm going to sign the denial, but if he wants my records later on, he can have them.

Boyle goes on to ask a few innocuous questions about my employment history, but eventually gets back to the question of sexual orientation:

"Was your current employer at the time or when you were in the co-op programs, were they aware of your sexual preference?"

Arlene again instructs me not to answer questions concerning sexuality.

"All right," says Boyle, "do you plan on disclosing that fact to future employers?"

Arlene, who must have been thinking she'd fallen into the Land of the Clueless, again advises me not to answer. I take her advice. To my left, Hansen shakes her head. This woman had been shaking her head all through the hearing. It bothered me. I kept wondering, "Is she shaking her head because I'm not answering the questions, or does she think I'm disgusting or horrible?"

Next question.

"Are you fully aware of the courses of action available to the U.S. government in relation to your case?"

Arlene offers, "He's not a lawyer, so—"

"No," I respond. "I'm not fully aware."

Ritchey covers the various scenarios: Boyle will make a determination. If he finds willful evasion on my part, then I will be called before a formal board. If Boyle finds no evidence of willful evasion, he will make a recommendation that I either be "disenrolled" without payback of scholarship, "disenrolled" with payback of scholarship, "disenrolled" and ordered to active duty as an enlisted soldier instead of an officer, or be commissioned an officer. The higher headquarters would then make the final decision, at which point I would be free to pursue any legal avenue I wished.

When Ritchey finishes, Boyle attempts to explain his position. "You see, it's my determination right now on whether there — of whether this warrants — I'm trying to dig up enough information to give me some kind of an idea on whether I should convene a formal board or not. That's my function. I'm trying to figure out what the hell I'm supposed to be doing or whether to go with a formal or not. If I determine that there is no need for a formal board, I will make a recommendation on what I think should be the proper course of action."

Arlene allows as to how she is "not terribly versed in this" and "wasn't really quite sure what sort of information you were looking for."

There follows a discussion on what, exactly, "willful evasion" means. I ask if a person's being homosexual represents willful evasion. Boyle says that's why he wanted me to read the DoD policy. The conceivably sympathetic Ritchey explains that Boyle "has the burden of proof to show that you are homosexual for willful evasion. We haven't done that, so this informal investigation will determine—"

I interrupt: "So an individual who is homosexual is not necessarily willfully evading his contract just by the mere—"

"No, it would have to be proven," says Ritchey.

"Correct," says Boyle. "It is not criteria for *enrolling* in the class."

Arlene: "Even meaning that if somebody might choose to be gay—"

Boyle: "I have no idea. That's why I'm—"

Arlene: "Even though he has said that he wants to be—"

Boyle: "I know you say you want to be commissioned. Let me ask the final question. Would you be willing to submit to a psychiatric evaluation or interview by a military psychiatrist in regard to your homosexuality? I have to figure out whether you are a homosexual or not."

Let's see if the witch floats, in other words. If the psychiatrist labeled me gay, I'm gone. And if the psychiatrist declared me straight, it would open up a Pandora's box of conceivable consequences, including a charge of willful evasion. And how would the psychiatrist determine my sexual orientation? Would I be shown gay porn to see if I got an erection? And exactly what happens to a gay man officially declared straight by a military psychiatrist? Arlene and I reject as absurd the idea of a military psychiatrist divining my sexuality.

The hearing comes to an end with a discussion on timetables for submitting additional documents. Arlene asks if Washington University will be asked for its opinion in the event a formal board is called.

"Yes," says Ritchey. "As to whether or not we were biased."

"Right," says Boyle.

# Rolla

A s I've said, my desire to become an engineer began early in childhood when I became fascinated with Legos, erector sets, and girder-and-panel building sets. I was always amazed by big structures — the large dams in the Ozarks and tall buildings in cities. I was also good at science and math. It seemed only natural, then, that I follow Mrs. Talley's advice and attend college at Missouri-Rolla. Once I got there, though, I found that the school fell short of my expectations. Actually, the worst thing was not the school itself, but its small-town location. Although I'd lived in a small town all my life, at eighteen I'd seen enough of city life to know I wanted to live in one.

But several aspects of the school bothered me. For one, the campus is 80 percent male. You might ask why a gay male would mind. Well, 80 percent of those males were engineering majors, which made for an intense and rather strange environment. Again, you might ask, why I, as an engineering student, consider a plethora of engineering students a drawback. I'll tell you why: Because most of them actually sit around and think of technical things all the time, and I never did. I was shocked to discover that these people actually *enjoyed* discussing the intricacies of engineering. I never did and don't today. I mean, sit around and *talk* about this stuff? Engineering? Get real.

I pledged Delta Sigma Phi fraternity at Rolla with two friends, Glenn and James. Within a matter of weeks, however, all three of us decided we had made a mistake, so we all de-pledged. It is embarrassing for me now to reveal the reason I didn't like the fraternity. But the truth is, we felt that when we pledged fraternity they had kept certain people away from us, then after we pledged, these people came out of the woodwork — students we considered "losers" and didn't want to be around. They were different. They weren't like us. As I've confessed, I was a little bigot at the time. I feel bad about it now. Sometimes I wonder if it takes being gay or being oppressed to make a person realize these things are wrong. I hope not, because not everyone is going to have something happen that compels them to put themselves in someone else's shoes. When I think about what I might be like today if I wasn't gay, it's scary.

Glenn became my best friend at Rolla. The other main person in my life at that time was my roommate, Robo. While everyone in Ava knows me as "Morris," my friends from my days at Rolla still refer to me as "James." It wasn't until I moved to Saint Louis that I became "Jim."

I have to admit that I had something of a crush on Glenn. I'm sure I would have slept with him if he had wanted to, but I was far too frightened of his reaction to ever mention it or make the first move. His friendship was more important to me, and I didn't want to risk ruining it. Sometimes it was awkward, because we used to joke around about gay things a lot, and I often wondered if a sexual relationship was possible. Sometimes Glenn would do some pretty overt things, but I was always too afraid to respond.

Robo, who was a year ahead of me in school, was my roommate for three years. We met by the luck of the draw when we were paired in a dormitory room. We got along so well that we continued living together for three years — the second year in a one-bedroom apartment, the third year in a two-bedroom house in the country.

Thomas Jefferson Hall, the main residence hall at Rolla, is an eleven-floor red brick monolith, the tallest building in town. It sits on a hill, next to a Pizza Inn. Robo and I bought wood and constructed freestanding loft beds in our dorm, putting our desks underneath and freeing up a lot of space that was needed for my computer and Soloflex. It turned out well — we had one of the nicer rooms in the dorm.

*Robo works as a medical physicist. He's soft-spoken, good-look-ing, and tall, with dark blond hair. Lounging on a couch in jeans and a Surf Shop t-shirt in the French-style house he shares with his girlfriend, Karen, he was eager to talk about Jim despite feeling jet lag from having just returned to Saint Charles, Missouri, from Paris the previous evening. Karen — openly friendly and unaffec-tedly attractive — also took an active interest in discussing Jim, appearing to find the whole story fascinating and wonderful.*

*"Rolla is one of the toughest schools in the state," Robo says, when asked what college life was like. "It required a lot of studying, which is what we did most of the time. Then we would party real hard one night a week, or maybe one night every two weeks. A typical party was usually sponsored by a fraternity. We weren't members but we always had friends in fraternities, so one way or another we always ended up being invited to their parties. There are about four men for every woman at Rolla, so right there we were at a handicap. It wasn't like at a big university where it's pretty much equal. They were basically just college drinking parties."*

*Saint Patrick's Day is treated as a major holiday at Rolla. Classes let out Thursday and Friday, and the party lasts through the weekend. People come from all over the state to drink green beer and act crazy. The premiere event features dunking in-dividuals into a huge vat of garbage. Oozy, slimy garbage, at that.*

*"It's kind of a privilege to be elected to be thrown in," says Robo, as Karen laughs, cheerfully bewildered by the concept.*

*There's also a contest to see which team can put the most sweatshirts on its man in a minute. Robo reports that when he and Jim were on campus the record was twenty-seven sweatshirts.*

*"Believe me," says Karen, "as silly as it sounds, people do travel from all over Missouri to do this. It's a party."*

*Robo and Jim developed and explored several interests over the three years they lived together.*

[56]

*"James liked a lot of the same things I did — outdoor activities such as canoeing, camping, and hiking. By our second or third year we had developed a taste for backpacking. We kind of grew into it together. One spring break we went backpacking in the Smoky Mountains. I'm very fond of that trip. We learned a lot about what it takes to do that. The first couple of days we carried too much, but then we trimmed it down. We liked it so much that the next year we did a trip to Mount Magazine, the highest mountain in Arkansas."*

Robo also accompanied Jim to Ava on a couple of weekend trips:

*"I met several of his high school friends, so I got to see where it all started for him. But I know, from what James has told me, that he was pretty much by himself for the last year or so in Ava because he did nothing but work."*

According to Robo, Jim was also pretty much alone when it came to his family.

*"I've seen a father and son closer before than James and his father. I think it might be just their personalities. James's father — he believes in hard work and the person working for everything he gets. He doesn't believe in handouts. That's why James had to work for everything he got. His father wasn't going to try to help him. I think James told me that his father's father was the same way.*

*"His relationship with his stepmom was probably even more strained. Sometimes he'd have to fall back on his father's help to resolve a problem with her. When I'd visit, it always seemed like she would have to force herself to be nice to James. I could sense it, and he always knew it. He'd just blow it off and say that's the way it is."*

Mr. Holobaugh concedes that he did not help much with Jim's college expenses, but thinks it might have been a mistake if he had.

*"With me being a schoolteacher, and having been through the expenses of the death of a spouse and the medical expenses of my second wife, who was in the hospital four or five times, Morris felt a need to pay for most of his education, which he did. I paid for my education totally. It sometimes looks cruel, but I really have a feeling that if a parent had the money to send a child through college without [the child] working, it would be a mis-*

[57]

take. I don't think anything can have much meaning to you unless you have to work for it. That may sound again as if I'm justifying the way I raised my son, but I didn't have the type of money to give him six thousand dollars a year to go to school. He knew that, of course, and that was part of his interest in ROTC. Although it wasn't just money — he was interested in the military, very interested. And I think they were interested in him. They were grooming him for a career in the military and he was doing well. He excelled, certainly."

By the beginning of their third year together, Jim and Robo were becoming creatures of habit.

"At our house in the country," Robo recalls, "James got a Labrador retriever puppy — Dixie. James would come home after classes and spend at least an hour every day training her to retrieve and do all those things a Labrador likes to do. Unfortunately, we could only keep her one year. After that she stayed with his sister.

"We also had the weekly grocery shopping ritual. We'd sit down and plan out a week-long menu. There were several dinners that we knew how to cook that we could fall back on. We knew how to make the basic spaghetti, chicken, hamburgers, and several casseroles, so we'd plan out the menu and make a grocery list from that. We always had a great time shopping together, and we'd just split the bill down the middle. But that year out in the country we got into this habit. We'd come home, and James would cook this baked chicken and these baked potatoes — a very good meal, but we ended up eating it every night. We'd sit down and watch "Wheel of Fortune" and eat chicken. Finally, after several weeks, we'd sit down, look at each other, and just start laughing, because we were so sick of this chicken."

Jim and Robo both decided that three years of living together was enough.

"By that third year," says Robo, "we'd gotten on each other's nerves so much that we were ready to go our own ways. I got sick and tired of him after that third year, I really did. But after we split, we were good friends again. We got back together the following year and did a nice hiking trip together. He's still one of my best friends."

[58]

Robo never had a clue that I was gay, even though during our first year together in the dorm I was involved in a month-and-a-half affair with a guy living down the hall.

I'd had no sexual contact with another male between eighth grade and my freshman year of college. But one night during my first semester at Rolla, I was with this guy named Pete and I got so drunk that I couldn't get up in my loft bed, so I ended up sleeping on Pete's floor. Pete was an attractive guy. I wasn't sure exactly how much we had in common, but he seemed nice enough, and I was definitely interested in him physically, although I hadn't allowed myself to think about it. But when you're drunk, your inhibitions disappear, and as Pete got undressed that night, I raised up from the sleeping bag he had put on the floor for me and just stared at him until he completely undressed — completely nude.

I wasn't even thinking about what I was doing. I must have made it pretty obvious that I was interested in him, because in the middle of the night he crawled down beside me. I was lying on my stomach, when suddenly I felt his hand on my butt. He was lying beside me jerking off. He must have been pretty drunk himself to have the nerve to do that, because — aside from the fact that I might have objected — his roommate was asleep on the top bunk.

I listened to Pete jerk off for a few seconds, and quickly became excited by his touching me. It had been a long time since I had sexual contact with a guy, and I was crazy to experience it again. I knew Robo was gone for the weekend, so I reached over and grabbed Pete and said, "Let's go to my room."

The next day I was excited about the prospect of having a male sexual partner again, but I also felt guilty. I guess Pete didn't know what to think, either, for neither of us mentioned the incident for nearly a week. But as the next weekend drew closer, Pete asked if I wanted to go to Saint Louis to see a Cardinals game. When I told my friend Glenn of our plans, he said, "I want to go." This was awkward, because I liked Glenn a lot more than I liked Pete, but I didn't want him to go because I knew he would get in the way. So I had to say something like, "Well, Pete didn't ask you." He didn't push it.

After Pete and I watched the Cardinals, we went out to a straight bar across the river in Illinois, because the drinking age there was nineteen at the time. Pete was having a good time, taking turns dancing with several women. Some women asked me to dance, too, but I didn't want to. It confused me that Pete was dancing with women. I kept thinking, "Well, maybe he doesn't want anything more to happen between us and this is his way of telling me he's straight."

As we drove back to his parents' house early in the morning, I was pretty bummed out. But then a strange thing happened: Pete stopped the car by this fountain, we got out and were walking around it, and he just fell in. He did it on purpose, for two reasons, I think. First, getting wet gave him an excuse to get partially undressed. Also, it broke the tension of the evening.

We went back to his house and went to bed. He was on the floor, I was in bed. We talked for a while. Then he reached up and started rubbing my arm and said, "Come down here."

After that, our relationship developed quickly. We'd go to Lions' Club Park in Rolla and have sex in the backseat of his Toyota Celica. I can't believe the balls we had, doing these crazy things. But we didn't have many options if we wanted to have sex. The cops came by once and shined a light in the car. Luckily we were in the front seat and weren't doing anything. That could have been the end. But we managed to keep our affair a secret, even though everyone was wondering why we were hanging out together so much.

I'm the one who called off the relationship. I began feeling guilty about the sex and worrying about AIDS. Pete told me he'd never done anything with a guy before, but I wasn't sure I believed him. Nobody was talking about safe sex much at that point — and we had not had safe sex. But it was more than guilt and worrying about AIDS. The main reason I ended it was that it occurred to me one day that I was spending all my time with a guy I really didn't like, just for the pleasure of sex. I had come to dislike him as a person, for he frequently failed to tell the truth and he was extremely materialistic. It began to dawn on me that I was hanging around this dude simply because I liked his looks and enjoyed sex with him. I definitely would rather have been involved with some other guy, like Glenn, but Pete was all I had at the time.

I think I told Pete once that I loved him, but it was nothing but the passion of the moment. It was stupid. I was not in love with him, although there was a certain amount of bonding. I remember going on a field training exercise with ROTC, and lying out in this field in the cold thinking, "What am I doing here? I miss Pete. I want to be with Pete."

I should have sat down and talked to him about my feelings, but I didn't. I just quit talking to him about anything. During Christmas break, he sent me a present and I didn't even call him. Back in Rolla, he asked me what was going on, and I told him I just didn't want to do this anymore. He cried and asked, "Well, can I have one last kiss?" I refused. I was a total jerk about it. I could have handled it much better.

For the next couple of months I was consumed with guilt and convinced I had AIDS. Several times a day I felt my lymph nodes and checked my skin for spots. I was going berserk. It became clear that if I didn't get tested, I was going to drive myself over the edge from worrying about it. So, I did, and it came back negative. I still worried. The test had just come out, so how could I be sure how accurate it was?

The emotional trauma of that experience with Pete drove me back to women. I knew I was attracted to men, but they just didn't seem worth the turmoil. I began dating girls again, and I didn't have sex with another guy until Brent.

I did, however, have sex with women. My most meaningful sexual relationship during this period was with a pom-pom girl named Erin. I'd get excited thinking about having sex with her, but after copulation, as we were lying on the couch watching television, I'd be attracted to the guy on TV and wish he were lying under me instead of her. Although I made a major effort to suppress the feelings that had been reawakened with a vengeance during my affair with Pete, I couldn't. Still, I kept hoping that my relationship with Erin would be the beginning of what I thought of as my heterosexual adulthood. But even though I told her I loved her, and thought that I meant it, I couldn't seem to convince her that it was true. To me, still naive, saying it was enough.

My relationships with females always began and ended the same. The first and last moves — asking them out and deciding to call it quits — were mine. I know I've been lucky. I've never had to go through the hurt of being dumped. I never even had the fear of someone breaking up with me until I met Brent. Before that, I didn't care; it was no big deal. But after I met Brent, I thought back to my relationship with Erin and realized that she had been right — I wasn't in love with her. Once it dawned on me what I had put her through, I felt awful.

*The fact that Jim was dating females when he came to Rolla, and continued dating them during the time he lived there, is one reason his roommate never had a clue he was gay.*

*"When James came to Rolla he had a girlfriend back home," Robo recalls. "When that broke off, he dated regularly with girls around Rolla. I never had any idea he was gay. No sign whatsoever. I know I made jokes about gays but James was right there doing it with me. I try not to be a person who's prejudiced, but sometimes I get caught up in it."*

*In any case, says Robo, Rolla was not the place for Jim to come out of the closet.*

*"A group of gay people tried to come out once, but they were severely suppressed. The student population at Rolla is very conservative. They're all engineers, mostly Republican. They all dress alike, they all drink the same beer, they all do the same thing — so when some different group of people tries to move in on their world, they don't like it. One day somebody put a personal ad in the school newspaper saying if you're gay and interested in forming a group, write to this address. It was an anonymous ad, unsigned, with a P.O. box for replies. The next issue of the paper, there were all these letters to the editor saying, 'How could you print this?' People got very upset about it. Nobody ever heard about the gay people again. They probably decided this is not a town to come out and try anything, and just went back in the closet.*

*"It's kind of a love-hate relationship with that school. You get a very good education, but you hate it while you're there because you have to study so hard — and the social life is so bad."*

[62]

That's Rolla all right, where you can't even run an ad. Even with my self-hating homophobia eating me up at the time, I thought that incident was ridiculous. My attitude was, "Come on, lighten up." But that's how the place was.

A gay organization has finally been formed at Rolla by Wendy Pelton, a therapist who saw the need for such a group from the students she was counseling. Pelton says BI-GALA is more social than political, but that forming the group was hindered nonetheless by administrators in the Student Activities office. But the group was formed, and residence halls like Thomas Jefferson were persuaded to post notices on bulletin boards announcing the group. BI-GALA also obtained new students through an ad in the *Miner*, the campus newspaper.

So there has been change at Rolla, according to Pelton. "But that's not to say that administrators aren't discouraging."

When Pelton returns calls left on her answering machine relating to BI-GALA, she begins by asking the caller if they did, in fact, leave a message. A lot of the calls she receives are prank calls from students leaving the name and number of an unsuspecting friend or enemy.

But just the fact that a group exists is a big step forward. I'd love to speak there sometime.

In the summer and fall of 1985, I began working with Burlington-Northern Railroad in Springfield, Missouri. The job was part of a competitive co-op program for ROTC students majoring in science or engineering. The program provides salaried employment in a high-tech facility. Students work for a semester, then go to school a semester for as many years as they're in the program. I worked in a nine-state area with Burlington-Northern, assisting in the construction of inter-model hub centers. These are facilities designed to transfer trailers from trucks onto flatcars and vice versa. Railways carry the trailers on trains for long hauls, then transfer them to trucks for short hauls.

My job was mainly surveying for quality control. One week I'd be in Dallas, the next week, Florida, and the next week, Kansas City. I traveled all over the Midwest and South to various Burlington-Northern construction projects. It was a lot of fun. I knew all along that I never wanted to live in Ava again, nor, most likely, anywhere in southern Missouri. My co-op experience reinforced that feeling. It made me even more dissatisfied with Rolla. I'd be out in the world having fun, then I'd have to go back to school for a semester in this tiny little town with all these engineering students. I never did like that school.

The following summer I worked again with Burlington-Northern. I also made one last try at a relationship with the opposite sex. Everything went fine until the woman's shirt came off one night while we were making out. She obviously wanted more to happen, but I didn't. She said something like, "I think good-looking guys like you don't think women are attractive enough."

My reluctance to have sex with her cooled off the relationship pretty quickly. Still, I liked her a lot, and I liked her family, too — even though they were right-wing Christian fundamentalists. It's wrong to dismiss people just because they have very conservative views. If you exclude everyone from your life who doesn't agree with you, then you limit your opportunities to make a difference in the world. You can't teach tolerance if you're not tolerant yourself. If you treat people with respect and show patience, a lot of people will come around eventually. It would be especially hypocritical for me to dismiss people; after all, I was a bigot once myself.

In 1987 I lost another person close to me when my Aunt Barbara died of liver cancer. I had drifted away from my mother's side of the family over the years. Although I was close to my grandmother and my Aunt Barbara, we could have been closer. When I was working for Burlington-Northern in Springfield in 1985, I had stayed with Aunt Barbara a lot. She was very religious — I mean *very* religious. She owned a gospel radio station in Springfield and was one of these new fundamentalists who believe it's okay to have money. She never spoke in tongues around me, but I'm sure she did it when I wasn't there. Because of her, I went through a brief religious spurt.

I've often wondered if I would have come out in the ROTC if my Aunt Barbara were alive. I guess I still would have gone public with it, because the thing that forced the issue was Brent, and her existence would not have prevented my falling in love with Brent and the military's inevitably finding out about it. But I would have been very concerned about her feelings.

I remember her doing radio shows on homosexuality. I think she just didn't understand it. When I think of her now, I wish that she was alive so I could talk to her about it. I don't know if my situation would change her mind, but it would make her think. Being the owner of a gospel radio station, she could have made a difference.

I spent the entire 1986–87 academic year at Rolla, living with Robo. Although the co-op work delayed my graduation from college, it was worth it. It gave me an advantage later when I was job hunting.

Part of the money I made from co-op work went toward a new red Jeep pickup. I had driven a '79 blue Chevy Monza for years — a crappy car, too small for me and my dog and the laundry. The truck was nice because of my dog, and because I move a lot. Some people think only rednecks drive trucks, but I think those stereotypes are stupid. Anyone can drive a truck. You don't have to be a farmer. They are extremely practical vehicles.

I have moved around a lot. Although I get tired of moving furniture, I always like the change. I've never stayed in any apartment through more than one lease. Never. I like change in just about every aspect of my life. Brent is the first thing I've ever wanted to hold on to forever.

During the summer of 1987 I got another co-op job working near Saint Louis for the Corps of Engineers. I also went to ROTC Advanced Camp at Fort Riley, Kansas. At the camp I had another opportunity to have an affair, this time with a cadet from a military academy in Missouri. He was exceptionally cute — gorgeous, in fact — and he made it clear he was interested in me. He moved to the bed next to mine, and even followed me to the bathroom once in the middle of the night when I got up to use it. It was an awkward moment. He didn't have to say anything; it was obvious what he wanted. But I was too scared to do anything, so I just went back to bed. Neither of us ever mentioned that episode, but he didn't give up that easy. A few days later six of us had a weekend pass, so we went into town and got a hotel room. He told me he wanted to get a room just for him and me, but I was so stupid that I went along with our buddies when they suggested three to a room. Nothing ever happened between us.

God, I was stupid. Passing up that cadet just proves how frightened I was. It's not every day you meet someone as handsome as that guy.

In the fall of 1987, I took twelve hours of classes at Saint Louis University (SLU). I lived with Craig, a friend from high school who was also going to SLU, and four other guys in a house across the street from a gay bar — Nites, at Vandeventer and Pine. Craig had moved to Ava from California. He was a nice-looking guy but had been picked on a lot when he first came to Ava, I guess just because he was a new kid. That was hard on him because Craig cares a lot about what other people think of him. I always liked him and still do.

Living across the street from a gay bar at this point in my life was strange. It was exhilarating, in a way — but also depressing: a constant reminder of what could be and what I was denying. I remember staring out my bedroom window into the middle distance at the patrons going in and out across the street. I always wanted to go in, and I hated it when people around me made comments about the "fag bar" across the street. On the other hand, sometimes I'd see these outrageously flamboyant guys going in the club and I'd think, "God, no." I was young and insecure and saw flaming queens as a threat to my identity. But the knowledge that there was, in fact, a gay bar that close, and all I had to do was cross the street — that was exciting.

I never gathered the courage to go to Nites by myself, but one night Craig and I and a guy named Dave who had become my best friend at SLU decided to go slumming and "see what it was like." We crossed the street, walked in, and I was pleasantly surprised to find myself surrounded by some pretty good-looking guys. When we got a table, several of these guys came up and started talking to us, very casually and very amiably. I think Craig said something that made it sound like we weren't gay, so one of these guys asked us. We said we weren't, but I stood up and whispered in his ear, "I'm not gay, but I may be back." I'm sure Craig wondered what the hell I was whispering to this guy, but he didn't ask. A little later, after we'd had a few drinks, Dave went to use the restroom and ran into one of his classmates, which embarrassed Dave to death. I don't know if his classmate was embarrassed or not.

Although I never gathered up the courage to go back to Nites by myself, I did reply to a gay personal ad in the *Riverfront Times*, Saint Louis's alternative newspaper. I was incredibly nervous, but I went through with it and met the guy. He was friendly, but even more nervous than I was. We met for dinner, ate, drove around and talked a bit, then went our separate ways. I think we were too much in the same situation to be of much use to each other — both scared and confused, still wondering if this is what we wanted. Neither of us got back in touch.

Because Craig was a member of Sigma Chi fraternity, and because more than a few of the friends I was making in Saint Louis were Sigma Chis, I decided to give fraternity life one more chance. As it happened, Brent had helped to start the Sigma Chi chapter at SLU.

*Brent, a trim young man of medium stature, with dark brown hair and deep-set blue eyes, had graduated and was in medical school at SLU, but was still active in the fraternity, coming back for various ceremonies, initiations, and parties. His influence was still felt.*

*"I was always very much against fraternities," says Brent. "One of my biology instructors was trying to start a chapter of Sigma Chi on campus. I said I'd never do it, but I went to the introductory meeting and thought, 'Well, we have a chance to do something different here — we could get away from all the hazing, and make it something positive. So I decided I would help start the chapter. Of course, it always turns out to be what the others are eventually, despite one's good intentions."*

*Because they were not in school at the same time, Brent and Jim did not know each other well.*

*"I'd gone back to the fraternity once to give a talk," Brent recalls, "and I distinctly remember Jim sitting out there with his*

*arms crossed, his legs stretched out, looking bored as can be. No matter what I did to try to interest this guy in the fraternity, he seemed totally unimpressed."*

I didn't know Brent very well at the time, but I knew that he was a founding member of the chapter, and he knew my face from teaching some pledge classes. As for the lack of hazing, that surprised me. I was expecting to have some fun as a wild fraternity guy, and thought this chapter was disappointingly tame.

At the end of the semester, in January 1988, shortly before returning to Rolla, I finally gathered the courage to go to a gay bar alone. In fact, I went to several.

It was very scary. I darted into Left Bank Books, grabbed a copy of the *Gay News-Telegraph*, which is free, and darted back out. If I'd had to stand at a counter and pay for a copy, I'd never have made it. It's amusing to me now how self-conscious I was, but it wasn't funny at the time.

I drove all over Saint Louis locating the various clubs listed in the bar guide. But each place I went to struck me as gross and scary, so I'd walk in then walk right back out. A lot of the patrons of these places fit the stereotypes I'd learned to hate, and I didn't feel at the time that I had anything to say to a drag queen. As the night wore on, I began to despair. I didn't know how to react to these places. I was afraid there were no other gays in the world like me. I drove down Forest Park Boulevard crying because I didn't know what I was going to do. I knew I was attracted to guys and I wanted to act on it, but I didn't know how.

Finally, I asked someone coming out of Nites if there was a bar around with people my age. He said, "Yeah. The Upside Downtown Club." So I went there. It was on Jefferson Street, just west of downtown Saint Louis. I was so happy when I walked in there and saw people my age. They looked like people I could connect with. But it was still scary. I didn't talk to anyone; I just sat on a stool. There was an old guy staring at me, making me uncomfortable. Then this guy named Steve came up and said hello. I would come to learn that this was

[68]

uncharacteristic of him. He's a nice guy, but he's usually not forward and bubbly. He's the guy who dresses in black and stays in the corner. But that night, he could tell I was scared. I think he knew that the old man was ogling me, so he came to my rescue. We talked a while, I told him I was new at this, and he offered to take me around to some other bars. Among those he showed me was Faces, across the Mississippi in East Saint Louis, where we watched a drag show. I had taken another step.

Although I had decided during my semester at Saint Louis to transfer out of Rolla, I had committed myself to living with an ROTC friend named Tim that spring. I didn't want to let him down and force him to pay double rent, so I went back to Rolla for one last semester and began the paperwork to transfer to Washington University.

Because I had pledged Sigma Chi at SLU, I was also a member at Rolla. So when the Sigma Chi chapter at UMR voted to kick out a pledge whom several members felt was gay, I was a silent witness to the crime. Several people stood up in his defense and said, "First of all, we don't even know if this guy's gay, and even if he is, it really shouldn't matter." But I was too scared to say a word.

A couple of days after the pledge was officially booted out, I went with several fraternity brothers to hear Caspar Weinberger speak. I saw the former pledge sitting off alone, and I felt *so* bad for him. Only a couple of days before, this guy had sixty so-called friends. Now he had none, simply because people thought he was gay. I wanted to go sit by him and say, "Hey, what the fraternity did was wrong." But I didn't. I was such a coward I wouldn't even be seen talking to him. This bothered me for a very long time. Although I wasn't yet ready to call myself gay, a part of me knew the truth, and I felt like such a hypocrite, not supporting this poor guy.

My attraction to men was tested again during my final semester at Rolla. It came from what I considered a most unlikely source: a fellow ROTC student who, like me, was considered a "top cadet." He was attractive, intelligent, and the sort of guy who is everyone's friend because he's just a great guy. He came on to me while we were sleeping in the same tent during field training exercise. Although he never came out and said it, he made it plain he wanted to have oral sex with me. I would never have dared to be so obvious. For me, it was a repeat performance of my reaction at camp. I was so scared I couldn't do anything. And, like before, I kicked myself several times afterward for passing up the chance.

The following summer found me once again working for the Corps of Engineers. I officially transferred to Washington University, and again moved in with Craig. This time, though, Craig was living in a two-bedroom apartment in the central West End with his girlfriend, Nancy.

I also began seeing a therapist. The idea that I was gay was getting to me. The therapist helped me in some ways, but she also said something that confused me: She thought I was bisexual since I had previously had sex with both women and men. I misinterpreted that to mean that a year from then I might be attracted to girls to the same extent I was attracted to guys.

My previous taste of Saint Louis gay life had left me eager for more. When I got back to the city, I phoned Steve and told him if he was ever going out to the bars to call me. Steve said, "Sure," and we went out a few times in May 1988. It turned out Steve knew Brent and knew that Brent was gay. When Steve found out that I was a Sigma Chi from SLU, he arranged for Brent and me to meet at Faces, the gay bar in East Saint Louis where we'd seen the drag show. But he didn't tell me about his arrangement until we were on our way to the bar. Our conversation went something like:

"Well, Jim, there's someone I want you to meet tonight."

"Oh yeah? Who?"

"A friend of mine who's also a Sigma Chi from SLU."

"No way! Turn the car around!"

I had a few ideas who it might be and I didn't want them to know I was gay. But Steve insisted. So, I reluctantly agreed.

When we arrived at Faces and went inside, there was Brent! I've rarely been so surprised, or so happy, in my life. Brent was surprised, and, I think, happy, too. That meeting changed my life forever.

# Brent

**B**rent was born April 20, 1963, in Toledo, Ohio. His father is an engineer who moved the family from place to place across the Midwest — Ohio, Michigan, Wisconsin, Illinois, and Iowa. The family is Polish Catholic.

"I had always thought Saint Louis was nothing but asphalt," says Brent. "But a friend from high school went to college there. She sent me a clipping of grass one time, and convinced me to come for a visit. I enjoyed it a lot. Saint Louis University has a good pre-med program, so I decided to enroll."

Brent did not come to terms with being gay until he was in med school.

"By the time I met Jim and Steve, I was accepting it pretty well. That was in my junior year of med school."

Like Jim, Brent had experimented with both sexes and had been dating a woman.

"She was a terrific person. But I had a major coming-to-terms with things one night after we attended a formal dance. I could either ask this woman to marry me and do that whole thing, or I could choose another route. I realized that I could have kids and do everything I was supposed to do in a marriage, but I couldn't be totally fulfilled that way. I realized marrying her wasn't what I wanted to do.

*"She and I have remained close friends. In fact, Jim and I just went whitewater rafting with her."*

*Steve was going to Washington University Medical School when he met Brent. They were doing rotations together at the local Veterans Administration Hospital, and started going out to eat together. During one of their restaurant visits, the people at a nearby table peppered the air with homophobic remarks. Brent could tell from Steve's reaction that he was gay. They became good friends, and even had a brief relationship.*

*"Steve is very uncomfortable with relationships," Brent says. "I think that's why he introduced Jim and me."*

*Brent's reaction to meeting a gay fraternity brother was much the same as Jim's:*

*"Steve was telling me he had someone he wanted me to meet, but I told him I didn't want to meet anybody. He said, 'Well, he's in a fraternity,' and I was like, 'Oh great, we're going to have like a million things to talk about.' Then he told me the guy was in my fraternity. I didn't have any idea who this guy was. I always hated to go to bars, but because Steve really wanted me to go, I did."*

Faces is an unlikely place to meet the love of your life. East Saint Louis itself is a dive, and it's difficult to say whether Faces is better or worse than its surroundings. There aren't many places in the United States with higher crime rates than East Saint Louis. The parking lot of Faces has armed guards. On the ground level there's a dance floor reminiscent of the seventies — very glitzy, with disco music and people jammed together doing poppers. Upstairs is the drag show, reputedly the best in town. Downstairs is a square bar with a video screen in the back showing hard-core skin flicks. Later, a dark room was added, but it wasn't there at the time I met Brent. It's what I imagine gay bars were like before 1982 — before the crisis — and it's sleazy even by those standards.

I had been working as a doorman at a straight bar called Tops. At Faces that night, I ran into two people from work I hadn't known were gay. I was happy because suddenly, for the first time, I had several people in my life who were gay — Steve and these co-workers.

[72]

Plus, I met Brent. We found that we actually did have a lot to talk about, and we felt remarkably comfortable talking to each other. We discussed being gay and what guys in the fraternity would think if they knew. Brent said, "I don't care what people think." I said, "I do." We both talked around getting together again, but neither of us was brave enough to suggest it. I did ask him for a ride home. We exchanged phone numbers — and he called the next morning.

Craig answered the phone. At that point Brent knew Craig better than me, but they certainly never called each other. Craig was like, "Well, *Brent,*" obviously surprised that he'd phoned. Brent said, "We're having this party. Why don't you come over — and bring your roommate." Craig asked me if I wanted to go, and I was like, "Yes! Yes! Let's go!"

*Brent: "We talked throughout the evening at Faces and enjoyed each other's company. Jim needed a ride home, so I dropped him off. It turned out he lived pretty close to me. The next day I changed my running route. I was running about six miles a day at that time, so I ran by his building to see if I could spot him. I was living with five other guys in a house with a pool and barbecue grill in back. It was Memorial Day weekend, so I called up Jim, not knowing who his roommate was. When Craig answered the phone, I recognized his voice, so I said, 'Craig, why don't you come on over for a barbecue or something?' I hadn't talked to Craig in a couple of years. Then I asked, 'Why don't you bring your roommate, too?' They came, and that's what got things rolling.*

*"Then Jim and I started going to Cardinals games and movies, spending a lot of time together. It was totally a nonphysical relationship for quite a while. But we quickly became close friends. It wasn't unusual for me to come home and hear my roommates say, 'Oh, Jim's in the backyard swimming.' He'd jump the fence and go swimming. He made himself totally at home.*

*"One thing that helped build our relationship — and this is odd, because neither of us drinks much at all — was going to a Cardinal baseball game one time when it was very cold and getting drunk. We stopped in at a bar next to the stadium and had*

*a few shots to get warmed up. Then there was an hour-and-a-half rain delay, when we kept drinking and talking at the stadium. We kept seeing people we knew all over the stands, so we'd go talk to them. Some of them were fraternity brothers, and we could tell they were thinking, 'Why are you two together?' But we didn't care. We had a good time drinking together."*

In the beginning I thought I was more interested in Brent than he was in me. Brent is a very handsome man, and one of the nicest people you could ever meet. It was clear from the beginning that he was someone you could plan to spend your life with. He obviously had his life together, his priorities in order. He was just the sort of person I'd been searching for.

In the beginning, though, I didn't know what was going on between him and Steve. But one night at this little bar, I was forward. I told him I certainly wouldn't be sorry if something happened between us. At that point, I had to say something to him because I was going nuts. I was thinking about him all the time, and I was really scared — afraid he wouldn't like me or that it wouldn't work out. I wanted to be with him every day, all the time. I didn't dare push it, but I was obsessed with him.

One day while I was working at Tops, Brent came by and asked if I wanted to go to a movie after work. I suggested we rent one and watch it at my place, since Craig and Nancy were out of town. So we did. I guess Brent was expecting stuff to happen — he brought things to stay all night. Just as the movie was ending, Brent put his hand on my hand — and that's all it took. We stayed in bed until two the next afternoon.

As the relationship with Brent developed, things got complicated on the home front. Craig, aware that Brent and I had not known each other very well, found it odd that we became such close friends so fast. When Brent began staying all night in my room and I started sleeping over at Brent's, Craig knew something was up. Eventually, Craig asked Brent if I was gay, and Brent said, "Well, you better talk to Jim about that."

When Brent told me about Craig's question, I decided it was time for Craig and me to talk. But I still wasn't ready to come out of the closet. I told Craig that I wasn't gay but that Brent and I were messing around and I assumed a lot of people did. The

[74]

news didn't seem to bother Craig much. But he said, "Well, we can't let Nancy know what's going on. I've got to tell her that you're not." I said fine. But Nancy soon knew, because Brent was spending so much time there.

The tension with Nancy turned into a crisis when Glenn, my best friend from Rolla, came to visit. He brought a friend with him, and at one point during their visit, while Glenn and I were out of the apartment, Glenn's friend was talking on the phone to his girlfriend in Arizona. After he hung up Nancy asked, "You have a girlfriend? You mean you're not gay like Jim?"

Glenn's friend, who had no clue what was going on, later asked Glenn, "Did you know your friend's gay?"

Glenn said, "No way! There's no way!" Glenn didn't say anything to me about it until the afternoon they were leaving. He and his friend and I were at a restaurant having one last meal together, when Glenn suddenly says, "You know, Nancy's been saying that you're gay."

I was stunned that Nancy had said that, and I couldn't believe that Glenn was bringing it up in front of this friend of his whom I hardly knew, and in the middle of a restaurant. If it had just been the two of us I might have told him the truth. But I said, "No, I'm not. Nancy's full of shit. We fight a lot, and she's just saying this to get at me." Glenn seemed to believe me, and they left. Then I confronted Nancy.

I was *so* angry. We really had it out. When I called her on it, her face told everything. I could tell she despised me and wouldn't think twice about doing me harm. She said whatever she could think of to hurt me, threatening to tell my parents that I was gay, and threatening to tell my friends. I was really afraid I would lose control. Eventually, on another occasion, I did. She was again threatening to out me to everyone I knew, and I became so enraged that I just grabbed her and started shaking her. At that point I realized I had to get out of the apartment before I did something crazy.

I'm not sure why Nancy had such a big problem with my being gay, unless she was afraid something would happen between Craig and me. If so, it was an irrational fear since, as far as I know, Craig is straight.

After moving out, I didn't talk to Craig for two years. Only recently, though, Brent and I called Craig's mother and asked her to have Craig call. He did — and he apologized for what happened and said he and Nancy had broken up. I apologized too for the way our friendship had crumbled. Craig said he never had any problems with my being gay. I'm glad we patched up our friendship.

I had to find a place to live in a hurry, so I contacted the university's roommate service. I immediately found a home with this neat woman who was renting a condo in the West End. Carolyn Lang, a nurse anesthetist, was terrific. I liked both her and her place. She seemed like an open-minded, easygoing person who would have no problems with Brent and me. I decided not to tell her I was gay because I didn't think it mattered, and I got the impression that it wouldn't matter to her. She figured it out, though, soon enough.

*Jim moved to Carolyn Lang's place in February 1989. He lived with her during the spring and fall semesters of that year, but spent the summer in Connecticut with Brent. Carolyn has short, dark auburn hair with a streak of white. Wearing gold hoop earrings and sitting cross-legged on her couch, she discusses Jim, obviously missing her old friend.*

*"The place I was living was nice, but expensive, and I was having financial troubles," Carolyn says. "I didn't really want to advertise, so I called the university's roommate service and left my name. I had several people call, but Jim was the right one. He mentioned that he had a friend, and later he brought him over for me to meet. I thought they were both very nice."*

*"Carolyn's funny," says Brent. "She's an incredibly open, intelligent, vivacious person. She kind of goes through life seeking something, but I don't think she knows what it is. I hope she finds it, because she's a very nice person."*

*Carolyn called Jim's basement bedroom "the little cave."*

*"It was a place he could have some privacy," she says. "The walls were rough, and there were only two little windows, so it wasn't very light. That's where he had his waterbed, his TV, and his stereo. He had a very nice waterbed. And books — he had a*

lot of schoolbooks. He had a half-bath, but no shower, so he had to come upstairs to shower."

Jim recalls that there was a water leak in "the cave," and that once, after it had been raining for several days, water began spurting "like a fountain" from the limestone blocks that made up his walls.

How long did it take Carolyn to figure out that Jim and Brent were lovers?

"I kind of guessed it right away, but I didn't want to say anything because, gee whiz, it's his life. No girls ever called, and he never called any girls. I just thought, Oh well, o-kay. Of course, Brent was always sleeping over. They were always very quiet, very discreet. They never made any noise. I thought, O-kay. And he spent a lot of time over at Brent's, too — about half and half. They seemed to get along well — never had any problems.

"I never brought it up. He brought it up. It was before he went east to work that summer. He came to me and said, 'Carolyn, how would you feel if you found out your son was gay?' It was kind of heart-wrenching at the time, and I thought, 'I have to say just the right thing.' Then I thought, 'Well, I'll just tell him what I really think.' I said, 'It really wouldn't make any difference, I'd still love him.' He seemed to accept that. I could tell there were big problems with his father because his father is sort of — right wing. His sister seemed to be the opposite, and he was close to his nephew.

"You just couldn't tell his sexual orientation by looking at him or talking to him. He and Brent really didn't like flames. Jim said, 'They just give gays a bad name.' I think Jim believed that he's a person first — with a mind and a body and a life to live like anybody else, and sexual orientation shouldn't matter. But some people's views are — not always fair."

Carolyn says the Jim she knows is a complete, multifaceted individual, with many interests:

"He was independent, conscientious, hard working, industrious, a hard studier. He'd sit at the table for hours and hours and hours working on his assignments.

"Jim was very into Saint Louis life. It isn't as cosmopolitan as other places, but there's always Forest Park, or Balloon Day, or

[77]

*Saint Patrick's Day. He loved to eat at the 94th Aero-Squadron by the airport, and he really liked Trotters, a restaurant with an all-you-can-eat barbecue smorgasbord. He liked to go to concerts and see plays at the repertory theater. He really liked getting things for his nephew — he'd have a blast buying things for special people. He loved the Sunday morning newspaper.*

*"And get this — Jim loved to clip coupons. I'd get the newspaper and he and Brent would be like, 'Can I have that one?' over the coupons. He's very thrifty. He would buy a turkey and use it for umpteen meals. He liked to barbecue chicken a lot on the grill. Jim's a cooker, whereas I'm a nuker. He'd fix a stir-fry sometimes and ask me to eat with him, but it seemed like our schedules never worked out. We rarely ate together."*

I don't mind cooking, and it doesn't surprise me that Robo and Carolyn tell these stories of my umpteen meals with fowl. But cooking is not something I love. I don't sit around thinking, "I'd rather be cooking." As for thrifty — yeah, I am. I guess I get it from my dad. When it comes to things like computers and cappuccino makers, I like to buy the best. But I'll admit, I was really excited when I moved to Connecticut and saw that phone calls were only a dime.

As for the theater, I like plays, but I'm hardly a fanatic. Before I met Brent, Broadway shows were something I never once thought about. Brent buys all the original-cast CDs. I like them if the songs are good enough to stand on their own. But I don't like these singing conversations — "I'm going to the store, I'm buying some bread" — things that you would normally just talk about.

*"Jim loved music," says Carolyn. "He bought himself a CD player and just loved it. He loved to work out at the gym, and was very conscious about what he looked like. He was sort of like a health nut — very much into healthy eating, healthy everything. Low-calorie healthy. He'd have a beer every now and then, but didn't drink much. He's more of an afternoon and evening person than a morning person. He'd rather sleep in if he can. He didn't really have a lot of friends over. He's pretty private. Not a lot of calls, either. Sometimes one of his classmates called about studying,*

*getting together for this or that. He's probably a lot like me — he had special people that he talked to, but not a lot of gibberish. He seemed to stay busy with school and didn't have a lot of extra people around. But he did go to some lesbian and gay get-together. He said that was kind of fun. That was his last semester.*

*"Jim had some 'dreaded stepmothers,' who, he said, were not real good to him. I believe he has a need for mothering. I didn't mother him; I was just there. Still, I think that deep down there's some insecurity there, because he didn't have that when he was growing up.*

*"As for his father, there are definitely differences. They seem to be distant. He tried to talk to his dad several times on the telephone when I was in the room. It was a strained conversation — I don't know why. He may be able to talk to him better now, since he's more vocal and something of a national figure.*

*"It was very unusual for his dad to call."*

I felt that we had the appropriate relationship for a father and son, that things with my dad and me were just where they should be, no more, no less. When I was a child, I was comfortable talking to my dad about things of little importance. But we never had any in-depth talks. When I was in the eighth or ninth grade, he asked me if I needed to talk about sex, but by then it was much too late. Still, I thought our relationship was fine. It wasn't until after I left home that I began to wonder if perhaps the traditional role between a father and son in America isn't quite enough. The things I needed to open up and talk about were important things I couldn't talk about: such as being gay. That's when I felt a lot of space come between us, when there were so many things going on in my life that I couldn't discuss with him. But I don't think he ever felt that.

As a child I wasn't very close to Melanie. I saw her as an adversary. It was the same relationship I saw in a lot of brothers and sisters — just picking on each other a lot. When she was in high school, our paths just didn't cross that often. She was popular and dated a lot. I remember being attracted to quite a few of her dates.

In a way, I was lonely in high school because I was never close to any girls. I had some crushes on guys, but that can be

[79]

very lonely, too — having those feelings and not being able to do anything about them. I think it would be so terrific if homosexuality was as accepted as heterosexuality. To me, that would be the ultimate — to be in high school and be able to walk up to a guy and ask him out on a date, with no more anxiety than you would have if the person were female. Now *that's* exciting.

When my dad and Kay divorced, Melanie — who was in college in Springfield — started coming home a lot, and we became close for the first time. We were even closer once I went away to college. I always felt comfortable talking to her — until lately. Now I'm not sure what's happening. Things change from one conversation to the next.

*Carolyn recalls that Jim and Brent did eventually have an argument — over whether or not to combine their checking accounts.*

*"I just wasn't totally willing to give up my independence," Brent admits. "It was selfish on my part, because Jim was always pressing for a joint account. We kept them separate until Jim moved to Connecticut. It's worked out perfectly, and now I can't imagine doing it any other way.*

*"I feel very fortunate that I have someone like Jim. He's my best friend — he's everything. When I think of myself, I don't think of just myself, I think of us. Everything that we plan is for us. I feel lucky because I think a lot of people, gay and straight, don't get that."*

At first Brent thought a joint bank account would be a logistical nightmare. I explained to him that straight couples do it. Also, I felt it would be better if we stopped buying so many things separately — with this being mine and that being his, instead of everything being ours. I felt we should be proceeding under the conviction that we would never break up.

The one thing that bothers me about Brent is that sometimes he's insecure — about me. I think he worries about my going to speaking engagements, afraid I'll meet someone else. I just wish he'd realize how much I love him and not let things bother him.

While I had to change lodgings because of my relationship with Brent, the houseful of men living with Brent had no problem with my sleeping over. It was never discussed, but they knew something was going on because I slept there all the time. One morning I was trying to sneak out of the house. I crept downstairs, looked around, but failed to see John, Brent's roommate, sitting on the couch. I was slowly opening the door when John said, "Bye, Jim." It was funny. So, they knew what was going on. In fact, when that house sold, John asked Brent to live with him. Brent did and I stayed over there all the time. John never mentioned our relationship to either of us. He just accepted it.

# A change of heart

Sometimes people ask if I have any clue why I turned out gay. Even if you're never asked, it's a question you'd naturally ask yourself at some point. But it is a question without an answer. People once said that boys who grew up without fathers or were too close to their mothers had a good chance of turning out gay. I grew up without a mother. So, I have no idea why I am gay — or why anyone else is. If I was the only gay person in the world, I might be able to point to something that happened in my life, like my mother dying, and work out a theory. But because I know so many other gays who have virtually nothing else in common with me, and have very dissimilar backgrounds, it is impossible to figure out. Now scientists are studying possible genetic causes. Maybe that will explain it.

Whatever the reason, as I began coming to terms with being gay, I slowly divorced myself from my Reaganite youth. Part of it was knowing who was on my side and who wasn't. It was, after all, the Reagan administration that closed the loophole in military regulations, making the mere state of being gay grounds for dismissal, not just homosexual acts. Also, it doesn't take a genius to figure out which political party in America is most sympathetic to gay rights — and its symbol is *not* an elephant. But the change in me went much deeper.

As I began to feel bad about taking part in gay jokes in my youth, I also began to regret taking part in racist jokes, and I began to look at all minorities, anyone who was "different," in a new light.

The person who had seen my conservative side at its most extreme was Robo. When we were roommates, I would cuss Democrats when they were on television. I'd call them "fucking liberals." When I started changing my views, I was ashamed of the way I'd behaved and the things I'd said. Although I was not yet ready to tell Robo I was gay, I wanted to let him know that I had been wrong — that not only had I ceased believing all that right-wing nonsense, I was ashamed of buying into it in the first place.

*Robo first learned of his friend's political changes soon after Jim moved to Connecticut:*

*"After James left Rolla and was gone for a year or so, I was talking to him on the phone one day and he said, 'I've really changed. I'm not a Republican anymore. I've completely turned the opposite.' I didn't understand it. I thought maybe it was his being in New York, because everyone's more liberal there than in Missouri. Later, when he told me he was gay, I could understand the 180-degree flip in his political thinking."*

*Another friend who noticed Jim's changes was John Taylor.*

*"I still saw him quite a bit after high school," says John. "I was going to the School of the Ozarks and we'd see each other over holidays and sometimes on weekends. I always was and still am a Democrat. He was a Republican, and not your average Republican — he was staunch. Then he came back to town and we were discussing some things, and I realized his political views had done a complete one-eighty. I thought, 'God! What's gotten into you?'"*

My conversion was gradual. At first, I still saw myself as a Republican. Although I often came across policies I did not agree with, those issues were not enough to make me switch parties. I had this image built up in my mind of who I was, what I believed in, and the role I played in society — and Jim Holobaugh was a Republican. But when I could honestly say to

[83]

myself, "I'm gay," then I could honestly say anything to myself. I could examine any issue without worrying about what other people might think about me. That's when all of these Republican ideas started tumbling down like dominoes, one after the other. I started looking at things through the eyes of other people.

It is an interesting concept: Republicanism as a selfish facade, a state of mind, easily blown away by a good dose of honest self-evaluation. It's what makes former ultraconservative Republican party chairmen and Reagan campaign chairmen confess on their deathbeds that what they did was wrong. But does it have to take inoperable brain cancer or AIDS to make someone understand the fallacy of the politics of hatred? Does it take being gay? If I wasn't gay, would I be a different person today? Absolutely. I believe I would be much less sensitive to other people and their beliefs.

One of the influences in the Republican party that drove me away was the religious right. I see them as a bigger enemy than the Republican party. The Republicans just pander to these people, and that includes taking part in their antigay rhetoric. I don't understand why these people are preoccupied with the gay issue. Contrary to what they say, gays are not asking for any special rights; we just want an end to discrimination against us. It doesn't hurt anyone for a city to adopt an equal protection ordinance that includes sexual orientation. It simply means that some people can live with a little less fear and not worry about losing their jobs or being kicked out of their houses.

Yet time after time, these Bible-thumpers work up petitions and gather signatures to have antidiscrimination ordinances repealed. Don't they have better things to do with their time? What's their motivation? I don't understand their compulsion to persecute us, but it bothers me a great deal. I can understand having religious objections to homosexuality. That's fine. But I don't know how, morally or ethically, they manage to work it out in their minds that discrimination against gays is justified.

Brent, on the other hand, until recently still called himself a Republican.

**Brent:** *"I feel like I'm a moderating force on Jim. There's no middle ground with him; he has a hard time seeing gray. I think that has to do with my liberal arts education. Jim's was cut-and-dry engineering. He was a totally conservative Republican, and now he says he's the absolute liberal Democrat. I have problems with either label. I've always been pretty conservative, but, yes, I have changed my political beliefs. I campaigned for Ronnie and all that, and considered myself a pre-yuppie. As time has passed, I've seen there are problems with all of that. I guess I'm more of a moderate than anything else. I'm more conservative on economic issues, but when it comes to social issues, I'm very liberal — probably because I deal with it every day at the hospital.*

In some ways Brent is more compassionate than I am. He wouldn't have burned snakes and turtles when he was a child. When we watch a sad movie, he will be the first to have tears in his eyes. He works himself up about things. But when it comes to politics, I am the one who gets worked up. I think five years ago I was far more conservative than he was, but my pendulum of ideology just whizzed by him. He is a moderating factor, but it makes me quite angry sometimes. I think he does it on purpose to smooth out my rough edges. Every time we discuss politics, he's always a little to the right of me. Even when we watch a talk show, I'll be more to the left than Brent. But the thing that really annoyed me was his claiming to be a Republican. No matter how much he wanted to believe it, I knew that Brent was not a Republican. Brent and I each have our areas of expertise, and I feel that politics is something I know more about because I am more interested in it.

Sometimes I can be offensive. For instance, if we are standing in a grocery store checkout lane and I see a *National Enquirer* or some other sensationalist tabloid, I am likely to go off about it or about Bible-thumpers or something. Brent will say, "Jim, these people around you may be fundamentalists." But it doesn't bother me if they hear me.

A lot of gays have gone through experiences like mine and not been transformed. Leonard Matlovich remained a Republican and was campaigning for Republican candidates long after he was openly gay. When he opened a pizza restaurant in

[85]

California's Russian River area, Matlovich placed on the wall a photo of Barry Goldwater inscribed, "In your heart you know he's right." Although Matlovich's conservatism softened after he was thrown out of the Air Force and the Mormon Church, his politics did not change drastically until he was dying of AIDS.

Matlovich had tried to form a Republican gay think tank with several powerful gay officials in the Reagan administration and several of Reagan's personal friends who were gay. But the fact that all of these people were closeted (except Matlovich and Robert Bauman, the former Maryland congressman arrested for having sex with young hustlers) made it impossible. Shortly before his death, Matlovich did protest the Reagan administration's lack of action in facing the AIDS crisis by demonstrating in Washington with Dan Bradley, head of the Legal Services Corporation during the Carter administration, and 350 others. The former Reaganite was arrested while sitting in the middle of Pennsylvania Avenue and tying up traffic in front of the White House.

So, why did I change? I think because gay rights means more to me than it does to some other gays. Republican gays obviously feel that there are other issues more important than gay rights, and they agree with the Republican party on those issues. But I see gay rights as being extremely important, not just to me but to society. Being willing to look at people with tolerance, to accept diversity, is important to America. It affects a lot of things other than gay rights. The Democratic party is much more in tune with that.

I suppose I am an activist at heart. If I wasn't fighting for gay rights, I would be fighting for something else. Before, I was a conservative activist. I had bumper stickers on my car for various Republican candidates. I even gave money. Now, the people I admire are openly gay congressmen Gerry Studds and Barney Frank. But if there is anyone I would consider a hero, it is Martin Luther King, Jr. Imagine that little Reaganite bigot back in Rolla saying that, and you will see how completely my thinking has changed since I came to terms with my being gay.

Once we realized we wanted to spend our lives together, Brent and I decided to live in the New York City area. We knew Brent was going to finish school a year before me. Neither of us wanted to stay in Saint Louis, so we sat down and discussed the places he could go for his residency. We ended up with our first choice, which was the Connecticut–New York area. We knew I could get a job there and we liked the area a lot.

*"We looked at a lot of places," says Brent, who graduated from medical school in May 1989. "I remember the hospital in Peoria calling me. It seemed like a good program, but we didn't want to go there."*

*Jim, sitting with Brent wrapped in his arms on the floor of their apartment in Connecticut, recalls, "I gave him a card that said, 'I'll follow you anywhere except Peoria.'"*

*"Connecticut was my number-one choice," says Brent. "I used to come to New York a lot for vacations. It felt like the center of everything. Now I like the East Coast in general more than I like Manhattan in particular. I like the seasons, the beautiful scenery, being so close to history, and the ocean. I love being near water — and the Mississippi River doesn't quite cut it. We go to Cape Cod often, or anywhere we can, just to get to know the area. I think we both needed to get out of the Midwest for a while."*

*Jim's move east did not surprise his father.*

*"He's living in an area where he probably would have to live to be a pronounced gay," Mr. Holobaugh says. "But he educated himself out of a small town, anyway. You don't become an engineer and want to live in a small town. He told my dad when he was a tiny boy that one day he'd make his living sitting at a desk in New York City."*

I always enjoyed cities and knew I wanted to live in one. You can live in the city and enjoy outdoor things, too; you don't have to live on a farm to go outdoors.

My college transcripts show that I excelled in my ROTC courses. The transcripts from Missouri-Rolla list A's in all six military science classes, and in the speech class taught by the liberal professor who always argued with me. In the words of

[87]

my ROTC commanders, I was a "top performer." I became second in command of the entire ROTC battalion at UMR and I even appeared in a recruiting ad for the Army that ran in newspapers and magazines nationwide.

I enjoyed ROTC. In fact, because I was always coming home and telling him about all the fun I was having, Robo even took some ROTC classes. I was active in ROTC's extracurricular activities, such as Pershing Rifles, a drill-and-ceremony outfit, and Raiders, an organization that practices military tactics and fighting. I enjoyed Raiders more than Pershing Rifles. The drill and ceremony of the rifle unit was kind of boring, but I liked the camaraderie.

Although I was a "top performer," there were some experiences I would rather forget. Once, when the Pershing Rifles went to a drill-and-ceremony meet in Saint Louis, I was put in charge of the color guard for the first time. There are a lot of events in these meets, and we had practiced for all of them — except the color guard!

My commanders said, "Don't worry about it, it's easy. You already know the commands. Just watch the groups in front of you."

That seemed simple enough, but we got up there and guess who was going first? Missouri-Rolla. I was in charge and I had no clue what to do. I marched us onto the parade floor as if I knew what I was doing, then faced us toward the guy in charge. I didn't even ask permission to be on his floor — a major breach of etiquette. We just faced him — didn't salute or anything — then marched around aimlessly for a bit. I called out "right face, left face" a few times, while people looked at one another wondering, "What is this guy doing?" I didn't have the faintest idea when to stop or how to finish. Spotting a side garage door that was open, I maneuvered us through it and we casually disassembled. It was awful — like we were a bunch of fools who just showed up and marched around for five minutes and went out the side door. I felt like such an idiot. We finished a well-deserved last place.

Even though I enjoyed much of my experience with ROTC, there were some things I disliked. A lot of the traditions and regimentation seemed ridiculous. I was never into the haircut and dress bullshit. There were a lot of people in ROTC who felt like I did, but there were others who really got off on spit and polish. I hated wearing the uniform, especially to class. And I was constantly harassed about my hair. I thought, as long as my hair's neat, what's the problem? It was cut short, above my ears, off my collar, and my attitude was, "Leave me alone! I'm in college; I'm not in the Army yet."

I always considered myself a college student first and an ROTC cadet second. I didn't want to be an ROTC geek who did nothing but ROTC. People get so excited about the silliest things. Nevertheless, I was a very good cadet. I was honest, and I think a lot of the officers shared my views. The things that were important, I excelled in. So when I told them to fuck off about my haircut, it didn't affect my overall ratings.

People used to call me Rambo. I got the name because I nailed a tank with one LAW (light antitank weapon) rocket. This is the rocket that Rambo fired at the helicopter in the movie. It costs taxpayers about a thousand dollars each time one is fired. But I was tagged with the nickname more out of sarcasm than respect, for everyone knew that, like Rambo, I did not like the spit and polish of the military.

My work in the summer and fall of 1987 with the U.S. Army Corps of Engineers and the Department of Army Scientific and Engineering (DASE) co-op program landed me at the Melvin Price Lock and Dam in West Alton, Missouri. They were involved in a twelve-year, billion-dollar project replacing a lock and dam. My job was to review shop drawings and make inspections to be certain the steel was in the structure before they poured the concrete.

The work I performed with the Corps was apparently pretty good. My supervisor, Vick James, wrote a letter of recommendation that concluded, "Mr. Holobaugh's work constantly reflected sound judgment. He accepts responsibility readily and performs his duties with efficiency. I have found his character and personal reputation to be exemplary."

In any case, someone in the military thought I *looked* good doing the co-op work. Out of the blue, I received a phone call from Young-Rubicam, the New York advertising agency that handled the Army's account. They sent someone to the site to take my photo, then called me back and said they were going to use me in a recruiting ad. I wasn't sure what to think. Why me? This was a nationwide ad campaign, after all. I now think they chose me because I fit their image of what an ROTC cadet should be. I was what they wanted to project. The ad shows me perched atop steel girders in a bulky sweater, hard hat in hand, a smiling portrait of good spirits and good health. The lock and dam are in the background. They quoted me as saying, "The DASE co-op program is like a course in real life. The big thing it offers is experience, and that's what companies look for. There are things I've learned on the job that I couldn't learn in school."

It is an irony probably lost on the military that many of their advertisements, including this one, are homoerotic. The bodies they highlight, with their flexing muscles climbing ropes or bounding over hurdles, and their alternately boyishly grinning and sternly frowning faces, are most likely to excite the very youth they least want in their ranks — masculine gays. This is especially true of their television commercials. If the military wants an exclusively heterosexual force, they could start by using only homely boys in their ads — or, at the very least, refrain from making sexy, glistening bodies the focal points for their campaigns.

I signed a release giving permission to use my photo and quotation in the co-op ad in exchange for one dollar. I still have the uncashed check.

I also attended ROTC Advanced Camp in the summer of 1987. The camp is designed to test cadets' leadership skills. One interesting concept is that each cadet is matched up the first day with a "warrior buddy." For six weeks you and your warrior buddy do everything together. Your bunks are on top of each other, in the field you share a tent, and you are supposed to know where your warrior buddy is at all times. It sounds suspiciously like the Sacred Band of Thebes — the army of lovers. This is interesting, since one quarter of the ROTC shield is a Greek helmet, symbolic of the Greek concept of the warrior scholar. Again, to anyone with the slightest knowledge of ancient history, it is a concept steeped in homoeroticism of the most heroic sort. Luckily for the ROTC, most of their warrior buddies have little concept of history, modern or ancient. Still, I wonder who decided to base an element of ROTC training on the ancient Greek concept of lovers-in-arms. The concepts *are* similar. Except the ROTC tries to build a strong bond between you and your warrior buddy without suggesting you have sex with him.

In my "Leadership Dimensions" evaluation from Advanced Camp, I was judged "outstanding" in physical stamina; "excellent" in planning and organizing, administrative control, problem analysis, decisiveness, technical competence, and "followership"; and "satisfactory" in the remaining categories. Mysteriously, my "Overall Camp Performance" rating was only a three, rather than a four or five, which would have meant I was in the top 30 percent of the cadets attending. My "Camp Performance" narrative gives nothing to explain the overall rating. It reads:

> Cadet Holobaugh came to Advanced Camp eager to learn and willing to accept leadership challenges that were presented to him. At the leadership Reaction Course, he issued clear instructions to his subordinates and quickly developed a plan of attack for his particular task. Early on during the execution phase of his mission, he determined that his original plan would not work so he immediately issued a fragmentary order which facilitated the near completion of his task. As squad leader for the squad defense, Cadet Holobaugh effectively utilized all available materials to shore up his defensive position to include mines, obstacles, pioneer tools, and all available cover and concealment. He coordinated interlocking fires with adjacent units and effectively covered deadspace with claymore mines and M203 grenade launchers. Cadet Holobaugh's efforts resulted in a solid defensive position that repelled the enemy's attack. As a patrol leader during the Tactical Application Exercise, he quickly and effectively maneuvered his squad-size patrol across a linear danger area. Cadet Holobaugh is definitely a team player and is fully supportive of his peers. His high personal standards of performance resulted in his achievement of RECONDO status. Due to his outstanding

map reading skills, Cadet Holobaugh was selected on numerous occasions during the Capstone Exercise to be the compassman while conducting patrolling operations over difficult terrain. His hard work, determination, and desire to excel resulted in Cadet Holobaugh being a definite asset to the platoon.

My "Leadership Potential" is then summed up: "Cadet Holobaugh possesses outstanding leadership potential. Strongly recommend him for active duty."

The evaluation seems to say I would make an outstanding officer in the United States Army. If my performance wasn't among the top 30 percent at the camp, the future of the American military would appear to be most bright.

My rating of "3" did not go over well with Lieutenant Colonel David Lexa, commander of my battalion at UMR. Knowing I would soon be transferring to Saint Louis, Lexa wrote a letter addressed "To My Successor," taking issue with the rating:

> Cadet Holobaugh's Advanced Camp evaluation score of 3 is totally unrepresentative of his ability level and actual demonstrated performance. He was and is one of the top performers in his class. His individual scores at Advanced Camp also suggest that his ability level is higher than 3. I strongly recommend that your write-up on the Form 4609 contain statements to the effect that he is a top performer, and that his camp score doesn't reflect his true abilities or level of performance.

My transfer to Washington University went smoothly, except that my new ROTC commanders seemed to expect more of me than I was by then willing to give. I had assumed a lot of responsibility in ROTC at Rolla. Along with my work in the Raiders and the Pershing Rifles, I was also second in command of my battalion. I thought I had satisfied my duty to ROTC while at Rolla, and now I was ready for it to play less of a role in my life. At Washington University, a greater concern was passing my classes. I had signed up for several difficult structural engineering courses — structural design, structural analysis, environmental engineering, transportation engineering,

engineering statistics — and I was working twenty hours a week at Western Union.

The ROTC people gave me grief because I was skipping a lot of ROTC events like physical training and leadership labs. Fortunately, one of the commanders, Captain Dawson, sided with me. He said that my grades were more important, and that if I showed up for two or three events, I'd be excused from the others. He was open-minded and I respected him. Soon, however, I found out I couldn't trust him.

*Because of his affair with Brent, it wasn't long before Jim began to question exactly what his role with ROTC should be. Carolyn Lang recalls:*

*"When Jim was 'coming out,' as they call it, he was having all these troubles with the Army."*

*She puts a finger to each temple, as if the memory is giving her a headache.*

*"He just didn't know what to do and was in constant turmoil. I could see that he had to do something. I remember his mannerisms. It reminded me of a little boy who is so frustrated, he just walks very intensely, and tries to figure out some way to manage the situation, but hits a stone wall. He could have been very indignant, but he didn't seem to be acting out at all. He'd ride his bike, take his dog Louie for a run. He was trying very hard to be honorable, and he just didn't believe he should be ostracized and punished — as they tried to do."*

*"We'd been together for more than a year before any of this started," says Brent. "Jim was really concerned that he would be court-martialed or that something else bad would happen. We talked about it. I was basically just there for support, as a sounding board. It was Jim's decision. At first he thought he could keep it quiet, but then he had second thoughts."*

Until Brent came along, I had never given serious thought to how my being gay might affect my ROTC commitment. Even when I was having sex with Pete, I never thought of it in relation to ROTC. I guess I thought I could go through life being attracted to men without anyone in the military finding out. I never stopped to think what would happen if I fell in love and

[93]

wanted to spend the rest of my life with a man. But after Brent and I began our relationship, I knew that this was how I was going to live my life.

The magnitude of the decision I would have to make hit me when I went for my pre-commission physical. The doctor asked me point-blank if I was homosexual. It was a routine question, but I knew I was lying when I said, "no," and I began to worry about what might happen if they found out. Even then I figured no one would find out because I was planning on serving in the Reserves, which meant a commitment of one weekend a month and two weeks out of each year.

But there was a chance I'd end up on active duty. Brent had already told me that if I got active duty he would try to find a residency program close to where I was stationed. But after that physical, I went home to Brent and told him how frightened I was. The next day I went to Lieutenant Colonel Bates, the commanding ROTC officer at Washington University, and asked, "Is there any way you can promise me I'll get Reserves? I really don't want active duty." I was assured I would get reserve duty, but I began to think, "Gosh, someone still might find out, even in the Reserves."

As my commissioning date of May 1989 neared, I worried constantly. I was afraid I could be in a lot of trouble if someone did find out — that I might even be court-martialed. I had no idea what could happen, but I knew the military definitely had a ban on gays. The only thing I was sure of was that I had to be with Brent.

I'm sure I drove Brent crazy talking about my fears. I wanted to make the right decision, but I didn't know what the right decision was. My worst fear was, if I told my commanding officer I was gay, everyone I knew would find out. That's what happened eventually, of course, but at the time it was my worst nightmare. I also knew it would take all the courage I had to just walk into Colonel Bates's office and say, "I'm gay." But the more I thought about it, the more I felt I had to tell the truth. I kept asking myself, "What difference does it make? Why should it matter to them who I am in love with?" The injustice of it all, of having to choose between a surreptitious life or coming clean and probably getting kicked out, really made me angry. I couldn't see why my falling in love with Brent should put me in that position, when straight cadets could fall in love and not worry. But most of all I was just scared, and dreading what was to come.

*Brent remembers how afraid Jim was:*
*"To go before the Army and say, 'I'm gay' — he knew what the implications were and he was scared. We would lie in bed and talk. There were a lot of nights like that, when we'd just lie there and hold each other. Those were some very scary times."*

*Although Jim's father was not aware of these events, he bristles at the suggestion that Jim purposely waited until he was near graduation to tell the ROTC he was gay.*

*"Morris and I have never sat down and talked about much of this in detail, so I don't know when he admitted to himself or to friends that he is gay. I suppose the problem with ROTC would be not knowing what to do. That would have been a tough decision. If you know anything about Morris, you know he is a very honest person. Honesty is something that my family holds dear. Morris would have known he could have got his schooling in other ways."*

Brent finally said to me, "If you're going to do something, you need to do it soon."

I took his advice.

# SEVEN

# Telling ROTC

In January 1989, I decided to act. Because I didn't want to jeopardize my commission, I first tried to see a Judge Advocate General (JAG) officer for advice. I was told that I could not see one because I was to be commissioned an officer and the attorneys see only enlisted personnel. I then went to Colonel Bates and told him I was having some problems and needed to see a military attorney. He asked me why, puzzled by my sudden request. I started to tell him the truth, but he stopped me before I got very far, apparently sensing that I should talk to an attorney first. He said, "No, wait, don't tell me." He then tried to get the JAG officers to see me, but said they refused.

Captain Dawson told me later that after I met with Bates, Bates called him. Bates told him about my visit to his office and asked Dawson if he knew whether I was in any kind of trouble. When Dawson said he had no idea, Bates said, "Well, I thought maybe the little son of a bitch was going to tell me that he's gay."

Colonel Bates, a big man with a Texas drawl, is the type of man who goes around talking about women and cussing, but when it comes to something like homosexuality, cites the Bible. Take the stereotypical Texas redneck who's a military officer and has enough religion to be dangerous — that's Bates.

Not knowing what to do, for several months I did nothing. But the problem would not go away. By March of 1989 I knew I had to get advice from someone. Since he had helped me when I first came to the school, Captain Dawson was my choice. I had also taken a class of his in which we discussed the Uniform Code of Military Justice, so I knew he was familiar with military law. I also knew he had a master's in psychology, which meant he wouldn't be entirely ignorant about homosexuality. He was from California, too, where gays are more visible than in Missouri.

I made an appointment to see Captain Dawson, fully intending to tell him I was gay. The night before, Brent and I rented *The Boys in the Band*. Neither of us was very familiar with gay-themed books or films at that point, but we had both read John Reid's *The Best Little Boy in the World*, which often mentions *The Boys in the Band*. It was a depressing movie — the last thing I needed to see — so we stopped the video about halfway through. To this day, we have never watched the end of that movie. I spent the night with Brent at his house. Being wrapped in his arms was more comforting than any movie could have been.

The next day I told Captain Dawson I was gay. It wasn't as hard as I was afraid it would be because I knew I had to do it. I had gone over the words in my head so many times that I probably sounded like a robot, though a very nervous robot. I just walked into his office and told him, and he just sat there staring at me. Before he had time to respond, I also told him that I wanted to be commissioned, and asked him what he thought I should do, if anything.

Once he'd collected his thoughts, Dawson advised me to come forward about being gay. He said I would be in better shape if the military found out then rather than later. He also said that he didn't agree with military policy on this issue, that a person's sexuality is something he or she should be able to express. But a policy is a policy, Dawson said, and he had to go along with it. Then he told me about Bates calling him and saying, "I thought maybe the little son of a bitch was going to tell me that he's gay." That did not surprise me too much, because I had never trusted Bates.

[97]

Taking Captain Dawson's advice, I wrote a letter to Colonel Bates in April telling him in my own words that I was gay. At Dawson's request, I called him first and read him the letter. He had me completely change the wording. The changes were bad for me because the final product said nothing about my wish to be commissioned and serve. I shouldn't have listened to him, but his was the only advice I had, and I thought he had my best interests at heart.

The letter, addressed to Colonel Bates, April 12, 1989, read:

Dear Sir:

This is to request a termination of my scholarship because I feel I must decline commissioning on the grounds of homosexuality. I have changed a great deal since I accepted my 4-year scholarship five years ago. If I had felt then like I feel now, I would have never accepted the scholarship. I did not accept the fact that I am gay until this past year. Until recently I thought that I could serve in the reserves with a good chance that no one in the military would know. However, I now feel that it is in my best interest to speak up and not accept a commission rather than to take the risk of the military finding out at a later time.

Sincerely,
James M. Holobaugh

I made an appointment to see Colonel Bates and deliver the letter personally. When the day arrived, I took the letter, handed it to him, and sat there. I was extremely uncomfortable sitting there, watching him read the letter, wondering what he was thinking and what was going to happen. Although the situation was not the least bit funny, it was so ridiculous that when I gave him the letter I was smiling from embarrassment. When he finished reading the letter, he said, "I kind of thought this is what it was."

Bates then mentioned calling Dawson after I'd first come to him. I made no comment. Then he said that Dawson had called him after I'd met with Dawson. This stunned me. Bates said that the same day I told Dawson, Dawson had called him and said, "Jim Holobaugh has given me reason why he should not be commissioned, and if he doesn't come and tell you what that is before he's commissioned, I will have to tell you."

I understand Dawson's actions to a certain extent. It could have meant trouble for him if I hadn't gone to Colonel Bates, and then later the military found out I'd told Dawson I was gay. Officers are obligated to come forward with that information. But that's the only credit I'll give him. He also might have done it for brownie points. Either way, I felt betrayed. But in front of Bates, I did the best I could not to show it.

I tried to hide my shock by arguing my position, telling Bates that the military policy was wrong, that gays should be allowed to serve. Bates told me he had to uphold policy whether he agreed with it or not, but that in this case he did agree with the policy. As soon as he said that, something inside me tightened up — I knew he was going to cause me problems. He confirmed this seconds later by saying that he would try his best to make sure I didn't just walk away from the ROTC. I left the meeting knowing that I had an enemy — someone who would do all he could to ensure that I repaid my ROTC scholarship. He came across as so homophobic that I immediately sought the counsel of a private attorney in Saint Louis — Arlene Zarembka.

When I explained the situation to Arlene, she said, "Well, this letter doesn't say what you're telling me. You're telling me you're gay and you want to be commissioned. And that you want to be up-front and honest now because you're afraid of them finding out later. We need to rescind this letter and send another stating exactly what you mean."

So, we did. The second letter, dated May 19, 1989, and also addressed to Colonel Bates, read:

> Dear Lt. Col. Bates:
>
> I am writing this letter to correct my previous letter to you of April 12, 1989. I wish to withdraw that letter and to supersede that letter with this letter.
>
> I am gay and have recognized this in myself recently. However, I do wish to be commissioned as an officer in the United States Army, and am specifically asking that the Army

commission me as an officer, so that I may carry out the terms of my Enlistment Contract.

I therefore am asking that the Army stop the disenrollment proceedings that have been initated [sic] against me. The Army should not disenroll me based on any anticipatory breach of my contract, as I fully intend to accept a commission as an officer in the Army if I am offered such a commission.

The reason I wrote the letter dated April 12, 1989 was that I was mistaken as to my legal position; I thought at that time that I had to decline a commission and therefore thought that I had no choice but to request a termination of my scholarship and to notify you that I would decline a commission. Since writing that letter, however, I have had an opportunity to consult with an attorney, and realize that it is up to the Army whether or not it chooses to commission me. Therefore, I am revoking my letter of April 12, 1989, insofar as that letter requested a termination of my scholarship and declined commissioning.

To reiterate: I am gay, but I wish to be commissioned as an officer, and to continue my status as a scholarship student.

Sincerely,
James M. Holobaugh

Although other ROTC cadets who have been kicked out for being gay — Robert Bettiker and Robert Schwitz are two — privately received support from some of their commanding officers, I did not. In fact, if I hadn't gotten a lawyer right away, things could have been very bad for me — as they have been for gay cadets and soldiers in similar situations. Attorneys, however, cost money, and I was certainly not wealthy. I was paying Arlene with cash advances on my VISA card and raking up a huge debt. She was flexible about the money, though she could have been more helpful by sending me to, say, the American Civil Liberties Union. She didn't. If I had gone to the ACLU first, they might have taken my case and assigned Arlene to it. She's not with the ACLU, but they use local cooperating attorneys in many cases.

One of the things Arlene arranged to help me save money was my doing some of the research for my case myself. Once while I was out hunting down information, I found myself standing in front of a JAG officer. I told her that I was being kicked out of ROTC because I was gay, that previously I had been told I could not see a JAG officer, and I wanted to know why not. She seemed shocked. She said, "They should have allowed you to see one of us. Give me your name. I'll give it to the secretary and she'll get back to you." Although I left them my name and number, they never got back in touch. This particular attorney, however, did seem sympathetic. It's possible she was told by higher-ups not to pursue it.

My worries were just beginning. An immediate concern was what to tell my father. I knew he was expecting me to be commissioned at the end of the semester, so I had to think of something quickly. I also knew that I was not ready to tell him the truth. Telling Captain Dawson I was gay was one thing, but telling my father would be the hardest thing I'd ever done. I felt like I had enough stress in my life at the time without adding more to it.

So, I lied. I told my father I had decided the military wasn't for me and that I was going to pay back my scholarship to avoid being obligated to them. He seemed to buy the story. I got the feeling that he was even relieved in some ways, because I don't think he ever really wanted me to be in the military in the first place. He had always been neutral on the subject, never putting the military down, but never talking it up, either. He didn't seem disappointed that I planned to repay my scholarship.

Repayment *is* something a person can do, and it was an idea I'd tossed around in my mind — just paying it back and never telling anyone why. I knew as soon as I talked to Captain Dawson that I wasn't going to get commissioned. I didn't know what was going to happen with the scholarship. But at that point I would have sooner paid back half a million dollars than tell my father I was gay.

I then went to Connecticut to join Brent. The ROTC told me to check in every two weeks during the summer to see what was happening with my case. But the person I had been told to check in with was never there. He was at ROTC Advanced Camp in Fort Riley. The biweekly calls went on for a while. Then, feeling ridiculous, I quit calling.

In Connecticut, I got a call from my old friend Robo, who was in New York on business. I was excited about seeing him again and invited him to visit. But after I hung up the phone, I thought about what Robo would find when he arrived: two men living in an apartment with one bed in it. For a panicky minute, I tried to think of some likely story to explain my living arrangements. But nothing sensible came to mind. Then I thought, Why not tell him the truth? The thought of coming out to one of my best friends scared me to death at first. But as I sat there awaiting his arrival, I found myself *wanting* to tell Robo. The time had come.

*Robo:* "I drove up to Connecticut, to his apartment. Brent wasn't in when I got there, so I walked in and started checking out his place. One peculiar thing that stuck out was that there was only one bedroom, and one bed. I began looking in all the other doors for the other bedroom, and just as I was about to ask him, he said, 'Well, I have something to tell you.' Then he says, 'Brent and I are gay.'

"I didn't believe him at first. It didn't want to sink in. I'd known James for so long that the kind of voice he was using almost sounded like his joking manner. So I said, 'No, you're joking,' and he said, 'No, I'm serious.' All of a sudden it hit me and I had to sit down. We started talking about it. He said he expected that, of all his friends, it would be hardest for me to accept it — I think because we had been roommates for three years. James kept telling me, 'I'm not a different person. I'm the same person you always knew.' I asked him about all those times we would joke about gays, and he said, 'Well, that's just the way people are.'"

Why did I think it would be hardest for Robo to accept? Because I had lived with him for three years and he had no clue. Also, I thought he might be afraid people would wonder about him since we had lived together that long. It *was* hard for him to accept. The next day he told me that he woke up in his hotel room thinking, "Did I dream that?"

*Karen remembers the day well:*

*"Rob called me from New York and said, 'You're never going to believe this. James is gay.' He was just floored. He couldn't believe it."*

*"That night I went back to my hotel," says Robo, "but the following night we were meeting in New York. James showed me around all the places I wanted to see. Then we were walking through Greenwich Village and he said he wanted to take me to a gay bar to show me that these guys were not out of the ordinary, just normal guys that you might see in a fraternity down at Rolla. But I was so nervous that I said, 'No, I don't think I'm ready yet. Maybe some other time.' He was cool about it and said, 'Okay.' We had a good time that night."*

*While they were walking around, they needed change for the phone, so they made a deal with a beggar — a dollar for seventy-five cents. According to Robo, the beggar was saying, "You just don't see good people around this place anymore. Now it's all these gays everywhere."*

The city was weird that night. There was a car on fire in Times Square, causing a mob scene. There were two Asian guys making out with each other in public. Then we took a subway and the station we used — Bloomingdale's — had more homeless people than I've ever seen in New York. It was completely full of homeless people. There are always a lot of homeless in New York, but it seemed like this subway stop had an inordinate amount. Robo was really taken aback by this anarchy he was seeing. I think his finding out I was gay, and then me wanting to take him into a gay bar in this insane city was more than he could handle. I had wanted to take him to Uncle Charlie's. Now, New York has the worst bars I've ever been to in my life. People won't talk to each other — especially at Uncle Charlie's. It's a "stand and model" bar. But I thought it would be the best crowd for him to see — a bunch of college guys. I thought he would be more comfortable there than in the other bars I'd been to.

*"We were afraid everyone was going to think Rob was gay since he lived with James for three years," says Karen, laughing.*

[103]

*"Yeah," Robo agrees, "that was an initial fear, but after a while I just didn't worry about it. It's no big deal."*

*One other thing Robo remembers about that trip to New York:*

*"James told me that as a boy he would be spending the night with other boys and they might get each other excited. But he didn't think about it as gay, he thought it was normal. I thought that was kind of odd."*

In the fall, I returned to Saint Louis and Washington University, still having heard nothing from ROTC. In fact, nothing happened with my case between May 1989 and January 1990. That period was hard for me and for Brent. At this point few people knew I was gay, let alone involved with Brent. Although I was scared to death that everyone was going to find out, I did come out to a few people, including some ROTC friends who had been commissioned lieutenants. They were surprised. Before, many of these guys would have said, "Of course we don't want queers in the military." But after I told them I was gay, they realized how wrong the policy is. They knew I would be a good officer.

Brent and I had to be apart for a semester, which was hell. I hated it. I didn't want to leave Connecticut, for the idea of being without Brent for a semester was almost more than I could handle. It wasn't just that I loved him, although that was the main reason. It was also because I had come to count on him for support. He was the one person in my life who knew everything that was going on.

But I returned to Saint Louis and lived with Carolyn again. It felt strange being in college and not being in ROTC. Instead, I was in the process of being disenrolled — and no one would tell me what was going on.

*Brent says there was no concern that their relationship would not survive a semester apart.*

*"I never thought there would be a problem. We were both very committed, and it was just something we had to endure. It was forever," he says, his voice dropping almost to a whisper, "it really was. Either I flew there or Jim flew to Connecticut once a month, which is all we could afford. But our phone bills were*

*astronomical. Together, we were each spending about $600 on phone calls every month. I think only one day went by the entire semester when I didn't talk to Jim on the phone."*

The Labor Day following Jim's departure for Saint Louis, Brent visited his family, with the intention of coming out to them.

*"I guess Jim and I had been together about a year, and it got to the point where I just didn't feel like talking about the weather or about Jim as my roommate or friend, so I finally told them. I'd told my sister, who was fine about it, though at first she said, 'Don't tell Mom and Dad.' I went for a visit and tried the whole weekend to say something but just couldn't get it out. But the night before I was leaving we were sitting up watching videos, one movie after another, and it was really getting late. There never seemed to be a good time to discuss it, but finally about one or two in the morning I just kind of blurted it out: 'I've got something to tell you: I'm gay.'*

*"They didn't believe it. They were totally shocked because it had just come out of nowhere. They said they had no idea. They said they loved me. They cried. They said they didn't understand it.*

*"I slept on it that night; they didn't sleep very well. The next day they said they still loved me. I had a copy of Betty Berzon's* Permanent Partners *with me, which has a list of books to help parents, so I wrote down some titles. When I left I gave them the list and said, 'Maybe this will help.' They had no idea, except what they saw on TV, of what a gay person was.*

*"About four days later I got a call. They apologized. They said, 'We're sorry, we didn't know.' I guess my dad had gone to the library and checked out these books. I mean, that was a lot for my dad to do. So they read the books, and they accepted it; they realized it wasn't some weird thing. And they've really come to know and love Jim. He's become a major part of the family. We've gone to see them together several times now. He gets as many Christmas presents as I do."*

A few weeks later, I too decided it was time to let someone in my family know what was going on in my life. The reaction of Brent's parents had boosted my morale. I still did not want to face my father, but I decided to tell Melanie.

When I first told her, I was surprised. It was almost as if she knew what I was going to say and had planned the best way to react — hugging me and telling me she loved me. In truth, she reacted that way because that's the kind of person she is. Melanie instinctively knows the right thing to do in those situations. She had never had any idea I was gay.

As time went on, though, Melanie was much less supportive. She's become much more religious since she's been married. One of my biggest concerns when I told her was that she wouldn't want me around Heath, my nephew. But she told me, "No, I would never think that. The only thing that bothers me is that Heath may never have any cousins."

As it's turned out, I haven't been around Heath much anyway. I don't think my being near Heath is the problem for Melanie. I think she doesn't want Heath to see Brent and me together in a healthy gay relationship. At first she was okay with it. But after everyone else found out, I think she caught a lot of criticism from people. I'm sure it's been hard on her, but I was counting on her to stand by me. I needed someone in my family to accept me like Brent's parents had accepted him. I thought Melanie would be that person.

*"Melanie took it pretty hard," says John Taylor. "After I found out, we talked on the phone about it. It was a long conversation and Melanie literally talked until she could no longer form words. Then she just cried. Melanie's husband, Danny, wouldn't care if he never saw Morris again and he damn sure doesn't want him around the kids."*

Danny is like a lot of American men. My guess is he thinks homosexuality is bad because it's bad, but has never really thought about it. He probably doesn't want to be embarrassed by me, and he doesn't want his son to be embarrassed by me. Melanie had a daughter in May 1991, so now I also have a niece I rarely get to see.

*While Jim received some initial support from Melanie, he received most of his support from the daily telephone conversations with Brent, and from some new Saint Louis friends.*

One of those friends, Andy Katz, has a perfect memory of the night he met Jim:

"It was Saturday night, October 22, 1989. I remember it distinctly."

An eyebrow goes up as Andy says "distinctly." He's wearing gray shorts, a green polo shirt, and white socks, sitting in his stylishly decorated Saint Louis apartment. Andy's hair is cut short and parted in the middle. He has a moustache, and works out at a local gym. He seems to have a slightly embarrassed twinkle in his eye when discussing Jim.

"We were at Magnolia's, and met thanks to this drag queen who's about seventy years old and works in the city government office. They call him Betty Davis. Everyone knows about him. Betty's an actress, though — she's not drunk like she pretends to be. It was about midnight and I guess I was at that stage in my life when I didn't have anything else to do but go to a bar, then leave around midnight since I'm not a night person. I don't smoke, I don't drink, I'd be kind of depressed, and I'd leave."

Magnolia's looks as if it was once two townhouses. It has wood floors and several old stairwells — the kind you find in old townhouses. The club is a maze of rooms. There's a restaurant attached and a newspaper room upstairs. The dance floor decor is weird. There are huge black tubes large enough to be drainage pipes along the ceiling, but they seem to be connected to nothing. Incongruous with fake black pipe is the pink neon along the walls. There is also a silver reflecting ball in the middle of the ceiling. The clientele, like the decor, is eclectic and contradictory. There are steroid guys in muscle shirts, arguing queens in just about anything, and a lot of men wearing designer blue jeans that look uncomfortably tight.

"I'm just standing getting ready to leave and all of a sudden Betty comes walking in," Andy recalls. "I was wearing blue jeans with red suspenders, and one of the people who turned out to be with Jim pulled my suspenders. I turned around, took one look at Jim, and thought, 'I'm not leaving this bar.'

"So, there was Jim. My first vision of him was like, here's the most young, innocent-looking boy I've ever seen, wearing blue jeans, a t-shirt that's hanging out, and a jacket that's shorter than the t-shirt. He had no idea of fashion — I loved it. He was just this

[107]

real, natural person. I said 'hi' to Jim, and I don't think I even gave him a chance to say 'hi' back before I asked, 'Are you dating anyone?' He immediately said, 'I have a boyfriend who lives in Connecticut and I'll be moving there at the end of the semester.'

"I've found that with other people I've met, if they had a lover, they just didn't want you around. So I was ready to turn around and go my merry way, when Jim said, 'But I'd like to meet some people for friendship.' I was really surprised. I know he gave me his number because I still have the card that he wrote it on. I went home and stared at this card.

"I was a supervisor at General Motors at the time, and I guess I called Jim first. We started talking, and talked for about an hour and a half nonstop. We talked about everything and I thought, Oh my gosh, there's someone on this earth who can talk as much as I can. I realized something right away — that he couldn't complete a sentence without the word Brent in it. I knew this was someone who was really in love. One thing he told me as we were getting to know each other is that every time he thought of Brent, he ate.

"We started doing some things on weekends. We went to a great play, Some of My Best Friends Are. Again, here I am trying to be friends with this person, and I couldn't get my mind off the fact that he was stunningly handsome. I mean, every guy in the audience was looking at him. Jim has this butch red truck. I remember he picked me up in it at GM and I'm thinking, 'This guy has everything — good looks, this butch truck.'

"Jim went to a lot of parties with me. We went to a Thanksgiving party that I remember well. A couple I know have an annual party and every year they have this game you play where they put a name on your back, then you ask yes-or-no questions to figure out who you are. Jim's first character was Zsa Zsa Gabor. It took him a little while to get it. Jim knows a lot about a variety of subjects, but Hollywood entertainment isn't one of his best. Jim's next name was Jay Leno. He's asking the usual start-off questions: 'Am I dead? Am I male?' Feelings were starting to develop in me that I'm holding in at this point, so when he asks, 'Would you have sex with me?' I just thought, Oh, I'd love to say yes, but instead I asked, 'You're talking about your character, right?' He just started laughing. We joke about that a lot."

*Andy isn't alone in thinking Jim is pretty darn cute. Reading through the mail he's received, an impression forms that well over half of the correspondents were using his ordeal with the military as an excuse to write to someone they'd like to become involved with. How does Jim see himself? It's a question that doesn't get a quick response.*

"One thing about myself is, I don't want to ever come across like I'm bragging or the least bit conceited, and that's why it's hard for me to answer this question. It's something I've always been conscious of."

*Does he hate it when people comment on his looks, as people often do?*

"I don't feel like my looks are that great. I know that I'm better than average looking or else people wouldn't tell me that. But if I had a twin and saw that twin in a gay bar, I don't know if that would be my idea of the perfect guy, or the guy that I'd want to go after. Part of it is that I don't know how to respond. It really bothers me to see good-looking guys who are conceited. Brent and I were in Provincetown and we saw this guy who was just gorgeous, but when we got up closer to him, he does this thing with his hair that just said, 'I'm gorgeous and I know it.' He just didn't seem like someone I'd want to be around."

*Andy saw how strong Jim's devotion was to his nephew, Heath, when he and Jim went to see* Driving Miss Daisy *at the Galleria.*

"Jim was shopping for a book for his nephew. He's so in love with this little kid, and the neatest thing is that Jim gives 100 percent to whatever he's doing at the time. He found this book about teaching kids how not to be prejudiced. I think he would have bought the store for his nephew if he could have. It was a really neat thing to see how much he wanted to teach this kid and help him."

*Another thing that impressed Andy about Jim was his commitment to Brent. When they first went to a bar together, Andy asked Jim if he would like to dance. Jim said he couldn't. Confused, Andy asked if Jim did not know how, or if he was physically unable. Jim replied that he had never danced with Brent before, and the first time he danced with another male was going to be with Brent.*

"I can't tell you how many comments he got," says Andy. "I guess because Jim didn't go out to bars a lot he was like a new

[109]

*face in town. But all these people were coming up to me and going, 'Oh, he's so straight-acting!'"*

When I first started going to gay bars, one of the biggest compliments anyone could give me was to tell me I looked straight. But once I was comfortable with myself, I began to see what was wrong with that "compliment." Now, I hate it when people use that term, "straight-acting," because it implies that most gays act abnormally.

I was never enthusiastic about the bar scene. The bars treated me well in the sense that I met Brent and Andy and Steve in the bars, but I don't feel I missed out on anything by escaping the hunt for a mate in the bar scene. I don't find it exciting. I find it scary and frustrating.

But bars serve their purpose. They are places to meet. What bothers me a lot are the people who meet in public places for sex. I don't even consider these people part of the gay community. Most of them are married, or closeted, or both. When people have sex in public restrooms in parks and at rest stops, it doesn't do anything good for gays. It's also dangerous from the standpoint of AIDS. Some gay leaders who defend this stuff get so concerned with being politically correct that they forget how people think and how they're going to react. I don't think it's a practice we should be trying to defend.

*In late December, Jim returned to Connecticut. He sent Andy a Hanukkah card with a nice message: "Meeting you has reinforced my philosophy of following up when meeting someone new. I am really glad I gave you my number that night at Magnolia's. It makes me wonder how many people pass by each day who have the potential to be a good friend ... I want our friendship to last. 1500 miles means nothing if people genuinely try to keep in touch."*

*Before Jim left Saint Louis, during finals week, ROTC called and told him to report for an informal investigation.*

After the hearing, Arlene and I sat in her car a long time discussing what had happened and what we should do next. I felt good, mainly because Sergeant Ritchey had explained everything to me, and for the first time I understood what was happening. I was, however, depressed about some of my answers, particularly my inability to articulate why I wanted to be an officer.

Arlene and I decided the submission of supporting documents was necessary, so I asked several acquaintances to write letters testifying in my behalf. People who had known me prior to 1988 were asked to verify that they hadn't a clue I was gay until recently. Those who met me after 1988 would verify that now I was, in fact, gay. This would make it virtually impossible for the Army to prove willful evasion — that I had knowingly entered ROTC as a gay person, or that I was in fact heterosexual now and only pretending to be gay.

Melanie wrote the following:

> I am writing in regard to the problem my brother, James Holobaugh, is having with his commission to the Army.
>
> When my brother came home for a visit near the end of October (a few weeks ago), he told me he is gay. This came as a considerable shock to me, as he has always led a "normal" lifestyle. He has dated different girls, and visited in our home with them on numerous occasions in the last several years.
>
> I do not understand his recent choice of lifestyle, but I do understand it is in conflict with his entrance to the Army, and I think he felt the only right thing to do was to be up-front about it with you.

This is from a pre-1988 acquaintance letter:

> I have known James Holobaugh since August of 1986. We were in ROTC together and became good friends. We lived together from January to May of 1988. During this time he had relationships with girls and was normal in every way. I had no indication that he was gay.

And this from a post-1988 acquaintance letter:

> I was first introduced to Jim Holobaugh through work in May of 1989. Jim and I formed a friendship in which we have on several occasions met at various Gay establishments: i.e. the

[111]

beach, various bars, and with several mutual friends, we participated in the 1989 NYC Gay and Lesbian Gay Pride Day Parade.

Glenn also wrote a letter, although it was not included in the packet we sent to Captain Boyle. Glenn wrote, "I never had any indication, either overt or subtle, that James was a homosexual, and can only conclude that he became a homosexual after May 1986."

His accompanying note to me read:

Here is the letter you requested. I hope it is what you had in mind ... If CPT Boyle has any questions have him call me. Honestly, I can't say I approve of any of this. I hope you know what you're doing. Sorry, I don't mean to preach. Please be careful.

Glenn

P.S. Friends till the end, right?

I wrote a letter to Boyle myself to further clarify my previous letters to Colonel Bates:

Dear Cpt. Boyle,
    This letter is to clarify some facts about the letter I gave LTC Bates dated April 12, 1989. Prior to April 12, 1989, I tried unsuccessfully to obtain advice on the Army's policy regarding homosexuality. I was not allowed to speak with a JAG Officer since I am not an enlisted man. As the end of spring semester 1989 was nearing, I decided that I had to get some advice from someone. I went to see Cpt. Dawson. I told Cpt. Dawson I am gay and asked his advice on the best course of action. He suggested that I write LTC Bates a letter stating that I decline to be commissioned because I am gay. He told me to call him before I gave the letter to LTC Bates and we would go over the letter on the phone. I called Cpt. Dawson and he dictated over the phone what I should say in the letter. I wrote exactly what he told me to write. I took his advice because it was the only advice I could get. After giving the letter to LTC Bates I decided I should consult an attorney. My attorney

pointed out that I did not have to decline commissioning just because I am gay. For this reason, and because I wished (and still wish) to be commissioned, I sent the second letter to LTC Bates dated May 19, 1989 rescinding my first letter dated April 12, 1989.

Serving as a commissioned Officer would give me the opportunity to serve America and gain valuable experience at the same time. My engineering education would be an asset to the Army as well. I sincerely hope I will have the privilege of serving as an Army Officer.

Sincerely,
James M. Holobaugh

# EIGHT

# "Come after me"

After Arlene and I made plans, I loaded up my Jeep truck and headed east. With me were a friend, who was hitching a ride to Queens, and her two cats. I dropped friend and felines off, and then, following her erroneous directions to the Whitestone Bridge, I got on the Long Island Expressway and ended up in the middle of Manhattan on a Friday night. I'd never driven in Manhattan before and had no idea how to get to Connecticut. It was a nightmare. My truck was loaded, with my bike on top, and I just knew someone was going to rip my bike off and rob the back of my truck. I kept pulling over to curbs asking anyone who looked halfway friendly, "How do you get to Connecticut?" I might as well have been asking for directions to Utah. Nobody I asked had any idea how to get to Connecticut. But I eventually found my way, cargo intact.

I had worked at the Federal Reserve Bank the previous summer training new employees on word-processing equipment. My supervisors liked me and asked me to work for them again during Christmas break. They paid me seventeen bucks an hour, which wasn't bad. If anything about the Federal Reserve surprised me, it was the number of gays who worked there. One guy was a total flame.

Another guy asked me to go to Jones Beach. I accepted, and he told me where to meet him. Of course, he wanted to meet in the gay section. I didn't even know Jones Beach *had* a gay section. But when I got there and looked around, I immediately made the observation, "This is a gay section."

"Yeah," Eddie agreed, "in this area there are a lot of gay people."

"Are you gay?"

"Yeah."

"So am I."

Coming out to people was getting easier for me all the time. But it was much easier for me to come out in New York City — hundreds of miles away from my family — than in Missouri.

One of the executives at the Federal Reserve was homophobic. He liked me, thinking I was straight. He even took me to the Officers' Club once. It must have been a shock when he found out I was gay. But that's great. It probably made him think.

Meanwhile, Brent and I enjoyed being together again.

*"Jim's funny," Brent says, with Jim sitting behind him, arms wrapped around him, grinning. "When he comes home from work, he just totally lets go and acts out and tries to be really weird."*

*Jim stands up as Brent continues.*

*"He can't believe I'm saying this. He's got all this excess energy. He'll jump around or sing — something that he can't do in public. He enjoys doing that, and he's funny."*

*"I'm leaving the room," says Jim — and does.*

*Brent laughs and continues, "Yesterday when I came home the screen door was open, and I see this head bobbing up and down because he's excited that I'm home. He's very affectionate and very caring — not just to me but toward other people in his life. He really is a good person — and very honest. You get what you see."*

*Returned from hiding, Jim says of Brent, "He can be kind of weird, too. In our old apartment he insisted on keeping the windows shut and the blinds down all day long. I do not understand why. It's like he doesn't want people looking into our apartment. It drives me nuts. He'll open them up when we get home — but we come home from work and it's like an oven."*

[115]

Like most couples, Brent and Jim have developed certain roles. Brent balances the checkbook, sets up the VCR, and makes the pastas. Jim does the laundry, plans their itineraries when traveling, keeps up with the Frequent Flier miles, and mans the outdoor grill.

"You just follow these roles and get stuck in them," says Jim. "I mean, the VCR — I'm perfectly capable of doing it. But for some reason Brent's in charge of maintaining the cable connections. That's his job," Jim says, laughing.

Jim reads the New York Times *every day on the way to work, feeling guilty if he skips a day, afraid he's missed something going on in the world. His favorite sections are the front pages with the national and international news, metro, science (on Tuesdays), and food (on Wednesdays). He looks at the sports section to see the standings, but doesn't read the articles.*

"I like watching these games on TV, I like playing them, but I don't want to read about them," he explains.

Other than the newspaper, Jim's not a big reader, and until recently did not like fiction at all.

"I've been actively trying to go back and read some of the classics I missed out on. With my major, I never had to read a lot of these books that everyone else has read. I just read Catcher in the Rye *for the first time."*

Jim and Brent have an eclectic music collection, with each claiming his tastes are broader than the other's.

"Don't put on the Traveling Wilburys, or any of that other neutral, nonoffensive stuff you put on when guests are here," Jim yells at Brent, who has gone to change the compact disc. Without responding, Brent puts on R.E.M.'s Green.

Aside from Brent, the real love of Jim's life is food. As a result, he's constantly watching his weight, and goes on a diet anytime someone says he's gained a few pounds.

Jim and Brent buy groceries at Stew Leonard's, the self-described "Disney World of supermarkets." The store features an actual glass-enclosed dairy. A live cow moos in the parking lot. A plastic cow stands guard at the entrance. A mechanical cow sings nursery rhymes inside. And mechanical dogs serenade customers from above the frozen peas. There is one winding aisle down which all buggies roll in the same direction, sometimes resembling bumper cars.

[116]

While finishing up the final credits for my engineering degree, I sent out 150 resumes to structural engineering firms in New York and Connecticut. After a number of interviews, I received three job offers. I agreed to take a position with a small engineering firm in midtown Manhattan following graduation. Although I was finishing my courses at the University of New Haven, my degree would come from Washington University. Unlike most schools, which require you to finish your last thirty hours in residence, Washington has a more intelligent system — you must complete more than thirty hours of classes in your major above the 300 level in residence. The idea is to take the more important classes there. With that system, I was able to finish off my electives at New Haven and still satisfy Washington's residency requirement.

It turned out to be a very hectic semester.

I had flown to Connecticut a couple of weekends during the fall to be with Brent. On one of these flights I sat by an outgoing businessman based in New York named John Dallas. John has blond hair, a round face, and a deep voice. He is Mr. Marketing — everything he describes always sounds perfect. Whatever he's talking about — a restaurant, a film, whatever — he's always trying to sell you on it. We started talking on the plane, and I got his address. When I returned to Saint Louis, I wrote him a letter. So many times you meet people and say, "Yeah, give me a call some time." But people never do. I've made myself start following through. When I meet someone interesting and I say I want to keep in touch, I make an effort to do just that. I've had a lot of good experiences from getting to know these people.

I said nothing about being gay in my letter to John. But while I was in Connecticut that December, John and I met for lunch. As we were walking back to my office, John asked if I had a girlfriend in Connecticut. I said, "You remember I told you about my roommate, Brent? Well, Brent and I are gay, and we're partners." John, taken aback by my being so up-front about this, didn't say anything for a couple of minutes. We crossed the street, and then he said, "Well Jim, I'm gay too." Brent had already decided that John must be gay, otherwise a forty-year-old man wouldn't be interested in me. But I think that's kind of cynical.

When I told John about my situation with the military, he asked if I'd heard of Joe Steffan, the cadet who had been kicked out of the Naval Academy for being gay. John went on to say he knew the attorney representing Joe — a man named Marc Wolinsky, who was a partner in the firm of Wachtell, Lipton, Rosen and Katz. As it happened, John was going to a New Year's Eve party at Marc's, so he volunteered to tell Marc about my case. Much to my surprise, Marc called me from the party and asked me to come by his office the following day.

The first thing that impressed Brent and me about Marc was his work ethic. We knew there had been a party the night before, but the office of this big New York law firm on Park Avenue was filled with people working on New Year's Day. We couldn't believe it. Brent and John Dallas had drinks across the street in the Algonquin while Marc and I talked. I felt very comfortable with Marc. We talked for about an hour, and I showed him the co-op ad. For some reason, I'd never shown it to Arlene. I just didn't think it was important. But Marc loved it. He was like, "This is great!" He told me to call him as soon as I received news about my case.

Things were beginning to piece together. Soon after talking to Marc, I got a call from Bill Rubenstein of the ACLU. I had written to the ACLU when I first told the ROTC I was gay, and had met with Bill soon after. Now, Bill was calling to see what had happened with the case. We met again, and I told him about the board and about meeting with Marc Wolinsky. Bill explained that the reason the ACLU hadn't taken my case earlier was that they didn't want to step on Arlene's shoes. But I got the feeling he might be interested in taking the case after all. He said the ROTC issue was becoming hot, and I think he saw Marc's interest as an opportunity for the ACLU to do something without offending Arlene. Like Marc, Bill told me to get in touch with him when something happened with the case.

On January 11, Captain Boyle sent his recommendations to Colonel Bates, titled "Results of Informal Investigation, RE: HOLOBAUGH, James M." It read:

1. Forwarded for your action are the results of my investigation by use of informal board proceedings pertaining to Mr. Holobaugh.

2. Under the provisions of paragraph 3-43a (8), AR 145-1, I recommend that Mr. Holobaugh's scholarship be terminated and that he be disenrolled from the Army ROTC program. Further, that he pay back the U.S. Government for all scholarship benefits that he has received.

3. Based on the evidence, there is no willful evasion that can be proven. However, there is a strong indication of an attempt by Cadet Holobaugh to manipulate the scholarship system to his advantage. This should not be tolerated.

4. I am also troubled by Cadet Holobaugh's refusal to be examined by a military psychiatrist and also by his apparent lack of understanding of the importance of a commission. There is sufficient indication that Cadet Holobaugh was aware of Department of Defense policy on homosexuality, yet he continued to collect scholarship benefits despite this knowledge.

5. I recommend disenrollment based on Mr. Holobaugh's failure to maintain requirements for enrollment, specifically his claim of homosexuality, and, that he be required to pay back all scholarship money that he has received.

The results mentioned in item one were as follows:

Cadet Holobaugh was aware of Department of Defense policy on homosexuality, yet willingly entered into a contract with the United States Army. This fact is shown by his letter, dated 12 April 1989, where he indicates that there is a "risk" to his commission if the Army found out he was gay.

Cadet Holobaugh is unwilling to subject himself to a psychiatric examination by a military psychiatrist to verify his sexual preference.

Cadet Holobaugh shows little evidence of appreciation of what it means to be an officer in the U.S. Armed Forces as shown by his equivocation towards questions pertaining to officership. He has not internalized any of the values which are necessary to perform as a [sic] Army officer. He only considers it a "privilege."

Cadet Holobaugh willingly collected scholarship benefits despite the fact that he supposedly changed his sexual preference while on scholarship, specifically some time in 1988. He did not notify ROTC authorities until 12 April 1989 on this supposed change of sexual preference.

On January 16, Colonel Bates sent the following recommendations to the commander of the U.S. Army Second Region ROTC Cadet Command in Fort Knox, Kentucky:

1. Forwarded for your action are the results of the board proceedings pertaining to Mr. Holobaugh.

2. Under the provisions of paragraph 3-43a (8), AR 145-1, I recommend that Mr. Holobaugh's scholarship by terminated and that he be disenrolled from the Army ROTC program. Further that he pay back the U.S. Government for all scholarship benefits that he received.

3. Disenrollment is based primarily on Mr [sic] Holobaugh's failure to maintain requirements for enrollment, specifically homosexuality [sic], and on Mr [sic] Holobaugh turning down the original commission that was offered him on 19 May 1989.

4. I agree with the findings of the informal board held by CPT Boyle and his recommendation that Mr. Holobaugh pay back scholarship monies.

5. Recommend that Mr. Holobaugh's scholarship be terminated and that he be disenrolled from the ROTC program and that he pay back the U.S. Government for scholarship money received.

Through a lapse in grammar, Bates said in paragraph three that homosexuality is a requirement for enrollment and I had failed to maintain my homosexuality. Imagine that.

When I got the word from Colonel Bates, I was furious — I don't think anyone wants to pay back $35,000. My attitude was,

"Come after me. Try and make me repay it." After all, it wasn't as if I had flunked out of school or quit ROTC; I wanted to be commissioned. They were forcing me out, and still wanted me to repay my scholarship. I was ready to fight. More than anything else, Boyle's contention that there was evidence I may have tried to manipulate the system pissed me off. That was his own opinion, and I don't know where he came up with that conclusion — he just pulled it out of his ass, and contradicted himself in doing so. He'd already stated that there was no evidence I had attempted to defraud the military.

When I received a copy of Bates's recommendations, I immediately called both Marc and Bill. Marc's law firm, Wachtell Lipton, took my case *pro bono* along with the ACLU. Bill was still concerned about offending Arlene, but he needn't have worried. Marc assumed that burden by writing her a letter referring to me as "my client." But Marc was in a much better position to help me than Arlene.

Bill and Marc decided that the best course of action was to put pressure on the military through the press and public opinion. The ACLU would handle the publicity, while Marc dealt with the legal work.

Brent and I were relieved — partially for financial reasons — when the ACLU took the case. I was graduating deeply in debt — a combination of food, school, rent, and legal fees. About $10,000 of that was on VISA cards at 19 percent interest.

Marc, Bill, and I decided not to litigate unless the military pursued the scholarship repayment. Joe Steffan's case was already in the courts, and it was very likely we would have lost anyway, given all the Reagan and Bush appointees in the federal judiciary.

Marc sent a letter to the ROTC commander at Fort Knox dated January 30, 1990, taking issue with Bates's recommendations and the board's "findings." Although Marc ignored Bates's *lapsus calami* where homosexuality turns into a requirement for ROTC enrollment, he pointed out that Bates's insistence that I failed to maintain the "requirements for enrollment" did not jibe with the ROTC's requirements for enrollment listed in Section 2 of Cadet Command Pamphlet 145-4. The "requirements for enrollment" regulation does not mention homosexuality in any context. Marc then lit into the board:

The implication is that Cadet Holobaugh gained admission to ROTC through false pretenses. There is no evidence whatsoever to support this conclusion. To the contrary, all of the recorded evidence is to the effect that Cadet Holobaugh recognized his homosexual orientation in 1989, shortly before he sought the advice of Captain Dawson.

Second, the Board concluded that Cadet Holobaugh had "not internalized any of the values which are necessary to perform as a [sic] Army officer" going on to belittle the fact that Cadet Holobaugh considers it a "privilege" to serve. Nowhere does the Board explain why it is not significant that Cadet Holobaugh considers serving his country a privilege. Nowhere does the Board reflect any consideration of Cadet Holobaugh's December 18 submission. And nowhere does the Board reflect any consideration of Lieutenant Colonel Lexa's evaluation of Cadet Holobaugh's performance or the fact that Cadet Holobaugh had virtually a straight "A" average in his ROTC courses. These facts belie the findings of the Board and demonstrate that its conclusion is based upon prejudice against gay men and women and not upon any assessment of Cadet Holobaugh's commitment to service.

Marc then points out that refusal to subject oneself to a psychiatric examination is an improper basis for a recommendation of dismissal since such right of refusal is guaranteed under Armed Forces regulations. His final point:

Fourth, the Investigating Board found that Cadet Holobaugh willfully "changed" his sexual orientation. That finding is without any support in either the record or in the scientific literature in this area. To the contrary, all learning is to the effect that while an individual may not come to recognize his or her sexual preference until a later age, sexual preference is neither chosen nor changed at will.

It was a good letter. I have nothing but good things to say about both Bill and Marc. Bill went to Yale, then Harvard Law

[122]

School. I'm sure he had many options, but he chose to work for the ACLU and make comparatively little money. He's handsome, tall, thin, dark-haired — a lot of people think he resembles John Kennedy, Jr. He's got a great personality — and he's gay.

Marc is a lot of fun, too. Brent and I have become good friends with him and his lover, Barry. Besides representing me through the ACLU, Marc represents Joe Steffan through Lambda Legal Defense Fund. Marc is like the John McEnroe of law. He's got a lot of energy and loves to get to people. He goes for blood.

Marc wasted no time notifying Washington University of the ROTC's decision. The provost of the university, Edward S. Macias, came through for me in a letter to Bates dated February 20, 1990. The letter, at times, seems more than a little sarcastic:

Dear Colonel Bates:

I have reviewed the file of Cadet James M. Holobaugh and the recommendations which you will be forwarding to the Second Region Command at Ft. Knox. In my judgement, this case raises a number of significant issues. However, I think it appropriate to comment only on the specific issues presented to me.

As I am sure you know, this university is non-discriminatory in its admission of students and hiring of faculty and staff. Among many other things, this means that the university does not discriminate on the basis of sexual preference or orientation. Although I understand clearly that the action against the cadet being recommended in this case is consistent with present Army regulations, it is also clearly inconsistent with the non-discriminatory values of this (and I should think virtually all) universities. Some friction between ROTC and the university community should not be a surprising result.

Let me turn to the particular case and the three questions you raise in your letter of January 30.

1. Were the rights of the student observed? I have reviewed the file and hearing transcript which you provided and am satisfied that the procedural rights of the student were in large measure observed. It might well have been to Cadet Holo-

baugh's advantage if he had consulted an attorney earlier, but the Army was apparently not obligated to provide one. I do observe that he was represented by counsel of his choosing at the hearing.

2. Does the evidence and finding support the recommendation? In fact, there are two recommendations — to "disenroll" and to require payback.

First, I do not find the term "disenroll" to be understandable. While the term may be suggested by Army regulations, in fact the issue is whether Cadet Holobaugh will be commissioned. As I read the record, he has completed the educational pre-requisites for commissioning. Although an assertion of homosexuality would not preclude a student here from participating in a University program, I recognize that the Army has exercised the right to establish its own standards for commissioning. There is evidence in the record of an assertion of homosexuality by Cadet Holobaugh. Letters submitted on his behalf do not resolve this issue. However, I am advised by our General Counsel that under Army regulations the assertion of homosexuality could be regarded as a sufficient basis to support the decision not to commission Cadet Holobaugh. Although I question the wisdom of current Army policy, I am aware that Army Regulation 635-100, para. 5 - 51 b, authorizes separation when one states that he is a homosexual.

However, I do not concur that the evidence and finding support the demand for repayment of scholarship funds received by Cadet Holobaugh. He has completed his course work and had demonstrated a willingness to serve in the Army. Thus, he is not seeking to evade his service obligation. It is the Army's stance on homosexuality, not evasive action by Cadet Holobaugh, which prevents his commissioning. We do not find he was fraudulent or mendacious in obtaining his scholarship. Thus, we do not conclude the evidence supports a decision to require repayment of the scholarship funds.

3. Was the student evaluated without prejudice? This is not an easy question. It is difficult for me to judge from the evidence in the record if the military personnel involved in this case were prejudiced. I do not find evidence in the record indicating that a prejudiced evaluation occurred. However, the

absence of substantial evidence to support the conclusion reached concerning repayment suggests that those making the decision might not have been open-minded.

I trust that you will forward these views together with your recommendations to Second Region Headquarters. Again, I appreciate the opportunity to comment. Please keep me informed of the progress of this case.

Very truly yours,
Edward S. Macias
Provost

Once again, someone had come through with a good letter on my behalf. "First, I do not find the term 'disenroll' to be understandable" — I love that.

The ACLU wanted to drum up as much public support as they could. They thought that by appearing on television and on the college lecture circuit, I could play a major role in the fight to force the Pentagon to reverse its policy, while helping my own case. Meanwhile, Marc began pressuring me to tell my father what was going on before the publicity hit.

It hadn't been much earlier when I would sooner have paid back half a million dollars than tell my father that I was gay. But my mind had gradually changed as the situation became more and more ridiculous. Here I was, perfectly capable, *more* than capable, of serving in the military and doing a fine job, and just because of who I lived with and slept with, I couldn't. When they demanded that I repay the scholarship, they added insult to injury. I felt like I was down and then they kicked me one more time. I wanted to fight back. It's ironic, because getting booted from ROTC has made me a soldier for life. The Army trained me to be a warrior for four years, never thinking I would wage war against them. But they forced my hand. I am a career soldier now, and my cause is equal rights for gays and lesbians. I feel that I'll be fighting for something for the rest of my life.

While I was as ready to tell my father as I would ever be, it would still be the hardest thing I'd ever done in my life. Unfortunately, there wasn't enough time before the media blitz to go to Ava and tell him in person. My choices were telephone or express mail, and I decided on the latter.

*Jim's father: "I received a letter from Morris by Federal Express. I was in the hallway at school when the delivery person gave it to me, and I was walking down the hall opening it and reading it. It's about as shocking a way as you can find out. I didn't become emotional or anything at that point. I do become emotional when I talk about it with some of my friends."*

Dad,

There is something I have wanted to tell you for some time. I have often wondered how I would tell you, and this is not how I planned it. I would prefer to say this in person, unfortunately circumstances have forced me to say something now. I am writing to tell you that I am gay. I really have no idea how you will react to this. Maybe you had no idea, maybe you did. I hope that if you do not understand now, that you will in time. I am the same person you have always known, it just happens that the person I choose to spend my life with is male. That person is Brent. I can imagine that many thoughts must be running through your mind right now. Sorrow or anger that your son is gay, guilt that you did something (or failed to do something) as a parent, fear of AIDS. There is nothing you could have done as a parent to prevent (or cause) my being gay. There is no reason for guilt. There is no reason to be sorry for me. I am happier than I have ever been. There is no reason for you to worry about AIDS. I am HIV negative, Brent is HIV negative, and we are monogamous, therefore there is *no danger*. I hope you are not angry with me. This was not a choice. Although a person may not come to recognize his or her sexual preference until a later age, sexual preference is not something that is chosen or can be changed at will. Maybe you think it is just a phase. It's not. I have had numerous relationships and sex with girls, I know this is not a phase.

I want you to be involved in my life. I do not want to cut you off like some lesbians & gays do when they are afraid to tell their parents. Those parents go through life wondering

[126]

why their son or daughter is so distant. Over the last few months, a wall has been going up between us because so much has happened that I could not tell you. Every time I have been home or talked to you on the phone it has been so business-like because I have had to edit out large chunks of my life. I want us to be able to discuss something other than the weather. I want you to know what is happening in my life.

I have wanted to tell you for some time, but I did not feel I was ready, nor did I want to tell you over the phone or in a letter. The reason I chose to say something now is that I have been afraid that you might find out from someone other than myself. After Brent and I had been together for some time, I began to fear that after I was commissioned an officer, someone who was homophobic might find out about our relationship and cause me problems with the Army. I thought that I might be better off telling the Army before I was ever commissioned. I tried to get advice from an Army lawyer (JAG officer), but they refused to see me since they only counsel enlisted personnel and I was going to be an officer. I called an attorney in St. Louis who specializes in gay issues, but she charges $70/hour so I could not afford her. I decided that I had to speak to somebody about the Army's policy toward homosexuality, so I went to see Cpt. Dawson. Cpt. Dawson is an officer with Wash. U. Army ROTC whom I trusted. He told me that I would be better off if the Army found out before commissioning rather than after. He advised me to resign my scholarship on the basis that I am gay. I gave a letter to LTC Bates declining to be commissioned because I am gay, as Cpt. Dawson advised. LTC Bates is a very homophobic Baptist, and after talking to him I decided I should see an attorney regardless of cost. I went to Arlene Zarembka (the attorney I mentioned above). She pointed out that I did not have to voluntarily decline commissioning just because I am gay. We sent a letter to LTC Bates rescinding the first letter. This all took place last spring. I have spent a great deal of money on legal fees. Fortunately I met a prominent New York lawyer who has taken my case free of charge. We are being backed by the A.C.L.U. LTC Bates has recommended to higher headquarters that I be forced to repay the Army all the scholarship money in addition to not commissioning me. We are fighting this on the basis that the Army is kicking me out, I am not quitting, therefore I should not have to repay them. I don't want to go into all the details here because I can explain them later, but rest assured that I have one of the best attorneys available (he normally gets $350 per hour) and the power of the American Civil Liberties Union behind me.

I know I am throwing a lot of stuff at you all at once. The last thing I want to do is embarrass you or cause you any problems. I hope you will understand. I have told Melanie everything also. She has several books for parents who find out their son or daughter is gay. They are very good and I hope you will take a look at them. I am not expecting you to accept all of this right away, after all it has taken me a long time. I saw a therapist for several months. I know you probably have a lot of questions, I will try to answer them the best I can.

I love you Dad,
Morris

My father didn't call the day he got the letter, but he did call the day after. I could tell he was extremely upset. There was no sense talking about the weather at that point, so I asked straight off, "Did you get my letter?" He said, "Yeah." He said he hadn't slept at all that night, that he was a wreck. I suggested he talk to someone about it, and told him that doing so had helped me. That didn't go over well. He said something like, "Well, that's probably part of the problem. You've gone to some psychologist who has talked you into believing you're gay, and to be proud of it, and you shouldn't be."

Over and over, my father kept telling me he didn't think I was gay: "I can't believe that you're biologically gay," was the way he put it. The sound of it was defensive — saying I didn't get it from his genes or whatever. I made it clear that I would give him time to accept it, and I hoped he would. But he was like, "I'll never accept this. You're doing the wrong thing. You're going to regret it. Blah-blah-blah-blah-blah."

The thing that bothered me most was his saying my being gay would hurt my nephew. He told me my nephew loved me

*After marching in an ROTC color guard for Rolla's holiday parade,
I posed for this photo in December 1986.*

These two buildings became familiar sights during my ROTC years. Above is the Army ROTC building at the University of Missouri in Rolla. It's no longer standing, and they've moved to a newer building. Below is the ROTC building at Washington University. The Air Force ROTC occupies the lower floor; Army is upstairs.

In 1988, ROTC used my photo in this advertisement to promote their co-op program.

Above: My family home in Ava, Missouri. Below: My dad, me, my nephew, and my sister Melanie after my graduation from Washington University in May 1990. I had just learned that I wouldn't have to repay my scholarship. This was also the first time I'd been around my family since I came out. If none of us looks very comfortable — it's because we weren't.

*Several things changed my life as the 1980s drew to a close. The most important, of course, was meeting Brent.*

Brent and I spent as much time together as we could. We skied in Yosemite in early 1991; later that year his parents joined us for sightseeing in New York.

*December 6, 1989, will always be clear in my mind. On that day, I walked through this door to the "informal investigation" that was triggered by my coming out.*

Fortunately, of course, Brent was with me during those difficult months — and he still is. These photos were taken on Cape Cod, after the worst of my ROTC battles had ended.

and that I shouldn't do this to him. He also said he thought my moving to the city did this to me. If he'd known this was going to happen, he said, he wouldn't have wanted me to go to college. Staying in Ava and working at Town and Country the rest of my life would have been preferable to being successful and gay. I don't think he still feels that way. I hope not. He was blaming things that were out of his control for my being gay. As if "The City" can make you gay.

One interesting thing he said, almost as an aside, was that he had a roommate in college who was gay. This was the first I'd ever heard about that.

*Jim's news took his father completely by surprise.*

*"I never suspected Morris was gay. I had no idea. To find out your son is the total opposite of what you thought is really a shock."*

*When Jim mentioned that he might be giving interviews on the subject, his father was very much against it.*

*"I probably encouraged him not to," Mr. Holobaugh says. "My words to him were that what you're doing to yourself is creating a situation where you're going to have to live within 10 percent of the population for the rest of your life, and that's going to create a lot of hardships on you. Of course, my first few phone calls were trying to convince him he wasn't gay."*

My father was sure my going public would hurt my career and ruin my life. I'm sure he believed that. But I also think he just didn't want people to know his son was gay. When he told me I'd be forced to live within 10 percent of the population, I said, "Dad, it's not that way at all. It might be that way in Ava, but I have plenty of straight friends, and New York's not like that." His argument was ridiculous. You're not relegated to living with 10 percent of the populace; it's not like a commune. In fact, the publicity surrounding my case brought me dozens of new friends, and more acquaintances than I could keep up with.

But I understood why my dad tried to talk me out of going public. A parent's normal reaction is "Don't tell Aunt Flossie or Gramma."

I was telling the world.

# Outrage back home

B efore the ACLU went public with my story, they asked me about any past homosexual conduct that might be unearthed and cause problems.

Pete, the guy from my first semester at Rolla, was my only concern. I knew none of the cousins or childhood friends I'd fooled around with would be volunteering information, and I didn't think Pete would, either. But just to be sure, I called him, told him what was going on, and asked him not to talk to anyone about our having sex. I didn't have to twist his arm.

The ACLU then sent feeders to the press. The *New York Times* called and asked for an interview.

I didn't want to tell my dad that I had agreed to do the article, so I called Melanie instead. She begged me not to do it, arguing that it would hurt Dad. I ignored her. I knew it was too late to back down, and the issue was too important to run away from. I hope my family eventually will understand that I never meant to hurt them, and that I did my best to protect them from the media. I never mentioned Ava. If anyone asked where I was from, I either said Springfield or southern Missouri. Even my recently acquired friends thought I was from Springfield.

The *New York Times* article appeared March 2, 1990. The night before, Brent and I had dinner at John Houston's house. Marc

Wolinsky and Joe Steffan were there, too, along with their partners. The early edition of the *Times* comes out before midnight, so Joe and I went to get a copy as soon as it hit the stands. I didn't know what to think when I saw it. I was both excited and apprehensive.

The article laid out the basics of my case, noting that Washington University supported me. A photograph of me in a dark suit and tie, looking straight into the camera, ran alongside the copy. A lot of people told me they liked that photograph, that I looked honest and sincere, and that could only help my case. I wasn't crazy about it, but I rarely like photos of myself. The headline beside the photo read, "Gay Cadet Is Asked to Repay R.O.T.C. Scholarship." The photo, with the words "Gay Cadet" beside it, was sure to attract attention.

The next day, I went to school as usual. But when I got home, Bill called to relay a pile of messages. Most were from the public, but some were from the media. That weekend I taped an interview for "ABC World News Tonight," Monday morning I was on "CBS This Morning," and that was just the beginning. It was strange and scary to talk about being gay in front of so many people, but I'd prepared myself for it, and I knew it had to be done.

During the first few months, I was bombarded with phone calls and letters. Bill and Marc told me I would be getting that sort of thing for about two weeks, then it would die down. Boy, were they wrong. It was almost overwhelming. I was going to school full-time, and it was hard to concentrate on studies when reporters were leaving messages on my answering machine every day. That whole semester I couldn't wait for the day when I'd come home from class and find no messages. It seemed to go on forever. Brent, of course, had to live with all of these distractions too.

*Brent: "It was a frightening time, especially for Jim. I was pretty much able to stay in the background, but Jim was really nervous. When things come out in public, who knows what's going to happen? You don't know who you're going to meet, what kind of weirdos will be out there. I remember being in John Houston's apartment March 1, the night before the* Times *article. We were all nervous. Then, to see it in print! But the weird thing is it just kept going and going. Now, it's been going for two years, and I'm just amazed. We thought a couple of months at most. We never thought there would be all these lectures, that he'd become a major force in the movement.*

*"I think at first all the attention in the press was kind of hard on Jim. Here you have a 23-year-old trying to deal with all this attention — radio talk shows, television talk shows. I especially remember the first show. He wanted me to stay with him the night before at Le Parker Meridien. He was nervous about it. So I drove down for the night, and then rushed to get to work the next morning in time to see the show. I was running through the hospital thinking, 'I've got to find a TV, but I can't tell anyone why.' I caught the last few seconds."*

*The reaction in Ava was even worse than Jim expected. Fortunately, his father was spared most of it.*

*"All of my close friends here know about this," says Mr. Holobaugh, "but it's not generally known in the community. For one thing, the news has never tied it with Ava. And the name — he was known by Morris, and they say 'James,' and when they say 'Holobaugh' it doesn't come out the way it should be pronounced. Probably more people know about it than I think. It's not something someone's going to bring up in talking to you. Ava is a town where no one gay has ever announced it to everyone. But all of my friends and the school people have been supportive. Several teachers and people in the administrative staff came and talked to me and offered support. They saw it as something we didn't understand, and we'd just have to accept it and go on.*

*"The biggest concern of some of my friends was that he would be hurting the family — including other members of the family in other states — by going so public. You know, if you're going to be gay, fine, that's your right. But to get on a stump and try to change anyone else ... And then there's the negative thing about being in the military. They'd say, 'If you're gay, fine, but don't try to force that on the military.' I don't see it exactly that way. You know, if this thing with being gay is a natural thing, then it shouldn't be a problem."*

[132]

*Jim had not talked to John Taylor for some time, so John had no idea what was going on. Mr. Holobaugh says, "It hit John pretty hard. They were great friends."*

*When Jim was on "CBS This Morning," the mother of his ex-girlfriend saw the program and arrived at work in tears. She works in the same office as John's father, who is also named John.*

*"After I picked myself off the floor," says Mr. Taylor, "I was hurt. I was hurt deeply. I went to the school to tell Janice, my wife. It broke her into tears. She had to leave the classroom."*

*Mr. Taylor then went home and called John.*

*"My dad called me about 4:30 that afternoon," says John. "I know it was hard for him to tell me. Homosexual was never in our vocabulary. Morris and I even made fun of homosexuals in high school. By the tone of my dad's voice I was absolutely positive my grandmother had died, because she'd been sick. He asked if I was sitting down. I said I wasn't and he said maybe I'd better have a seat. He said, 'Son, it seems as if your friend Morris is gay.' I started laughing. I said, 'Dad, you're full of shit.' He didn't change his tone of voice. He said, 'No, I'm serious.' It hit me pretty hard then. I started getting choked up."*

*"Johnny finally said, 'Dad, I've got to hang up. Let me get my wits about me and I'll call you back later,'" Mr. Taylor recalls. "It just tore him to pieces."*

*"After I was off the phone I started breathing hard like I was hyperventilating," says John. "Then I just cried. When my wife came home and asked me what was wrong, all I could get out was 'Morris.' She thought he'd died by the way I was acting.*

*"I called Morris's dad and asked him for Morris's phone number. He'd moved and I didn't have his new number. His dad knew by my voice why I was calling, but neither of us said anything about it. So I called Morris. I guess what I really wanted to say to him was, 'Hey, why didn't you ever say anything to me?' 'Cause we had been pretty tight. We weren't just casual friends. On a scale of one to ten, we were a ten. After I called, Morris sent me an eight-page letter explaining what was going on. I wrote his dad a letter, just to let him know I knew what he was going through, and that I'd always be there even if others weren't."*

*Jim does not think he handled John's phone call particularly well:*

"I could have been more understanding when he called. By this time I'd gotten comfortable with being gay and I really wasn't very sensitive to the things he was feeling. Later, I felt bad about that, and I also felt bad that I hadn't told him before."

When John is asked if it's true that the news is not well known in Ava, he replies, "Shit, no! Everybody heard it and people were literally in disbelief. There are about twenty-two hundred people in Ava, and I imagine everyone knows about it. It didn't go over well at all. Some people were outraged. My mom teaches at the school. People approached her asking what my link to this was. She broke down in tears at school because people were in-criminating me.

The reactions John heard from others in Ava were vicious:

"One mutual friend said, 'He will never set foot on my property again.' Danny, his brother-in-law, doesn't want him around the kids. A friend of ours who moved to Texas after his junior year came up in June [1991]. I showed him one of the articles on Morris and he said, 'Mother fuck! No way! Morris can't be a faggot!' All weekend he'd shake his head and say, 'This just can't be right.'

"Jean Parker, Chris Parker's mom, goes to the United Meth-odist Church where I went, and one Sunday she came up after church and said, 'John, all of this stuff about Morris isn't true, is it?' I said I was afraid it was. She said Chris and her husband didn't believe it, that they thought Morris just did it to get out of the Army and not have to pay back his scholarship."

"You've got to understand this is not New York," says John's father. "This isn't Chicago. People don't want to talk about it. If you do say something about the subject and someone comments, their opinion is the same as mine and Johnny's — not good at all."

Does John ever defend Jim when he's attacked by others?

"No, I do not defend him. Let me rephrase that. I defended him on every issue until the day I found out he was gay. From then on, I have not defended him. I tell gay jokes, I listen to gay jokes, and I laugh at gay jokes. In Morris's mind he is acting in a normal and acceptable way; in my mind he is misguided and needs to step outside himself and look at what he professes. He and I used to make fun of 'faggots' in high school. We thought the Eddie Murphy routine about Mr. T. was hilarious. You must understand that we grew up in a town with no blacks, no Asians, no big-city influences, and where Ku Klux Klan and paramilitary groups still exist. Ava, Missouri, is the heart of the Bible Belt, with churches on every corner. Gay behavior is not tolerated, period. I believe people would literally bring out the guns if a gay group ever tried to hold a demonstration in Ava. People around here have been killed for a hell of a lot less than that.

"Still, he was my best friend since 1978. I can't go back in time and choose a new best friend just because I found out he is gay. It has strained our relationship because I had to find out the way I did. That was hard to cope with. I regret the fact that we've grown apart in our beliefs. I fear that he will die of AIDS, and that is not the way you want to lose someone who has been a friend for so long."

Does John think what Jim did was wrong?

"You bet your bottom dollar what he did was wrong. I believe in a person standing up for themselves in whatever way is necessary, but he went too far. He should have kept his mouth shut and given his time to the Army. They trained him and shelled out the money for his education, and he was both contractually and morally obligated to fulfill his duties. If he knew he was gay, then he should have served his four years as an officer and put his feelings on hold or kept them secret until the four years were over. He made such a big deal about wanting to serve. Well, he could have if he wouldn't have been so bent on blowing everyone's mind and coming 'out of the closet.'"

Did John hear any sympathetic reaction in Ava?

"Sympathetic to Morris? Shit no! The only sympathetic reaction in the whole county would've been for Morris's father. His father is well liked; he's one of the few people in the school system who's held on. Usually principals offend someone and they're gone. But Jim's father is salt-of-the-earth. I think he looks ten years older. He aged ten years in a week. It's not just me that thinks that. People in Ava have said that."

"I wanted to talk to Jim [Mr. Holobaugh], but I didn't know how to approach him," says Mr. Taylor. "I still don't. When we see each other it's just, 'Hi, Jim,' 'Hi, John.' Very short. Since this happened, he's quiet. Reserved. He won't hardly talk."

But if Jim was well liked in Ava, didn't anyone — instead of saying, "Morris is gay. Morris is horrible" — say instead, "If Morris is gay, maybe gays aren't so bad?"

[135]

"Morris was extremely well liked by everyone," says John. "But there are some lines you just don't cross in Ava, and Morris crossed them. There's no sympathy for him at all. Probably only two of his high school friends have remained friends through this — me and Craig. Our graduating class is thinking about organizing our ten-year reunion. I would guess the committee would vote not even to send Morris an invitation."

Does John think Jim should come back for the reunion?

"No. I wouldn't say he'd fear for his life, but people would be hard on him. Morris doesn't want to come back to Ava. The people here don't want him to."

John didn't tell Jim of the reaction in Ava for well over a year. Finally, John wrote a letter, stating matter-of-factly:

"As for the reaction in Ava, most people would rather see you burn in Hell as to come back. You hurt so many people by coming out of the closet. People whispered in the hall while your dad and sister hung their heads in shame."

When asked what he thought would happen if Jim came back to town, John's father said, "He's liable to get the shit whipped out of him."

"My mom and dad love Morris like a son," says John. "But I don't know if my dad would ever want him in the house again. My mom says if he came to visit, she'd talk to him, but she's afraid my dad would get up and leave the room."

"In high school, Morris was an excellent kid," says Mr. Taylor. "It could not be detected. But when it did happen, it hurt us. It hurt us bad. I will not let that kid into our house again. I won't mess with that kind of shit."

Mrs. Taylor declined to discuss Jim, saying the subject was still too painful to talk about. "He hurt our son terribly," she said.

"It's been hard on my sister, Jana, too," says John. "She always idolized Morris. He was always what she wanted her boyfriend to be like. He was nice, intelligent, handsome. He always dressed nice and had a good haircut. Even when he was mowing the lawn or something, he still looked nice. Of all the guys I graduated with, if you lined them all up and said, 'Pick out the one who might be gay,' Morris would be the last one I'd have picked. To this day, I still find it hard. I can only liken it to death. When I found out, a part of me just died. It will never be the same no

[136]

matter how many moons go by. Every time I see a photo or anything that reminds me of Morris, it still hits me like a ton of bricks. But I'm certainly not ashamed of him. I can't hit rewind and go back and pick another best friend. When I look through my photo albums and scrapbooks, Morris is there."

John has written a sixty-page manuscript about Jim, and about learning that Jim is gay.

"My wife was gone one day. I locked myself in my room with my dog and just went to town on it. This may sound corny, but one thing I had always looked forward to was Morris being the best man at my wedding. I was looking forward to being his best man, too. I've even got little scraps of poetry about it. Morris and I were always really tight, but we never were touchy people. We never did pat each other on the back or hug each other like some guys do, especially on football teams. About two minutes before I got married, he was straightening my collar and making sure I looked all right, and he said, 'John, I'm really happy for you. I wish you the best.' Then he put his arms around me for the first time in my life and hugged me. That really took me. I kind of floated through the wedding ceremony after that, mumbling the words. It made me so happy that my best friend had finally hugged me and said he wished me the best.

"I don't know if he ever plans to marry Brent, but if he called me and asked me to be best man, I don't know if I'd have the strength for it. I've prayed to God not to ever be put in that situation."

I wanted to tell John the previous August that I was gay, but he was in the middle of getting married. I was his best man, and I didn't want him to have to deal with everything going on in my life, not to mention the fact that his best man was gay. I didn't want to upset his time of happiness, and I didn't want to tell him over the phone. John didn't have a clue I was gay. I messed around with all these friends when I was young, but John wasn't one of them.

I didn't know about the reaction in Ava until recently. I never got any feedback from my stepmother, Connie, either, though I'll bet this whole gay thing has just made her life. For her, it's probably more ammo to use against me.

*Before Jim received the letter from John describing the reaction in Ava, he admitted he did care how people thought of him back home.*

*"It's weird — there's something about your hometown that makes you care about what people think. I don't know why. I tell myself, 'Who cares?' I mean, I don't care what people in Connecticut think about me being gay. I don't care what people in America think when they read the articles. If they don't like it, so what? But people in Ava — for some reason I value their opinion. I don't like them thinking I'm being mean to my father by doing this, or that I've lost my mind. I want those people to understand. You tell yourself it doesn't really matter. But it does."*

*In a response to John's letter, which quoted scripture, Jim wrote:*

You said the Bible should scare me to death. Why should the Bible scare me? I am not a Christian. I consider the Bible fiction. Islam forbids eating pork. Does eating pork scare you? Unless you have converted since we talked last, probably not ... I was curious about the way people in Ava reacted to my being gay. Do I really care? Not really, but probably more than I should ... From your description they reacted about like I expected. I just hope that my coming out made at least a few people think a little before they completely closed their mind and shoved me into one of the comfortable, rigid, little categories they have segmented into their brain. I hope that at least one of the gay young people in Ava was able to feel a little bit better because it made her/him realize that they are not the only one in the world with those feelings. If that happened it was worth it. It doesn't bother me to write the rest of Ava off.

Your parents are a different story. I care a great deal about them and I won't just write them off. I just hope that someday they will understand what is important.

I did not hurt Melanie and my Dad. Ava did. The homo-hating society that you described did. I am guilty of nothing but honesty. If society didn't harbor this bigoted prejudice against gays my family would not have to "walk down the hall with their heads hung in shame."

*After receiving John's report of the reaction in Ava, Jim could only shrug and say, "What a place." As the Arkansas Gazette editorialized after the residents of Arcadia, Florida, burned down the house of a family whose three children had AIDS: "Pit bulls wouldn't be safe in this town."*

*Today, when asked what he misses about living in Missouri, Jim says: "Nothing."*

My appearances on television went well. The first appearance, which is still my favorite, was Monday, March 5, on "CBS This Morning," with Bill Rubenstein at my side. I liked the way I handled the questions, and doing the show gave a boost to my confidence.

The report on "ABC World News Tonight" followed, showing me jogging through Central Park wearing a Washington University sweatshirt. The people at ABC did one thing that irritated me, though: The narrator said that "an ROTC investigation," while finding no evidence of willful evasion on my part, "noted strong indications of an attempt to manipulate the system for his advantage." As this was spoken, the words "manipulate the system" appeared on the screen. The statement is inaccurate. The ROTC investigation report says nothing about manipulating the system. The words are from Captain Boyle's recommendations to Colonel Bates. They are one man's opinion and should have been identified as such. Unfortunately, this type of shoddy reporting seems to be common on the network newscasts. The more familiar I've become with some of the stories they report, the more I realize how inaccurate and distorted they are.

Later, I also appeared on "NBC Nightly News," the local newscast of WFSB in Hartford, New Jersey station WOR's "Nine Broadcast Plaza," PBS's "Livewire," ABC's "20/20," and "CBS Nightwatch."

The "NBC Nightly News" segment ended with the curious comment that the ROTC debate "has prompted many Pentagon officials to predict the armed forces will be open to homosexuals within a few years." *Many* Pentagon officials? A major development, if true. Most Pentagon officials still refuse com-

[139]

ment. Although invited to appear on the Hartford newscast and "20/20," Pentagon officials would not.

On the Hartford newscast I was sporting a new look, my hair grown long in the back. I was out of the ROTC now and could look the way I wanted. But now when I watch that telecast on tape, I think my hair was too long. And that I talked too much.

The New Jersey show was one of the most memorable. I appeared with Peter Laska, who had been kicked out of ROTC at the University of Pennsylvania; Tamar Pachter, Peter's attorney; and retired captain Tom Blomquist of the Coast Guard. The youngest of eleven children, Laska was on a Navy ROTC scholarship at the University of Pennsylvania. He was suspended a day after writing a letter informing his commanding officer that he was gay. The Navy later demanded that Laska repay his $26,000 scholarship. When he refused, the Navy sent a bill for the $26,000 to his parents, who were in their seventies. They hadn't even known their son was gay. Laska told *USA Today*, "I am bitter. They often talk about honor and character ... All through this, I was the one being honest and truthful."

The audience was obviously on the side of Peter and me, reserving its biggest applause for Tamar's statement: "This is discrimination, plain and simple." Only one audience member spoke in favor of the military. A chain reaction of support for me and Peter began when a woman who identified herself as "Gloria" stood up and said, "I've been in the Army Reserve for the last twelve years. I've been on assignments with gays, lesbians, and straights. I've had more men hitting on me than lesbian women. It doesn't matter if you're gay or straight, it's whether you can do the job." Her policeman husband then stood up and agreed, saying he'd served alongside gays in the police department and had no problems. A construction worker said he was not aware of working with any gays himself, but he agreed with Gloria.

Sandra Lowe, staff counsel for the Lambda Legal Defense and Education Fund, appeared with me on WNET–New York's "Livewire." Unfortunately, the show's objectivity was compromised in that it was moderated by a representative of the Gay Cable Network, making it too much of a gay love-fest. But

Sandra Lowe was great. Responding to the old myth that gays are more predatory than straights, Lowe said that in surveys, 75 percent of female soldiers reported more than one incident of sexual harassment from males in the military.

Given this statistic, together with the PERSEREC report indicating that heterosexual males have a lower preservice adjustment rating than women or gay males, and the studies showing that virtually all cases of espionage involve heterosexual males (see Appendix), it's logical to ask whether allowing heterosexual males in the armed forces is such a good idea. Certainly a better case could be made against allowing straight males than the military has made against allowing gays. The arguments would at least be supported by studies and statistics instead of by prejudice.

The "20/20" segment was, by far, the worst of my television appearances. I hated it. First, I was introduced as "Joe's friend, Jim Holobaugh," with a photo of Joe Steffan and me running together. This must have led some viewers to think we were lovers, or at least that we had known each other prior to our being kicked out and might have planned our actions together.

My main objection, though, was ABC's decision to tell the military's side of the story for them. The narrator told viewers that "'20/20' called every branch of the service several times asking, 'Will anyone speak about this for the record?' ... Since they won't talk, we'll try to make their case for them." This statement was followed by photos of soldiers in showers, a soldier getting dressed, and the reporter's remark to Joe: "If I were showering with women, I'd get turned on." Joe responded sensibly: "If you had been allowed to shower with women from the time you were five years old, I don't think it would necessarily turn you on. I've been showering with men since I was on the basketball team in elementary school. It's something I can deal with."

The reporter also said gays in the military weren't the same as blacks in the military because with gays it was a sexual question. The similarity, of course, is that both kinds of discrimination are based on ignorance and fear. If the military refuses to discuss the issue, why bring up these ridiculous arguments? The segment ended with a stupid comment from

[141]

Barbara Walters — something like, "Well, Hugh, there are two sides to every story and I guess both are valid."

ABC did the same thing when Joe Steffan was on "Nightline." Since the Navy refused to comment on Joe's case, ABC put on notoriously homophobic Representative Robert K. Dornan of California. He said homosexuality was a mental illness. Dornan also tried to make sodomy the issue, although Department of Defense policy makes no distinction between homosexual and heterosexual sodomy. In any case, Steffan had never been charged with sodomy.

I turned down an appearance on "Donahue," feeling I was not ready for that format. I also declined an invitation to appear on "Geraldo." The program topic was "outing," which had nothing to do with my case.

In the print media, I appeared on the cover of *Outweek* (New York) and *The Guide* (Boston). I was also featured in a two-page spread in the *Advocate*. Several publications ran editorials supporting me. A *Boston Globe* editorial said: "Holobaugh acted in good faith... The ROTC should drop its effort to recover Holobaugh's scholarship money."

I received editorial backing on both home fronts. The *New Haven Register* ran an editorial titled "Army policy denies humanity of gays," and subtitled "Ban on homosexuals grounded in ignorance, hypocrisy and intolerance." It said: "The anti-homosexual posture of the Department of Defense is denying James Holobaugh a basic right he has as a human being. If Holobaugh lived a lie and hid his homosexuality, he could receive his commission as a lieutenant in the Army reserves."

The *Saint Louis Post-Dispatch*, in an editorial titled "No Scholarship, No Commission, No Compassion," said:

> The effort to recover $25,000 from James M. Holobaugh ... is a travesty ... ROTC depends on cooperation from host universities, and its vindictive insistence that Mr. Holobaugh repay his scholarship money has brought opposition from some schools. That welcome stance should help the Army see how unfair its position is. An Army spokesman says the Holobaugh

case is the first he has seen seeking reimbursement; it should be the last, and it should be dropped.

And *Student Life,* the campus newspaper at Washington University, wrote:

The ROTC's request that a Washington University senior be denied military commission and be required to repay a $25,000 scholarship because he is homosexual clearly shows the discriminatory practices of the military. Such practices should be abolished, and — until they are — Washington University should not associate itself with such an institution.

I appreciated the press — especially the support — but was surprised that even the print media had a hard time getting the facts straight. The now-defunct *Outweek* was the worst. They taped an interview, then simply transcribed the tape, making an amazing number of errors. They inserted words I never said. They said I was from southwest New Jersey instead of southwest Missouri.

Then *Outweek's* photographer tried to talk me into posing for a photo with a flag in my mouth, as if I were being bound and gagged by the government. After a while I reluctantly agreed, stipulating that the photos couldn't be used until I saw them. They were terrible, and my attorneys were horrified. It wasn't the image they wanted to present — especially in the middle of the flag-burning controversy — and it wasn't something I'd do, anyway. Although I support the right of people to burn a flag, I personally would not do it. And I certainly wouldn't walk down the street with a flag in my mouth. Using the American flag as a symbol to get a point across is just a bad idea. It only makes people angry. We managed to obtain the negatives to the photos, and in the end no harm was done.

One thing I hated about many of the items in the mainstream press was that they said I was "homosexual" rather than "gay." *Homosexual* sounds so clinical, like a disease. Minority groups should be called by the names they choose for themselves, not scientific terms. It's like the press referring to blacks as Negroids.

[143]

Still, *homosexual* is at least better than *queer*. I don't like this movement to mainstream *queer*. It gives people the idea that it's queer to be queer. Queer Nation and ACT-UP have a very limited place as far as I'm concerned. They have a role to play — we're a diverse community, and standing in the street and shouting is sometimes necessary to make people aware of what's going on. But it's important that gay people be seen as more than just angry people in the streets. ACT-UP and Queer Nation are always the ones that get on TV, and that's too bad. Constant anger is tiresome. It's like reading the *Village Voice*. All the articles are so angry, and after a while it's more than you can take. It's also like burning the flag. You don't win too many arguments or converts by making people angry — at least not when they're angry at you. As a famous Beatle once put it, "If you go carrying pictures of Chairman Mao, you ain't gonna make it with anyone anyhow."

It was also odd the way the media identified Gerry Studds. "NBC Nightly News" introduced him as, "Congressman Gerry Studds, a homosexual," as if the standard way of introducing a member of Congress were by sexual preference. The host of WOR's "Nine Broadcast Plaza," a sympathetic woman who obviously found the military policy offensive, at first referred to Studds as "the avowed congressman from Massachusetts," as if Studds had called a press conference one day to say, "Yes, I *am* a congressman from Massachusetts. There's no sense in denying it!" She then corrected herself and said "the avowed *gay* congressman."

By the time President Clinton took office in 1993, editorials and columns calling on the military to abandon its petty policy had become a common thing. But in 1989, 1990, and 1991, only a few courageous journalists tackled the subject. The *Atlanta Constitution* on October 26, 1989, accused the Pentagon of suppressing the PERSEREC reports (see Appendix) because they found that homosexuals were no greater security risks than heterosexuals, contradicting Pentagon thought. An April 6, 1990, column in the same newspaper by Marilyn Geewax compared the military's arguments against admitting gays to its previous arguments against admitting blacks and women. And, on November 9, 1990, the *Constitution* asserted that homo-

[144]

sexuals should have the right to serve their country in any capacity, and that prohibiting them from exercising this right is absurd.

The *New Republic*, February 19, 1990, said:

> In the case of homosexuals ... the common justifications [to keep them out of the military] offered by defenders of the status quo do not make any practical or moral sense ... Of course, the admission of gays will no more eliminate homophobia than the integration of blacks cured racism. But irrational prejudices are bound to diminish over time if the isolation and ignorance they feed upon is ended.

The *Boston Globe* editorialized on September 6, 1990, that military policy should be based on individual behavior, not according to the sexual orientation of an entire group of people.

The *San Francisco Chronicle*, on January 14, 1991, found a reason for allowing gays in the service that might appeal to many heterosexuals: "There is no valid defense for a policy that says gays and lesbians should not be allowed to serve — or for that matter, be exempt from a possible future draft simply by declaring their sexual orientation."

*Spectrum* of Little Rock wrote in its May 8, 1991, issue:

> The U.S. military's ban on homosexuals is peculiar and unnecessary ... As a practical matter, its only effects are negative: it dissuades willing volunteers and/or enforces the closeting of those gays who have elected to ignore the rather silly regulation. Even a journal of such considerable imagination as William F. Buckley's *National Review*, which recently published an article in favor of gays in uniform, can find no serious reason not to open the ranks of the armed forces to gays.

Radio even got into the act. Los Angeles CBS Radio affiliate KNX broadcast an editorial likening the reasons for excluding gays to those used forty years ago to exclude blacks.

*Jim's father has seen a few of Jim's television appearances, but not many.*

*"I have them all on tape — all the ones I know about," he says.*

*"I'm going to sit down and try to analyze them one of these days."*

[145]

The newspaper in Springfield, Missouri, carried the Associated Press story on Jim. Other than that, Jim knows of no articles about him appearing in southwestern Missouri. Of course, word of mouth more than made up for the absence of newsprint.

Does the talk around Ava bother Mr. Holobaugh?

"No, that doesn't bother me. Being a principal, you're used to people who are mad at you one day and not the next. It didn't cause me to want to hide or feel ashamed. Never. The only problems I had were the emotions, for a while. But I stuck in there and toughed it out. I didn't resort to drugs to make me sleep or anything like that. But you can imagine, it was a tough thing to get hit in the head with a hammer. It's something I'm dealing with every day. I feel very close to Morris, and I'm sure he does me."

# New adventures

Aside from the reaction in Ava and a couple of nasty letters quoting the Bible, the response to what I've done has been encouraging. The messages left on my answering machine were mainly from the ACLU, passing along words of support. No one knew my phone number, so people could not call me direct. However, my old number in Saint Louis was still in the phone book under my name, and I expect that recording was worn out. There is also another Holobaugh family in Saint Louis — not related — and I've heard that they received a lot of calls. Someone who eventually got in touch with me said he'd called them first and they acted like they were sick of hearing my name. They said something like, "We don't know that person."

I didn't hear from my old fraternity brothers at first. But I've talked to a few recently, and none seemed to have a problem. A fellow engineering student from Washington University who managed to get my number called and came out to me on the phone. I barely knew him but he thanked me for what I was doing and said, "You're not the only one in civil engineering who's gay. I am."

My boss at the engineering firm read about me in the *Times*. His daughter, whom I did not know, went to Washington U, so he mailed her a copy and said, "This is the guy I hired." But he didn't say anything to me. I worried that entire semester about what he thought. My first day at work I was nervous. He was firing a lot of questions at me about engineering. I was messing up because I was too nervous to think. Then he left me alone for a while. I felt miserable, so I gathered my courage, went to his office, and apologized for being so inept. I told him I was nervous because I was wondering if he'd heard what had been going on in my life the past semester. He said, "Yes, I did. I wasn't going to bring it up because as far as I'm concerned it's not an issue. I'm going to judge you on your engineering abilities, not your sexual orientation." And that was that.

My boss was true to his word. His only concern was the possibility of my missing a lot of work for court proceedings. I told him not to worry, that we weren't litigating. I said I did want to do speaking engagements, though, and that I might need time off without pay to do that. He had no problem with that, as long as we weren't facing a deadline. As it turned out, he was terrific and let me have a tremendous amount of time off to speak. Otherwise, the issue never came up in the office again. I held the job until the recession forced layoffs throughout the industry.

*Jim's friend Robo has mixed feelings on whether or not gays should serve in the military, but he definitely supports Jim:*

*"Myself, I don't see anything wrong with gays being in the military. I can see the armed forces' point of view, but I can't see why a gay person can't do a good job in the Army. I know James, and I know what kind of job he can do. He's an excellent engineer and he could do a lot of good work for the Army. I wish they could just leave out his private life. But at the same time, the way they're structured, they really can't do that. You can't put all these male soldiers in this one sleeping area with some of them gay and some not gay. I don't think it would work out.*

*"As for all the publicity, from what I understand, the reason he is doing it is because he's pushing the issue of gays in the military, trying to either get them to accept gays or get the military off campus. Actually, I'm very proud of him for what he's doing.*

*"It wasn't too long after he told me that the whole thing heated up, and it was in the press. People who knew both of us were coming up to me and saying, 'Did you hear about James?' I'd say,*

*'Yeah, I know.' But people know that James and I are friends, and they know that if they say anything about James, they'll hurt my feelings as well. So if they had any negative opinions, they probably kept them to themselves."*

*One person who did talk to Robo was his and Jim's former speech professor in Rolla.*

*"He was surprised about James being gay, but he was more surprised about how the news was being suppressed in Rolla."*

*"He read about it in the* Chronicle of Higher Education," *says Jim. "I should call him. I'd love to speak there. It's kind of strange that UMR would go to lengths to keep students from finding out. It's not going to cause student unrest, that's for sure. They're not going to be rioting in the streets of Rolla, Missouri, because of this."*

*Jim finds the idea of students rioting in Rolla in support of gay rights hilarious and is rendered speechless while he laughs it off.*

*"When James's story came out," says Robo, "I think people in Rolla recognized him, but wouldn't say anything about it. They'd say, 'Well, he's gone; we're glad he's not here in Rolla anymore.'"*

*"After the CBS program," Carolyn Lang recalls, "there were articles in the local paper. He didn't know quite how it would all be taken. I spoke to some of the people where I work, and they seemed to think Jim was right and the government was wrong."*

*Andy Katz says the gay couple who threw the Thanksgiving party he and Jim attended are both Republicans and do not support Jim at all. They thought he should have repaid the scholarship because he'd broken the rules: Gays are not allowed in the military.*

That kind of reaction drives me crazy. First of all, even if somebody went into ROTC knowing he was gay, or even if he was planning to defraud the military — that's just too bad. It's the military's problem. It's their contradiction, not ours. In any case, that was not the way it was with me. I wasn't quitting, they were kicking me out. Most gays who get dismissed did not realize they were gay when they went in. That was my situation, too, and this couple, of all people, should understand that. Besides, they're "breaking the rules" themselves. Missouri still has a sodomy law.

The campus organization fighting the military policy at MIT put it this way: "Some students are unaware of their sexual orientation until later in their lives. They sign the statement in good faith. This type of 'contract' is irrelevant. If the military policy excluded Jews, the policy would not be justified in the least by a requirement that cadets sign a statement that they are not Jewish."

In the summer of 1989, I had flown to Washington to see Glenn. At this point I had written the letter to Colonel Bates stating that I was gay, but I had not yet been called before the board. I told Glenn that I was gay and explained what had happened. He was surprised but open-minded. When he told his friends at Fort Lee, they blasted me, saying stuff like, "Yeah, he's a fag." Then Glenn went to Germany and the publicity hit. Before he wrote the letter for me, he had talked to his commanders in Germany to make sure he would not be penalized for supporting me. So, when the story appeared in the *Army Times*, there were several people on his base who knew that I was his friend, and they really put me down. Glenn found himself defending me. He told me that after a while he realized I was right, that I should be allowed to serve — that the more he defended me, the more he knew I was right.

*For some people in the military and in ROTC, Jim's story made a difference. Karen Stupski, a Navy ensign, told "20/20": "I read about James Holobaugh, and I really respected his decision. That showed me that there is an option to serving in the closet, that you can come out and you can address the issue directly."*

*Karen told her commanding officers that she had come to the realization that she was a lesbian but that she had never had sex with a woman. She also said she would remain celibate if they would let her stay in. They would not.*

*At Washington University, Air Force ROTC Cadet Robert Schwitz couldn't believe it when he heard the news about Jim:*

*"My initial reaction was, 'Wow!' I knew he had been in a national advertising campaign, and I knew the command level he had achieved. It struck me as being a big injustice. What really bugged me was that he had told his captain, and then it came out*

*that his captain was going to tell on him before he graduated even if Jim didn't say anything. That made me totally not trust the military.*

*"I wrote letters about Jim's case to President Bush, both senators and my representative from my Mount Vernon [Illinois] address, and both senators and my representative from my school address. Paul Simon thanked me for making him aware of the case. Bush sent it to somebody who reiterated their stupid policy in a form letter. Jack Danforth was wishy-washy ambiguous.*

*"A lot of ROTC cadets thought Jim deliberately waited until a month before he graduated. Whether he did or didn't, I understand. A lot of people thought the whole thing was just stupid."*

I received letters of support from all over the world — England, Germany ... Montana. Some people sent donations to the ACLU in my behalf. Many wrote letters to Colonel Bates, the Pentagon, President Bush, and their congressmen. Those who wrote included ministers, doctors, lawyers, professors, a considerable number of heterosexual men and women, and more than a few former and current soldiers and cadets. The following are a few excerpts from the letters:

Dear James,

I really don't know where to begin. I guess I should begin with why I am writing to you. I don't want you to feel intimidated by this letter, I just need someone to talk to and you seem to be the perfect choice.

Like yourself, I too am gay. I have known since I was 16 — I am now 19. We are also alike in that I am also in ROTC. I am a sophomore at ———.

I admire you and respect you for your stand against discrimination against the homosexual community. You should be commended for your bravery. I am sure you have been the target and center of a lot of controversy. I only wish I could say that I have done the same, but my outcry has remained quiet and personal.

I come from a strict Southern Baptist family. I could only pray that my parents would accept me if I was to be honest

[151]

with them. However, I know they would be ashamed and disappointed. How did you tell your parents?

It's so hard to explain to you what I have been going through. It hurts the most to be living a lie to my parents, friends, and ROTC.

If you feel that you can give me some advice — please write back. It is so hard to find people with similar situations to talk to. (Florida)


Upon entering the University of Oregon, I joined the ROTC, in which I was a cadet for one and a half years ... I led a very straight life which included girlfriends, but I have come to the realization that I am attracted to other males.

I visited the Law School the other day, and a law professor had the article about you titled "Poster Boy" by Rick Harding on his door. I cannot tell you enough how moved I was. The article inspired me to fight this ridiculous injustice against us! For twenty-two years I have had to sit around silently while people slam us, and not be able to say anything, and pretend that I agree. Well no more! I will do my part to fight this bigotry.

In coming out, you have shown an incredible amount of courage! Your courage has given me the strength to do the same. I am writing a letter of protest to your commanding officer Lt. Col. Robert Bates, a letter to the Commander of my ROTC detachment coming out to him, as well as a letter of protest to General Arnold, the National Commander of the Army ROTC program ... I still plan to serve one day in the military. A military that does not discriminate against us. In my letters to the Army ROTC officers and N.C.O.'s, I stress that I love the military and that is precisely why I wish to fight its policy ... I feel exactly as you do about sexual orientation being such a private thing and not wanting to broadcast it, but that it is important to do it because people NEED to know about the injustice. (Eugene, Oregon)


I finished college last year knowing that I was gay. School was not much fun because in trying to cover this up, I made few

[152]

friends. Seeing your situation made me finally come to terms with my own sexuality and helped me decide to come out ... It will be hard for me to tell my family, friends and co-workers, but it will certainly be a lot easier than trying to cover up. It will also be much easier than what you are experiencing. All I can say is Thank You. (Durham, North Carolina)

Like you, I also joined the Army ROTC — my freshman year at the University of Texas at Austin. I loved it and did well. I earned the D.A. Superior Cadet award both my freshman and sophomore years ... I received outstanding reviews and was graded as extremely capable to lead troops in the field ... I've come out to most everyone I know and am constantly astounded by the phrase "But you are not like all the others." I guess having a gay person in the military engaging in "real tough guy" activity destroys the perception that we are all "limp-wristed sissies." I like to break down misperceptions ... I think we are making a greater contribution by speaking out than by being closeted military professionals. In a way I guess we are only doing what the system has instilled in us. When faced with adversity we dig in and fight. I guess I'm most upset about having to fight to be accepted and allowed to serve my country. (Austin, Texas)

I served as a reserve officer in the Navy when the issue was completely taboo; years later, I am still in the process of coming to grips with my sexuality. (Hartford, Connecticut)

Take it all the way to the Supreme Court if you have to. It's time the Establishment knew that gay men and women can be good service men and this bull—— that they are going to destroy morale is a crock. I was a sailor in WWII and lived in mortal fear I'd be found out. Still, I did a good job and didn't destroy my ship's morale. When I was on duty I thought only of serving my country and doing my job right. You hang in there. I'm not going to sign this because I fear it might fall in the wrong hands and I'll lose my pension. (place withheld)

[153]

I wanted to let you know what a real American hero you are ... One day this witch hunt will be behind us. Remember, for everyone like you who takes a stand, there are thousands like me cheering for you. (New York City)

My brother was a cadet at the U.S. Air Force Academy and was disenrolled for defending doolie female cadets in his squadron who were being sexually assaulted by first class cadets. Having blown the whistle, —— was seen as a threat and potential embarrassment to the Academy — he was consequently drummed out. At his disenrollment hearing he was denied sundry constitutional rights: the right to an attorney, to hear and face his accusers, to present material in his own defense ... in short, a Star Chamber. Even in the face of outraged U.S. Senators and an official U.S. Congressional inquiry the Air Force Academy still refuses to realize its culpability and recognize that it is not above the Constitution — the very document, as I am sure you are aware, Academy Cadets pledge to defend.

James, the Army has no more right to disenroll you or make you pay back your scholarship because you're gay than they have to disenroll a woman or person of color because of gender or race. (Connecticut)

[This] policy is not only unwarranted but has robbed the services of many fine men, of which you are now an example. There were many officers in the Navy during World War II who were homosexual and served with distinction. And, of course, enlisted men both in the Navy and Marine Corps ... The unfairness — or one unfairness — during WWII was officers who were found to be homosexuals were permitted to resign for medical reasons or for the "good of the service." Enlisted men, however, were given dishonorable discharges and, in some cases, prison sentences before discharge. It is high time all of this is reversed. (New York)

While I was serving in my [ROTC] unit, I really struggled with inner emotions and external influences for two years ... I was

[154]

honorably discharged this past August. I did not go through what you're going through. I am sure that would have been a matter of time. (Staten Island)

I am enraged and sad that you are being discriminated against so hideously. Not that it should matter, but I am a straight male who hates this kind of stupid, pathetic discrimination. You have my support, and the support of countless others.
(University City, Missouri)

I am sympathetic to your difficulties as well as those of other homosexuals. I am straight.

I was attached to one of the G sections of the Command Post of the ——th Infantry Division in May 1943 while the Division was on maneuvers in Texas. Since the Command Post was the heart and soul of the Division, only the best and brightest officers and non-commissioned officers were assigned to this leadership role.

I was a staff-sergeant in my G section, and the two sergeants above me were a master-sergeant and a tech-sergeant. These two soldiers were homosexuals. I served in the same section with these men for almost three years and found them to be intelligent, well-educated and gentlemen in every way. They served with distinction throughout the war.

The Division landed in North Africa in December 1943 and embarked for Italy in February. Early in March we entered combat along the Garigliano River. The Division subsequently participated in the capture of Rome, and from then on was used as a spear-head division to lead in the other battles as the Fifth Army forged up the boot.

We suffered bombings, artillery fire, strafing and the bitter cold of the North Apennine Mountains during the winter of '44–'45. During these times of human trial, the homosexuals in my unit, as well as those in other G sections, took everything in stride like the rest of us.

When danger came they sought shelter as we all did, and when it was over they went back to work. In other words, their military performance was no different than anyone else in the CP.

[155]

These men were quiet, efficient and never had a blemish on their records. As an example of how well thought of they were by their superior officers: shortly before the end of the war the Master-sergeant was given a battlefield promotion to 2nd Lieutenant, and after the hostilities he was awarded the Legion of Merit. The Tech-sergeant was awarded the Bronze Star Medal, and two other homosexuals (that I know of) in the G sections were also awarded BSMs.

In denying the military to homosexuals I believe the Army is closing the door on an excellent source of manpower. If we should ever get involved in a big shooting war again it would be tragic if this myopia over homosexuals excludes them from serving their country.

It might also be of interest that in a War Department survey after the war, it was found that the above-mentioned ——th Infantry Division was cited as the most efficient fighting unit of all American divisions, yet some of the leading non-commissioned officers in the CP were homosexuals. Figure that out!

(Saint Louis)


I could have been in your shoes. In 1982 I had an ROTC scholarship for Georgia Tech and believed myself to be straight ... I came out to myself with six months left in the Army at age 21, and first enjoyed gay sex when I was 22 immediately after discharge (what a waste of youth).          (Tucson, Arizona)


I enjoyed hearing you speak when you returned to campus last week. As an Army Officer and a former cadet, I feel a personal connection to your situation. But most of all, simply as another human being, I find the discrimination that you are suffering from alarming...

I know that I am not alone in stating that I would be proud to serve alongside you. And I want you to know that although you may be deprived of the opportunity to serve your nation in uniform, by fighting for an end to discrimination you are already providing a great service to this country. (Saint Louis)

The last letter was from Lieutenant Daniel Berger, who

[156]

enclosed with his letter a copy of letters he sent to President Bush, Senators Sam Nunn, Les Aspin, John Glenn, and eight other congressmen. Berger also wrote a letter to Duke University, which he attended while in ROTC, "urging that Duke set a deadline for reform after which the ROTC programs will be forced off campus if the discrimination persists." Berger's comments, of course, are his views as an individual, not as a spokesman for the military. From his letter to Bush:

> As a commissioned United States Army officer, I speak from a position of knowledge and authority in stating that the regulation preventing homosexuals from serving their nation bears no rational relationship to the accomplishments of the military's mission ... The time to change this senseless policy is now ... The issue is whether this nation is willing to sacrifice the service of talented individuals in the Armed Services simply because of blind prejudice ... Although I do not adopt Mr. Holobaugh's lifestyle, I would be honored to serve alongside such a distinguished leader and a fine person. His courage of conviction should be applauded, not condemned.

The president's office passed the letter along to the Department of Defense. A response came from Colonel Ted B. Borek, who stated policy, adding:

> Federal courts have upheld the military's homosexual exclusion policy and accepted its rational relationship to legitimate military purposes. In fact, it is noteworthy that since the current DoD policy on homosexuality became effective in 1982, every court that has ruled finally on the issue has held that the homosexual exclusion policy is constitutional. Accordingly, we do not plan to reassess the Department's policy on homosexuality, though we will comply with any final court orders on the subject.

Although a couple of people managed to get my telephone number and make nuisances of themselves, the consequences of what I did have been almost too good. It's been liberating. I was released from so many things that had been holding me down—everything from growing my hair long to being able to talk openly about Brent. If I hadn't done what I did, I would have had to suppress my homosexuality for four years on active duty or eight years in reserve. I don't think I could have done that. Even if I hadn't met Brent, sooner or later I would have started a relationship with someone — I'm just geared that way. My sexual orientation inevitably would have come out, so it's best that it happened when it did. Not being able to talk about the person who meant the most to them must have been hell for the lesbian and gay soldiers who served in the Persian Gulf. To go to work every day in the military and not talk about your spouse, to have that person be invisible — I just can't imagine.

*For Brent, the experience has been a roller coaster. Initially, he says, the attention Jim received was hard on their relationship.*

*"For a while it was very strained. Especially right after the news hit the press. Jim was meeting all of these people. I'm on call every three nights at the hospital and he's off doing these fun things. A lot of my insecurities came out then. He was meeting people who were very interested in him — I mean, Jim's very handsome and he could easily be swept away by anyone — and I wasn't able to give him the attention I wanted to give him. He was receiving it from everyone else."*

*One person definitely interested in Jim was his friend Andy in Saint Louis. Andy's admiration for Jim became an obsession. He even had Jim's photo at the side of his bed. Finally, he phoned Connecticut and told Jim he was in love with him.*

*"It was no big deal," says Jim. "It didn't bother me much. My reaction was almost no reaction. I was like, 'Andy, I'm glad you told me. I know you understand that I love Brent and only Brent, and he's the one I'm going to spend my life with, and I hope that this problem won't keep us from being friends.'*

*"Before he called, I knew Andy liked me but I didn't know he was in love with me. I don't want to sound cold and callous, but I didn't take it very seriously. I don't mean it like, 'Well, he fell in love with me, big deal, people fall in love with me all the time.' But I'd just moved back to Connecticut, I was happy to be back, Andy was in Saint Louis — I just told him that I wanted to be friends, that I wasn't in love with him, I was in love with Brent. And he knew that."*

[158]

*The important thing, to both Jim and Brent, is that the relationship has survived.*

*"We had to have total commitment to each other and to making the relationship work," says Brent. "There have been a lot of competing forces, with media coverage, family, jobs. You have to be completely honest with each other. If you feel there's something you can't tell the other person, that's bad, because you should be a unit. And, of course, love. There must be a lot of love there. I also feel strongly that a relationship must be monogamous to work. When they're not, there's just too much emotional stuff going on, and you can't feel that complete commitment that's necessary to make a relationship work."*

You have to expect the relationship to work. If you look at it in terms of, "Well, if we have problems I can always go somewhere or find someone else," then that's what will happen. I have never considered breaking up a possibility. If we have a problem, we'll work it out. Since divorce is not an option, we have to deal with anything that comes along.

According to Pentagon spokesman Major Doug Hart, nine gay ROTC students came out to their commanders and were forced to leave the program in academic year 1989–90. My case was the first to hit the press, and the first in which the ROTC asked for repayment of scholarship.

After deciding that I would be most effective speaking on college campuses, the ACLU wasted little time scheduling appearances. Within a month, I had delivered speeches at MIT and Harvard. Between April 1990 and April 1991, I gave approximately twenty-five speeches to various campus gatherings and alumni clubs.

It's hard to imagine I used to be terrified of standing in front of an audience and speaking, but for years I was. There were only ten students in my high school speech class, but giving a speech before that class was traumatic. I'd get up there and just shake. My greatest fear was that people would see I was nervous. I didn't want them to see that flaw in me.

I finally solved the problem when I was at Rolla. I had to give a class presentation, and I was nervous for weeks beforehand. I thought, "This is just ridiculous." So, I joined Toast-masters. Thank God for Toastmasters! When I saw the first video of myself speaking, I realized that no one could tell I was nervous. I couldn't even tell myself, so what was I worried about? Toastmasters helped me overcome my fear and even enjoy public speaking. When the opportunity came to speak at Harvard and MIT, I was ready. I accepted it eagerly and have enjoyed it. Educating people on the issue of gays in the military is very important to me. I meet so many wonderful people — courageous individuals who are standing up and making a difference on the campuses across the country.

*Many of Jim's friends, such as Robo, have seen him grow in self-confidence:*

*"With all the speaking engagements he's had all over the country, and all the television interviews, he's gained a lot of confidence. The person I knew in Rolla probably would not have had the self-confidence to do all this. But other than that he's pretty much the same person. The last time I talked to him I was telling him about this backpacking trip I was planning, and he was really excited about it. He said he wished he could go. He's the same person he always was, just a little bit more worldly now. And he's got that self-confidence."*

*Even those who don't agree with Jim's position have to admire his spunk. "I was telling my mom that in gay circles, a lot of people across the country would know who Morris is," says John Taylor. "If you mentioned the name 'James Holobaugh,' a lot of them would know who it was. She said, 'Morris always was a strong-willed person. Whatever he did, he gave it everything he had.' I guess if he's fighting for gay rights, he's going to be totally committed."*

*Jim's father sees his son as an adventurer, someone never afraid to try new experiences.*

*"Morris is a person who wants to explore all things in life," says Mr. Holobaugh. "He's done a lot of things. He's tried skydiving, which nearly drove me crazy. Hiking in the mountains in the snow — that scared us all to death. I believe there was a feeling in my family that Morris would do something big.*

[160]

*You just sense those things. He's one who takes on all things in life. He's a doer and a goer."*

Robo and I planned that trip six months in advance. We sent off for topography maps and back country maps. We planned our trail and sent the plan to the National Park Service for approval. The first day it was seventy degrees in April — great weather. But that night it began to get colder and started raining. We were near Clingman's Dome, about six thousand feet altitude, very cold, very wet, and out of water. We put pans outside our tent to catch rainwater. The next morning I woke up thirsty, so Robo unzips the tent to get the pan — and snow falls in. Our water was frozen.

We decided to go to Clingman's Dome because there were outhouses up there. I hoped we could break into the restrooms and get out of the cold. My feet were like ice — I couldn't feel them. I was freaking out, afraid I might lose my feet.

At Clingman's Dome, we ran into some men with a Jeep who had come up before the snow. They radioed a ranger and told him we were there and that our feet were frozen. The rangers came to our rescue and took us to a hotel where we thawed out and ate pizza.

But backpacking is fairly tame compared to skydiving.

Some people are afraid to fly, while others will pay money to jump out of a plane. The subject came up one day while Brent and I were in his pool. I said I had always wanted to skydive, and Brent said he had, too. The next day I made reservations. When I told Brent we were going skydiving, he was like, *"What?"*

But we went through with it and had a blast. They train you for two or three hours, then you have your first jump at four thousand feet. It's scary — oh, is it *scary*. You have to go out on the wing of a Cessna. First they open the door and the wind goes *whhhhhooooo*, and then you have to crawl out on this strut. Way out there are two little hand marks. You crawl along the strut, then drop your legs off the foothold so you are hanging on and flying along horizontally with the plane.

Then you let go.

[161]

The worst part is crawling out. Once you release your feet from the foothold, it's too late — you know you've got to do it. It's awful. For about two hundred feet, until your chute opens, you're free-falling and you feel like you're dying. But once the chute opens, it's great — you just float down. The chute is easily maneuverable, and you have a radio on so the instructor in the plane can guide you down. Unfortunately, the first time I jumped my radio wasn't working. I landed on my face in this cornfield. Brent was in the plane waiting to jump and the guy was telling him, "Your friend's drifting off way over there. He doesn't know what he's doing." We jumped four times. For some reason, the second time was the scariest.

After we had jumped a few times, someone showed me a newspaper article about two Washington University students who had been killed jumping at the same place we were jumping. That scared me. I'd purchased six jump tickets, but we only used four.

Compared to jumping out of an airplane, giving a speech before a couple of hundred people is not especially frightening. There is something to be said for scaring oneself to death so that all other daunting experiences pale in comparison.

*"Jim's usually very happy after a good speech," says Brent. "He doesn't like it when everyone agrees with him. He would rather go to a competitive audience and 'show those bastards,' as he puts it. He really hates — and this is a quote — 'those Bible-thumping bastards.' That's something he's adamant about — in fact, a little too adamant. He'll disagree with this, but I feel that he has little tolerance for religion. I try to be a moderating force in that, too. I have a very liberal Catholic background, went to a Jesuit school — very thought-minded."*

*Jim often listens to "Do You Hear the People Sing?" from* Les Miserables *to get him fired up before a speech. He sings along, changing the word* slaves *to* oppressed — *"who will not be oppressed again" — to better fit his subject. He is, after all, about to ask his audience, "Will you join in our crusade?"*

*The crusade, of course, is designed to pressure the military, the Congress, or the president to change Department of Defense* policy. The pressure has come from the media, members of Congress, and even former Pentagon officials.

Dr. Lawrence Korb, assistant secretary of defense during the Reagan administration, says, "What people can't seem to get through their heads is that [military officials] are not keeping lesbians and gay men out of the military. They're already there."

Korb has called on the Pentagon to change the policy, and has asked colleges to remove ROTC programs until the discrimination ends, even if it means losing federal funds.

"Rarely do you do anything good without paying a price," he says. "What we have to do is say, 'Okay, we're willing to pay the price. If that's the kind of organization you are, we don't want your damn money anyway.'"

Mainly, however, the pressure has come from college campuses — and it is there that Jim has made a significant contribution to the national movement.

# The crusade

My first speech was at MIT. Robb Bettiker had sent me a letter through Washington University saying he'd read about my case in the *New York Times* and the same thing was happening to him. Robb had been elected to the Navy's Nuclear Propulsion Program before disclosing his sexual orientation to his commanding officers. He had fallen in love with a fraternity roommate, although it had taken him a while to realize what was happening. At first he simply became physically ill whenever the guy was around. Eventually, he told another roommate, "I'm going to test your liberalism. I'm in love with 'x.'"

When Robb came out at MIT he got a lot of support from friends, fraternity brothers, fellow cadets, and MIT officials. Even his commanding officers sympathized, although they said their hands were tied by policy. Robb signed a statement acknowledging his homosexuality only after the phrase "my admission of being a homosexual" was changed to "my statement of being a homosexual." He felt the word *admission* implied guilt.

When his review board recommended that he not have to repay his scholarship and Navy officials at the Pentagon ordered him to repay it anyway, Robb wrote a letter to H. Lawrence Garrett, secretary of the Navy. It read in part: "Such

[164]

punishment is normally reserved for serious violations, such as misconduct or failure to complete the educational requirements. I am guilty only of coming forward with the truth. I do not acknowledge indebtedness ... in the amount of $38,612.00 ... I do acknowledge my commitment to serve as an officer in the US Navy, and request that I be reinstated in the NROTC program at MIT." It was a fine letter.

Robb, incidentally, credits his fraternity brothers at MIT with helping him get through this difficult period.

Professor David Halperin formed Defeat Discrimination at MIT (DDaMIT) in March 1990 and invited me to speak. I asked David if he'd like Joe Steffan to come along. Harvard called too, so I scheduled the speeches for the same trip.

MIT has studied the gays-and-the-military issue more thoroughly than most universities, thanks in part to DDaMIT. By April, DDaMIT had been enlisted in the ACLU's nationwide campaign. Their letter to gay organizations on other campuses said: "The U.S. military's exclusion of lesbians, bisexuals, and gay men is perhaps the single most important symbolic expression of homophobia at the national level. It is like a national form of heckling against sexual minorities, formalized and institutionalized as national policy."

DDaMIT reported that "a few members of ROTC who oppose the discriminatory policy joined us as unofficial advisors, and were helpful in educating us about official and de facto ROTC procedures." The group used a school newspaper story about Robb Bettiker and the resulting letters to the editor to educate students. The letter to other gay student groups also said: "Cadets who were in ROTC with Robb Bettiker were not affected by his sexual orientation. Many of his fellow students and his superiors supported him in his request that he be allowed to serve as an officer ... Many ROTC students support DDaMIT; certainly they do not feel that gay or lesbian ROTC cadets would affect their performance."

Among others, ROTC student Susan Raisty sent a letter to the campus newspaper in support of changing the policy.

Then, DDaMIT brought Joe Steffan, Bill Rubenstein, and me to speak, along with the local boy, Robb. I was ready. I had Toastmasters behind me and was anxious to get involved.

Although we were in a five-car accident on the way up there, we made it on time and spoke in a large lecture hall with at least three hundred people sitting on the steps and in the aisles.

The speech I usually give provides a brief overview of what happened to me, including how my relationship with Brent triggered it all. The first audience interruption is generally laughter when I mention my father's horror over the *New York Times* story. The follow-up line, "Then the next day my friends found out from Peter Jennings that I'm gay," generates more laughter. After that, though, it's time to get serious.

I give my reasons for going public, then read the current DoD policy followed by the 1942 policy dealing with blacks. If you read them together, it's obvious to everyone that tne reasons given for keeping out both groups are exactly the same. I then go through the list of arguments against accepting gays in the military, refuting each of them (see Appendix). I talk about the waste of resources and talent the policy costs America. Then I tell the audience what they can do to help change the policy.

I also give a lesson in consciousness-raising. I tell a story about how a friend and I were once in a supermarket and heard a checker repeatedly calling an adjacent checker a "fag." My friend told the checker that the word *fag* offends a lot of people and that she shouldn't use it. The checker was taken aback. After telling the story, I say that even though the checker may use the word again, she's at least going to think about it first. And that little things like that matter more than if I spoke at every university in the country. They need to know that they as individuals can make a difference.

I also encourage gay members of my audience to come out.

The speech is always followed by questions from the audience. Although the questions don't differ much from place to place, occasionally someone asks something truly off the wall. I don't mind, as long as it isn't so far-out illogical that I can't give a logical answer. I get a lot of personal questions about my relationship with Brent — which I'm free to discuss since we decided not to litigate with the ROTC. Everyone asks how my family reacted. Everyone asks if I'm still willing to serve. And for some reason people like to ask if I feel that I'm being used by the gay movement. I tell them no, that I went to the ACLU, they didn't come to me. And even if they *are* using me, I'm willing to be used because I believe in this struggle.

The speech at MIT went well. ROTC commanders and cadets attended, as did school administrators. One ROTC cadet stood up in full uniform and, as DDaMIT reported in its press release, "denounced the discriminatory policy, saying that if kicking ROTC off campus were the only way to get the military to change the policy, then it would be worth kicking them off." A letter appearing in the *Tech,* MIT's campus newspaper, April 3, 1990, written by Marc S. Block, said in part: "I am a member of the Air Force Reserve Officers' Training Corps ... I said at the talk that I felt all discrimination at MIT should be stopped. I meant that."

An editorial appearing a week later began: "Discrimination on the basis of sexual orientation is intolerable at MIT. No program that violates this principle should be allowed to remain on campus."

DDaMIT asked University Provost John Deutch, a personal friend of Secretary of Defense Richard Cheney, to become active in the debate, and gave him a copy of Macias's letter. Deutch agreed to write a letter to Cheney and to make the letter public. Dated April 10, 1990, and addressed to "The Honorable Richard Cheney," the letter said:

> Dear Dick,
>
> I am writing to you to express the concern of MIT about the ROTC policy not to accept gay or lesbian students into its programs and to require avowed homosexuals to disenroll and pay back scholarship funds.
>
> This policy discriminates against students on the basis of sexual orientation, in contradiction to the policy of MIT and many other universities. I believe the ROTC policy to be wrong and shortsighted. Individuals should be accepted into the military service without regard to sexual preference...
>
> However, my main purpose in writing to you is to point out the risk that this policy poses for the continuation of ROTC on the campuses of many of the leading US colleges and

[167]

universities. The contradiction between the university's principle of nondiscrimination against individuals on the basis of sexual orientation, and the presence of an ROTC that does discriminate, cannot exist on the campuses indefinitely. Many universities will withdraw from the ROTC program...

The letter closes with "Best regards, John." Copies went to General Colin Powell, among others.

On May 16, 1990, the MIT faculty passed a resolution calling for the ROTC to be booted from campus if their antigay policy was not changed. A follow-up vote October 17 got unanimous support for a five-year "action" program. Under it, ROTC would be unavailable to students beginning with the class entering in 1998 unless discrimination against lesbians and gays had ended. Many students enrolled in ROTC privately expressed their support. On May 7th and 8th, a student referendum was held, with those in favor of removing ROTC coming out on top.

MIT received $47.9 million in 1990 in DoD research money. If MIT does eventually remove ROTC from campus and then suffers the wrath of the military, it will be an astounding victory of values over dollars. So far, few universities have shown the willingness to be so courageous — especially those with as much to lose financially as MIT.

The next evening at Harvard we spoke to a crowd so large it spilled out the doors. Harvard had removed ROTC from campus during the Vietnam era but decided in 1989 to reinstate it. The university soon changed its mind, citing the antigay policy. Harvard students participate in ROTC, however, through an arrangement with MIT. One of them, David Carney, was dismissed for being gay and ordered to repay his scholarship. His case is similar to Bettiker's. Carney ranked second in his class of forty-one, and was appointed Battalion Executive Officer. Even though the Navy ROTC board found no evidence of deceit, and even though the board recommended that recoupment of scholarship money be waived, the Navy overruled the board and ordered Carney to repay $50,000.

After Massachusetts, I returned to Washington University to speak alongside Bill Rubenstein before three hundred people. It was nice to go back and tell my side of the story in person. My speech was scheduled for the same day as the student vote on whether to remove ROTC from campus. This upset me. I had no chance to affect the outcome. I think they held the vote far too early, with too little time for the issue to be explained to the student body. Even people who disagreed with the policy were under the impression ROTC did more good than harm. The fraternities were organized and lined up solidly on the side of ROTC. I can easily imagine the fraternity brothers getting up and saying, "You know, guys, I don't think I should lose my ROTC scholarship because some guy wants to fuck another guy in the ass." With that kind of logic going around, the fraternity boys voted against the referendum en masse.

Later, I got letters from people at Washington who agreed with me but said they voted to keep ROTC on campus because they didn't really understand the issue. They had failed to grasp the logic of removing ROTC, not because the university is trying to dictate Pentagon policy, but because ROTC is violating Washington University policy. If there was a scholarship available to everyone willing to sign a form saying "Jesus is not the son of God," there is no way it would be allowed. You can't think only of the students who would lose their scholarships. You have to think about the 10 percent of the students excluded from the scholarships to begin with just because they're gay.

Nevertheless, the Washington University Student Union voted sixteen to ten not to kick ROTC off campus. The student body went along, voting 871 to 509 not to boot ROTC. At the same time the students elected a student union president who had advocated booting ROTC. For its part, the university administration established a "Committee to Study the Relationship of ROTC to Washington University."

The committee consisted of four professors and three students, including Robert Christie, a member of the Gay and Lesbian Community Alliance, and Erik Trusler, a member of the Army ROTC. The committee consulted other schools that were studying the issue — particularly Wisconsin, MIT, and Princeton — and all the literature on the subject they could find, including the Crittenden and PERSEREC reports, Allan

[169]

Bérubé's *Coming Out Under Fire,* and Mary Ann Humphrey's *My Country, My Right to Serve.*

The committee also invited several people for closed door interviews. These included Provost Macias, Colonel Bates, and the president of the gay and lesbian alliance. Finally, the committee listened to participants at a university forum on November 4, 1990. The subsequent report said that "all but one speaker decried the discriminatory policies historically upheld by the Department of Defense and manifested on this campus ... by the ROTC." The committee noted that not many, if any, universities adopting antidiscrimination policies that included sexual orientation were aware "of the future implications these policies might have on their respective relationships with the Department of Defense."

In its findings the committee said the larger university community seemed against expelling ROTC. But it also noted that "with the exception of two letters addressed to the Committee, there is no evidence that the Defense Department's present policy of discrimination is considered rational, logical, ethical, or moral by any member of the academic community who contacted the Committee either in writing or orally."

The committee also "found it impossible to comprehend why a situation which could be retracted only with dire consequences should be thrust by the present regulations upon a young man or woman, especially at the age of seventeen or eighteen ... The possibility and indeed the inevitability (given what now is scientifically recognized about homosexuality) that a young man or woman might be trapped by external circumstances were human issues of great concern to the Committee."

Still, the committee's five recommendations fell far short of expelling ROTC. This was partially because it found little support on campus for such a move, but also because doing so "would make it impossible for many students to attend Washington University for financial reasons" and because such a move "would possibly be very unpopular, given the current Gulf crisis."

The committee's first recommendation instructed Chancellor William Danforth to write a letter acknowledging the conflict between university policy and ROTC policy, which he did.

The second aligned the university with others seeking to change Pentagon policy. The third instructed the university to put a statement in university publications, wherever ROTC is mentioned, stating that it discriminates. This was also implemented. The fourth concerned correcting "inaccuracies and ambiguities" the committee discovered in Washington University's contract with ROTC, and the fifth simply stated that the report should be made fully accessible.

After the report's release, several committee members speaking in defense of it said they felt the university would lose its clout with the Pentagon if it expelled ROTC. Erik Trusler, the ROTC student on the committee, said, "We've come out and said that discrimination is morally indefensible. There's nothing more that we can do." Those wanting the ROTC to be given five years to change its policy or be banned argued that if the university's clout hadn't accomplished anything within five years, surely a divorce might better make the point.

Editorials and guest columns in the campus paper took a dim view of the limited nature of the recommendations. In a joint "Student Perspective," Ben Jones and Andy Herzig argued that the university's stance was "morally repugnant ... By allowing ROTC to stay on campus we tacitly support institutional discrimination."

Michael Rothberg, the new student union president, wrote a brilliantly scathing column. He noted that the committee had discovered all the facts, but

> something funny happened on the way to the recommendations ... by explicitly stating that the military's policy towards homosexuals is unnecessarily discriminatory, and that it does violate the university's anti-discrimination policy, the committee leaves little room for interpretation. The Board of Trustees must either remove the element that is inconsistent with its policy, or it must change the policy to make it consistent with reality. What is the use of maintaining sexual orientation in the anti-discrimination policy if, in fact, homosexuals are not protected by it?

After comparing university officials to persons in the civil rights era who denounced segregation but lacked the backbone to end it, Rothberg attacked the committee for citing "economic discrimination" as a reason not to remove ROTC.

"Proponents of this argument," wrote Rothberg,

point out that however repugnant the exclusion of homosexuals may be, it is outweighed by the greater number of potential ROTC cadets that would be deprived of a Washington University education for financial reasons. This argument runs contrary to the basis of our economic system ... For instance, a miner in West Virginia generally cannot afford to own the same kind of automobile as a corporate attorney in Los Angeles. The miner makes less money than the attorney, and thus the miner is excluded from purchasing certain types of automobiles that the attorney can afford. Would most Americans classify the miner as a victim of discrimination? Of course not. He or she is simply unable to afford a certain product. We may feel sorry for the miner; we may even try to assist the miner; but we'd scoff at the miner if in a court of law he claimed to be the victim of discrimination ... Exclusion based on financial means is part of a capitalist system; exclusion based on prejudice is not.

(An MIT study found that it wouldn't cost the university much to replace the scholarships offered by ROTC, and that ROTC students at MIT whose scholarships were withdrawn usually did not leave the university. Said a DDaMIT spokesperson: "It must be noted that the financial aspect of the ROTC scholarship is a special privilege that participating students enjoy above the minimum standard that all other students are afforded. So, a given MIT applicant, without an ROTC scholarship as a possibility, will only be treated just like everyone else. If being treated like everyone else is being treated unfairly, then that would be a problem for the Financial Aid Office ... And even if we believe that removing ROTC will cause hardship for some individuals, we must certainly remember that economic benefits conferred on one group of students never justify the denial of rights to another.")

A few schools, such as Pitzer College and Rutgers, decided to remove ROTC immediately (see Appendix), but I don't advocate that. I'm glad those schools took some action, but in my speeches I advocate putting ROTC on notice while giving the policy time to change. The goal is not to rid America of ROTC, it is to end discrimination.

During my trip to Saint Louis, I ran into several old friends, most of whom were on my side. Among those in the audience when I spoke at Washington University was Cherrie Clausen, my ex-boss at the Corps of Engineers who had made such a difference in my thinking on racism. Clausen wrote a letter to me afterwards telling me she had never really thought about gay rights before, but she sympathized and supported me. Basically, she thanked me for educating her on the issue. That touched me because, although I'd never told her, she did the same thing for me on race.

Next I spoke at the Law School at American University with Joe Steffan. Joe and I got to know each other pretty well, and we've become good friends. I met another future friend at this engagement — Congressman Gerry Studds. He invited Brent and me to dinner, and we've been friends since.

My next speaking tour took me to the University of Chicago, the University of Wisconsin at Madison, and Northwestern University — all in the same trip, and all with Joe.

Marc Wolinsky, who attended law school at the University of Chicago, appeared with us at that stop. All seven law schools in the Chicago area, including the one at the University of Chicago, are terminating on-campus military recruiting because of the antigay policy.

The Wisconsin speech was on May 1, 1990, the day of the National Press Conference in which forty-eight schools issued a statement condemning ROTC discrimination.

The Wisconsin faculty, in its first full faculty meeting since the Vietnam War, had voted 386 to 248 in 1989 to have the board of regents sever ROTC contracts by 1993 if the policy is not changed. The board of regents, however, eventually decided only to "press" the military and government to change its policy. In April 1990, fifty-two students were arrested in Chancellor Donna Shalala's office after she refused to allow statements in university materials noting that ROTC discriminated.

At Northwestern, eleven posters advertising the appearance of Joe, Miriam Ben-Shalom, and me were defaced. Some were smeared with fake blood and covered with obscenities. Others were torn down.

More than two hundred people showed up at McCormick Auditorium to hear Joe, Miriam, and me speak. Afterwards, the *Daily Northwestern* interviewed several students in attendance:

Ken Valder said he had been discharged from ROTC his sophomore year. "I said I was a conscientious objector ... This presentation made me wish I had told the truth."

The debate at Northwestern has since been heated. Two student groups have demanded that ROTC be booted. A letter-writing campaign that began when we spoke demanded that Northwestern sever its ties with ROTC. The university's president, however, claims he has no jurisdiction over ROTC policy, leading some to wonder, "Who's in charge here?" If the military had staged a coup d'etat at Northwestern University, I think we would have heard.

My speech at Lynchburg College in Virginia was set up through an agent. I spoke alone, and to good effect. The college had a picture display of military leaders who were bisexual or gay — Alexander the Great, Julius Caesar, Napoleon, Richard the Lion-Hearted, Lawrence of Arabia, Nero, Augustus, Octavius, Alcibiades, Frederick the Great, Trajan, Hadrian, Lord Kitchener, Peter the Great, Phillip II of Macedon (the list goes on and on) — and a photo of me. It would certainly be difficult to argue that any of the men pictured with me were "incompatible with military service." The letters over the display said something like, "These people were gay and served in the military. Why can't he?"

I was introduced at Lynchburg by English professor Jere Real, who said, "The one thing that separates me from tonight's speaker is summed up in one word — honesty. He admitted what I didn't." Real had attended Virginia Military Institute and served as an officer in the military, but had never revealed his homosexuality to the military.

The crowd at Lynchburg was probably one of the straightest I ever addressed. They asked a lot of religious questions. At one point a guy got up and was spouting all this religious crap, and I said, "We don't want your approval or your hypocritical love. We want equality." That got a big round of applause.

I answered questions from the audience for almost an hour after the speech, and was interviewed by Jerry Falwell's Liberty College radio station, among others. The Lynchburg College newspaper said of the speech: "From the overwhelmingly warm response he received, it was clear to see that ... Holobaugh did indeed have his audience in support of him and that for which he was so strongly fighting." *USA Today* reported that students in the audience were "outraged" by my story. And the *News and Daily Advance* reported in September 1990 that the Lynchburg faculty had voted to give ROTC three years to drop its policy or face a possible phaseout. "Discussion of the military's policy toward homosexuals began this spring," said the paper, "when James Holobaugh ... came to speak at the college." When I received the clippings from Jere Real, I was very happy. It's moments like this that make it all worthwhile.

My next appearance was at George Bush's alma mater, Yale, where I am currently a graduate student. I was part of a large discussion panel that included Joe, Marc Wolinsky, and Sandra Lowe. It was a huge crowd and the discussion went on far too long, but it was fun. I also spoke at the Yale Club in New York City.

I spoke at the University of Minnesota during the "About Face" conference, a national strategy-planning session hosted by the ACLU. Other speakers included Gerry Studds and Randy Shilts. The conference went great, and the crowd was motivated, until Shilts spoke. He got up there and said the ROTC issue in itself wouldn't make any difference, that the Pentagon would let ROTC be removed from all campuses before they would change their policy. Shilts had not done his homework. He had no idea how important a strong ROTC is to the military, which gets 70 percent of its officers through ROTC. In 1988–89, 8,217 ROTC cadets were commissioned officers. It was a bad way to end an otherwise great conference.

The University of Minnesota student government on May 10, 1990, imposed a five-year deadline for the DoD to end its ban on gays or be booted. The university's president, however, said he had no intention of banning ROTC. Then the student senate voted in February 1991 that ROTC be given a deadline of June 30, 1993, and the university senate approved the vote

151 to 12. The board of regents will decide the issue. Their decision could be affected by the case of Mark Renslow, a former University of Minnesota ROTC "Cadet of the Year," who was discharged from the program in 1991 and ordered to repay his scholarship after disclosing he was bisexual.

At a May 8, 1991, University of Minnesota rally, a fight broke out between supporters and opponents of ROTC. On May 9, two hundred people — including a brood of "stern-faced ROTC cadets in military uniforms," according to the newspaper *Equal Time* — crammed into a board of regents hearing room to listen to twelve opponents and ten defenders of allowing ROTC to remain on campus. The opponents may have gotten their biggest boost when a local resident, Mary Jane Rachner, seized the microphone to scream, "Every act of homosexual intercourse is rape! We're talking about rapists on this campus!" The microphone was turned off and Rachner was removed by security guards. One of those speaking against ROTC policy was ROTC cadet Aric Nissen, chair of the student senate, who told the regents he had suffered considerable personal abuse over the issue. But, Nissen said, "if there is one thing that we must stand for, it is equal opportunity." A fellow member of the student senate said other ROTC cadets had made Nissen's life miserable with signs and chants proclaiming that Nissen was "queer."

The speaking engagements kept coming. The University of Pittsburgh, Duke, the University of Tampa, and the University of California at Los Angeles were next in line. At UCLA the undergraduate student government passed a resolution urging that ROTC be removed from campus, the school's chancellor wrote a letter to Secretary Cheney asking him to "abandon" the policy of antigay discrimination, and the university's gay organization held a protest to urge stronger actions than resolutions and letters. A column in the *Daily Bruin* by Steve Gonzalez, a former ROTC student at UCLA who had been asked to leave ROTC the previous year because he was gay, said: "Either the university means its nondiscrimination policy, or it isn't worth the paper it's printed on. By its inaction, the university tacitly endorses the continuing second-class citizenship of lesbians, gays and bisexuals."

A *Los Angeles Times* article on the ROTC controversy at area schools, published December 30, 1990, quoted Lisa Pantano, an Army lieutenant: "Personally, I don't think sexual orientation should have anything to do with it. There are already a lot of slime-ball heterosexuals in the service."

I then spoke at Ithaca College, James Madison University, the University of Colorado (the first event Brent was able to attend), Mary Washington College (Virginia), Duke again, and Cornell. Other engagements found me addressing the Dallas Gay Alliance's "Razzle-Dazzle" celebration, the Bay Area Physicians for Human Rights in San Francisco, and the Dartmouth Alumni Club. The fight to boot ROTC at Dartmouth received a boost at the 1990 graduation ceremonies when valedictorian Michael F. Lowenthal acknowledged he was gay and called upon the university to open its mind so that "lesbians and gays are not insulted by the college's sponsorship of ROTC and other agencies which discriminate against us." The audience of five thousand gave him a standing ovation. Michael's mother said his speech was particularly courageous because Dartmouth is a "hard-drinking party school, notorious for gay-bashing, anti-black, and antiwoman attitudes."

It was a busy year and I met many wonderful people through these speaking engagements. I found out, for one thing, just how many gay people there are out there. If I had only known when I was driving down Forest Park Boulevard just how numerous and diverse we are, I wouldn't have been crying. We're everywhere. I'm trying to keep up with addresses and stay in touch with people, but it's overwhelming.

There are others just as capable of doing this, but they haven't been given the opportunity. Since I *have* been, I plan to take advantage of it and use it as a chance to educate and, I hope, change minds.

# A big smile

M y case received its biggest boost when Congress became involved. Representative Studds drafted a letter — signed by twenty-three other members of Congress — accusing the Army of mean-spiritedness. The letter, dated March 7, 1990, was addressed to the Commander, United States Army, Second Region, Fort Knox, Kentucky.

> Dear Commander:
>
> We are writing regarding Mr. James M. Holobaugh, a Reserve Officer Training Corps member at Washington University in St. Louis, Missouri.
>
> It is our understanding that Mr. Holobaugh, notwithstanding his consistently excellent performance as a cadet, was suspended from the ROTC program last fall after acknowledging he is homosexual. It is our further understanding that Army ROTC is now considering whether to order Mr. Holobaugh to repay the $35,000 scholarship he received as a cadet over the last four years. We believe that to compel him to repay this money would not only be fundamentally unfair; it would also reflect an appalling mean-spiritedness which has no place in the ROTC.
>
> Throughout his career as a cadet, Mr. Holobaugh has compiled an enviable record of performance, with ROTC evalua-

tions describing him as "possessing outstanding leadership potential" and "strongly recommended for active duty." The Army has even held him up as a public model of excellence in ROTC recruitment advertisements.

Mr. Holobaugh has repeatedly expressed his desire to continue his training and to be commissioned as an officer in the U.S. Army. He does not wish to terminate his enrollment in ROTC. He is not seeking to evade his obligation to serve in the Army. The Army, however, intends to exclude him from ROTC and from any future service based solely on his status as a gay man.

In our view, it is wrong that private sexual orientation remains grounds for dismissal from the U.S. military. That ill-conceived policy is not before you today. The principal issue now is the proposed requirement that Mr. Holobaugh repay the scholarship he has earned as a cadet — and wants to continue to earn as an officer. This requirement, it seems to us, would be punitive, unjust and entirely unsupportable by any legal authority.

The ROTC has publicly acknowledged that it seeks retroactive recovery of scholarship grants only from recruits who have in some way deceived the service. There is no evidence of such deceit on Mr. Holobaugh's part. To the contrary, the Investigating Officer concluded that "there is no willfull [sic] evasion that can be proven." It is to Mr. Holobaugh's credit that he conducted himself in an open and forthright manner, directly informing his commanding officer as soon as he realized he was gay.

We do not understand why an ROTC Investigating Board would recommend that Mr. Holobaugh be ordered to repay his scholarship. What if Mr. Holobaugh had been dismissed due to some other disqualifying factor? Would they recommend he be compelled to repay the Army in that instance? We think not.

We believe that the Army has cheated itself out of the future services of a qualified officer. This unfortunate decision would be made only more egregious if Mr. Holobaugh were further punished.

Thank you in advance for your careful consideration of this matter. Please keep us informed as this case progresses.

The list of signatures included twenty-two Democrats and two Republicans. The Democrats: Gerry Studds and Barney Frank of Massachusetts; Patricia Schroeder of Colorado; Ronald Dellums, Tony Beilenson, Howard Berman, Don Edwards, Robert Matsui, and Nancy Pelosi of California; Alan Wheat of Missouri; Gary Ackerman, James Scheuer, Stephen Solarz, and Ted Weiss of New York; Les AuCoin of Oregon; John Conyers of Michigan; Sam Gejdenson of Connecticut; Bob Kastenmeier of Wisconsin; Peter Kostmayer of Pennsylvania; Jim McDermott and Jolene Unsoeld of Washington; and Lane Evans of Illinois. The Republicans: Bill Green of New York and Christopher Shays of Connecticut. A copy of the letter was sent to Dick Cheney.

Molly Yard, president of the National Organization for Women at the time, sent each member of congress who signed the letter a note of thanks, saying, "NOW shares your view that any attempt by the Army ROTC program to order Mr. Holobaugh to repay his scholarship would be 'mean-spirited,' 'punitive' and 'unjust.'"

Studds's office drafted a similar letter a few weeks later for Robb Bettiker and David Carney. Meanwhile, several additional congressmen had approached Studds's office offering support. The result was thirty-five signatures on the Bettiker-Carney letter.

The Bettiker-Carney letter, dated March 29, 1990, was addressed to Mr. H. Lawrence Garrett III, secretary of the Navy. Bob Kastenmeier did not sign the second letter; thus, twelve signatures were new. All Democrats, they were: Chester Atkins, Joseph Kennedy II, and Ed Markey of Massachusetts; Barbara Boxer, George Miller, and Mervyn Dymally of California; Peter DeFazio of Oregon; Eliot Engel of New York; Tom Foglietta of Pennsylvania; Bart Gordon of Tennessee; Steny Hoyer of Maryland; and James Traficant of Ohio.

*Jim's father was not entirely surprised that Congress got involved: "I believe people felt he was getting hit with a double whammy: not accepting him and then wanting him to pay back the money. I think that was looked upon as unfair. It was a pretty impressive list. There has been tremendous support for Morris, as you can see from the articles and editorials in major newspapers — the* Boston Globe, *the* New York Times."

On May 8, 1990, while taping an interview with Robert Bettiker, NBC News handed Robb a copy of a memo from the secretary of the Navy saying the demand that Bettiker and David Carney repay their scholarships would be dropped. The memo was dated April 27. Why it was withheld for several days, then given to NBC News before it was given to the cadets remains a mystery.

Just over a week later, on May 17, the Army followed suit in my case. The memorandum from Army ROTC Cadet Command Headquarters at Fort Monroe, Virginia, to Lieutenant Colonel John Hammann, of Cadet Command at Fort Knox, Kentucky, read:

1. HQDA has concurred in Cadet Command's decision to disenroll Cadet Holobaugh and not pursue repayment of scholarship benefits. This decision was based solely on the merits and circumstances of this particular case.

2. Cadet Holobaugh will be informed of this decision immediately ... The written decision will be provided as soon as it is received from Cadet Command.

The decision not to seek repayment apparently was made by ROTC Cadet Command at Fort Knox, then forwarded to headquarters at Fort Monroe on March 5. Why it took headquarters more than two months to review the decision is not clear. Fortunately, Hammann informed me of the decision right away. I didn't have to learn of my fate from a national television network.

ROTC officials at Washington University, predictably, were less than thrilled with the decision. But I was ecstatic. I heard the news when I went back to Saint Louis for graduation. When I called home from the airport to check in with Brent, he said that ROTC had phoned. When I called them back, they said I wasn't going to have to repay my scholarship but I wasn't going

[181]

to be commissioned, either. I immediately called Bill Ruben-stein. He was happy, too, but he kept saying, "We've got to have the memo! We've got to have the memo!" So I called ROTC again and said I wanted to drop by and get a copy.

When I walked into the ROTC building, I was *so* pumped. I saw the photo of the burned ROTC building, with the inscription "Lest we forget," and I rejoiced. I knew I'd given them something else to remember. I went in there feeling on top of the world. I knew that Colonel Bates wanted me to repay my scholarship, as did everyone else in that office. Especially Hansen, the secretary. I knew she hated my guts. I remembered her shaking her head during my hearing, and I expected she had taken a lot of calls from people giving them shit.

I walked in and said, "I'm Jim Holobaugh. I've been told that something's come in on my case." Hansen said in this snotty tone, "I know who you are." Then she turned to some other people and asked, "Did y'all hear of anything coming in?" They said no. I told them to check. Finally, I got a copy.

It was the best feeling, walking out of that building for the last time with that memo in my hand. I know I lost the case in that I wasn't commissioned. I was disappointed about that, but it was no surprise. I think it really got to them, though, that I didn't have to repay the scholarship. I remember vividly that day in Bates's office, when he said he was going to make damn sure I repaid my scholarship. Well, he failed. In many cases, gays being discharged go through hell with the military and never get their revenge. I did.

In a prepared (and obviously tempered) statement for the press, I said, "While I am pleased I will not have to repay the money, I am terribly disappointed that the Army has not seen fit to grant me a commission and to allow me to serve my country."

Many gay people — even some of the leaders — think people like Joe, Robb, and me are silly. They can't understand why we would want to be in the military in the first place. They think, "Why should the gay community be concerned about this? We should be working against the military." This bothers me tremendously. Even if you think the military is a horrible organization, you have to understand that this policy gives credibility to the idea that gays should be second-class citizens. This is one of the last U.S. government policies to officially sanction discrimination, and it affects a tremendous number of people. The military is this country's largest employer. There are thousands of Americans who have very little choice economically except to join the military. And a lot of these people are gay. I wish America would wake up to that.

Researchers believe that institutionalized discrimination against gays like the military's is a big factor in the development of homophobia. A 1988 report issued by the New York Governor's Task Force on Bias-Related Violence found that of all minority groups, "the most severe hostilities are directed at lesbians and gay men." It said that teenagers think gays and lesbians are "legitimate targets which can be openly attacked."

My favorite book about the future of the national gay movement is *After the Ball* by Marshall Kirk and Hunter Madsen. It is a book that has been widely praised by publications as diverse as the *Advocate*, *Christopher Street*, *Time*, *Newsweek*, *Booklist*, and the *Indianapolis News*, and sharply criticized by the gay movement's more separatist elements.

I agree with so much of that book. I read it and thought, "Yes! This is how I feel. I'm glad someone is writing this." Brent liked it even more than I did. I feel gays are presenting the wrong image to America in too many ways. Sometimes it isn't our fault, for when the media portrays us they use people who do not represent the bulk of the gay community. Most gays are just average Americans. Take the average American, if there is such an animal, and that person could also be the average gay. The media never shows that, and in a lot of ways, neither do we. When we have gay pride parades with drag queens and pedophile groups, that's who the media is going to show. They don't show the Gay Physicians walking down Fifth Avenue. They show Dykes on Bikes. I think gay America needs to work much harder at putting its most typical faces in front of the American people, rather than its fringe faces.

Another thing in *After the Ball* I agree with is their statement that gays put too much emphasis on youth and beauty, and just throw everyone else out the door. When you walk in a gay bar and you're not what everyone's looking for, you can be treated

[183]

cruelly. America's like that in a lot of ways. *I* was like that, but I'm not now.

We will win this battle. The man sitting in the Oval Office makes a big difference. George Bush obviously wasn't going to change the policy, but Bill Clinton said from the beginning of his campaign that he would abolish the ban on gays and lesbians in the armed forces.

If the military changed its policy and offered me a commission tomorrow, my gut reaction would be to say, "Fuck you. You had your chance." But at the same time, the idea of being one of the first openly gay people to serve in the United States military appeals to me.

*A year after Jim's case became public, his father still wasn't sure how he feels about gays in the military.*

*"I'm not sure that I know. I totally support Morris and his decisions. He's my son and he has 100 percent of my support. But if you probe deep into my mind about gays in the military, I don't have an answer for that."*

*Does his father still wonder if Jim is gay? Has he come to accept it?*

*"I can accept whatever he is, regardless. A parent accepts whatever deformity — whatever a child is, you accept that — totally. But I'm not equating being gay with a deformity or illness or anything like that. It's a tough issue. Religions are having trouble with it now. A lot of trouble. People my age have trouble with it. You can imagine how I flinch when I'm in a crowd and they tell a joke about a gay. In my mind I'm thinking, 'Hey, that's — that's my son. In my growing up, the word* queer *and all the derogatory jokes and terminology — that's what you thought of when you thought gay. I'm sure Morris thinks that since he is someone who seems unlikely to be a gay, his actions help win people's acceptance. And if he keeps plugging away at this thing through the years, then maybe there will be more acceptance. Maybe that's what he feels his niche in history is. I'm not sure I totally agree with that. Maybe I'm a selfish person. I want to enjoy the things in life. I'm not trying to change humanity that much. When I went to meet him at the airport one weekend, here comes*

a guy carrying a briefcase, with a short haircut and a tie and a sport jacket on. It's not the image Midwesterners have of gays."

Is his father proud of him?

"Oh, certainly. I guess if your son was a bank robber and he was an excellent bank robber, you'd be proud of him. That's a crazy statement, but, yes, you're always proud of your son's achievements. I don't suppose any son ever did and was everything that his parents expected and wanted him to be. Morris was a boy who my family had a lot of pride in, and that's why the hurt was so bad. He was intelligent, good-natured, fun to be around. He was liked by everyone. And with the problems he had with the loss of his mother, he was someone who I, as a principal, could use when discussing divorce. I could say, 'Hey, just because your mom and dad are divorced, that's no reason you have to mess up in school. My own son is in school at Rolla with an ROTC scholarship, and he's doing great.' He was an example.

"There is no loss of love between the father and his son, I'll guarantee you that. Maybe disappointment — and not understanding. Not because I don't want to understand, but because I was raised at a time and in a way that it's difficult for me to totally accept his decision. I can look back now and see that some people I went to college with were gay. I feel for them now, for I know they were fighting something they really weren't. Hopefully, someday all of them can live in acceptance of what they are. In my opinion, acceptance in the Midwest has changed more in the last five years than in all the rest of time put together.

"I think as a father you picture your children growing up and marrying and having grandkids, living somewhere close to you so you can visit. The 'little white house and picket fence' theory of life. And it's not that way, of course. I never harbored any ill will toward gays that I know of. I'm sure I've been part of the joke thing, but as I look back I think some of my best friends in college might have been gay — unannounced gays. That's true of anybody. Ten percent of the population is gay, and that's probably not all of them; it's probably a small estimate.

"Time heals all problems. Time heals divorce problems. Time heals death problems. Time heals everything."

A thoughtful, soft-spoken man, Mr. Holobaugh has conducted himself throughout the interview in the manner of a principal — formal, in control. But now he is sitting with his elbows on his knees, slumped forward, staring at the floor. He wonders aloud if granting this interview was such a good idea. He cites his inexperience and the possibility of his words being taken out of context. One can't help liking the man and feeling for him — he's had to deal with so much in so short a time. He seems to be making progress. Certainly, a lot of parents have had worse reactions.

When some of Mr. Holobaugh's comments — the positive ones — are relayed to Jim via telephone, there's a pause. Then Jim says, "I'm sitting here with a big smile on my face. He's never told me those things."

"The situation with his dad was never very good," says Carolyn Lang, "and from what Jim's told me, it still isn't. He was going to go visit, but they asked him not to bring Brent, so he didn't go."

Does that hurt Brent?

"It doesn't," says Brent. "What hurts me is that it hurts Jim. Quite honestly, I wasn't comfortable around his dad even before he knew anything. He's intimidating. I think it's because he tries to keep the air of a principal about him at all times. I'm just sorry that Jim feels he's being distanced. But sometimes Jim will say that he feels he should just stay away from his family, and I try to push him back. I tell him he should call his folks and call his sister. We were supposed to go back recently. I was willing to go there and stay in a hotel because I knew it would probably take them time. But Jim was adamant about our going only as a couple, and that was not possible. I wish Jim and his family had more contact, and I wish he would call them more often and try to make an effort."

In a letter to John Taylor written in June 1991, Jim said:

I love my family and I want to be a part of their lives and I want them to be a part of mine. I am willing to give them time to deal with all this, but I am slowly drifting away and becoming more of a member of Brent's family than my own. Brent's parents are terrific. They tell me they love me. They will call and talk to me for half an hour and never even speak with Brent. They fly us both home to Michigan to see them. In every way, they treat

[186]

me as if I am married to their son. I love them like parents. All this makes me resent the way my family treats Brent. My family acts as if he doesn't exist. Until he is as welcome at my parents' home as I am, I will not be back, because I will not go to Ava without him.

On Christmas Day, 1990, Brent and I exchanged rings. I had been around a gay couple who did this, and, reflecting on it, I liked what that said about their commitment. I suggested it to Brent and he agreed. We decided to do it at Christmas. We used to wear the rings on the left hand, the traditional marriage hand, because our philosophy was that we were just like any other couple. But when I rode to work on the train, it bothered me that I had this ring on my left hand and if the people around me happened to notice my ring, they would assume I was a married straight guy. I decided I wanted to wear it on my right hand, and eventually I convinced Brent. Now, if anyone sees the ring and thinks about it at all, it creates a little confusion. And if they ask me about it, I can tell them.

Brent and I have met a lot of different couples in the past six months. Our best friends are a couple we haven't known very long. What's most appealing about Daryl and Ramon is that they're in the same stage of their relationship as we are. We find ourselves talking with them about laundry detergent and supermarkets. I'd tell Brent, "I like these guys, they know what's important!" A lot of people you meet don't try hard enough to keep in touch and you find yourself doing all the work. But Daryl and Ramon make as much of an effort to see us as we do to see them.

I think people who are openly gay are some of the most comfortable, genuine people around. They don't have much to hide, so they can be themselves. By far, the best part of my life is Brent and our friends.

As for what I want to do with my life, that's a problem. I switch back and forth and think about different things. I want to leave the world a better place than it was when I came here. Maybe everyone feels that way and we all just have different ideas of what a better world would be. Sometimes I think that with Brent as a physician and me as an engineer, we could go to Africa and work for the Peace Corps and do some good in the world. We could help people rather than sit here in Connecticut and direct our resources toward a cappuccino maker and a new VCR.

Sometimes I think, "What's life all about? Why are we here?" I don't think it's to accumulate toys. I don't want to be a leech on this earth. Life would mean a lot more if you could make a difference by helping people. But I realize too that you don't have to go to Africa; you can make a difference in Connecticut. I struggle with that. For now, I want to continue to be active in the ROTC issue, and after that battle's won, to continue being politically active in the gay community and on other issues important to me.

*"We'd like to pay off our debt," says Brent, when asked about goals. "Med school is very expensive, so between us we've accumulated a lot of debt. We'd like to buy a nice home. I'd like to set up a good practice. I'm not certain if Jim knows what he wants to do yet.*

*"We'll have kids someday. Jim says we'll find two lesbians and do it that way. We have friends who have done it like that, and it seems to work. You have to find lesbians you're very compatible with. But that's not the only way it can be done. If we were in a better position, we could adopt one of the Bengali kids or the Romanian kids who are homeless. And God knows, there are people in the inner city who could be adopted. I'd have no problem with that at all. I think everyone would prefer to have a biological child, but for me it's not that important because what I will give that child is nurture and love, and that's what will be carried on, rather than genes. So maybe they won't have blue eyes or whatever. Who cares? There are enough people out there with blue eyes. That's not important.*

*"I used to have all these lofty goals — to be the best at this, the best physician or whatever. I think in a relationship your goals change. My goal is to grow with Jim and have our family, have a good life, and help folks around us when we can.*

One thing I do now is take chances. I used to stick to the safe road. But I took a chance with my relationship with Brent.

Although terrified of being hurt, I took the gamble. I took another chance when I went public with this issue. Both chances have paid huge dividends. I think you need to have a positive attitude. You've got to apply to the best schools and assume you're going to get in. You've got to go after that person you really like. If you play it safe because you're afraid to lose, you're not going to accomplish much.

There's a saying I like: "Some people are born on third base and go through life feeling like they hit a home run." I feel it applied to me; I've had a lot of advantages, and I've got to do something with that. Even before anything with the Army came up, I told Brent that I wanted to do something political, something that would help. I remember telling him that I felt like the line in that Ten Years After song: "I'd love to change the world, but I don't know what to do." I'm glad I was able to do something. Now, I want to do more. As for Ten Years After, they could begin by not using terms like "dykes and fairies," which they say in another part of that song.

This whole ordeal has been one of the best things in my life. I don't regret it at all. Probably the greatest benefit was my coming out — no longer having a weight on my shoulders, worrying about people finding out this big secret. It's a pleasure simply to be who you are. I was asking Gerry Studds recently if he was glad he was outed. I think the question surprised him — he was like, "Well, *no.*" I kept after him. I asked, "But aren't you much happier now? Aren't you glad you're out of the closet?" He said he was, but he wished it hadn't happened the way it did. I wish mine hadn't happened the way it did, either, but I'm glad it happened.

I'm not advocating outing people, but I think if people who are outed deal with it appropriately, they won't be sorry it happened. The biggest roadblock the gay community faces is its inability to come out and be visible. We aren't like other minorities. No one knows who we are when we're walking down the street unless we're one of the few who fit a stereotype. The only way things are going to change for gays is for gays to be open about their sexuality. If everybody came out, people would see how many of us there are and how normal we are. It would be eye-opening for most Americans to come face-to-face with the fact that their minister, or their best friend in high school, or their secretary, or their football coach, or their veterinarian, or the guy at the gas station, or their favorite waitress — or their lieutenant colonel — is lesbian or gay.

# Gays and the military

## AN OVERVIEW

Tonight thousands of men and women in the military are living in fear: fear that their careers could come to an end over something they had no choice about, and something that shouldn't matter. These gay men and women are putting their lives on the line for the freedoms this country stands for, yet they are being denied the freedom to be honest about who they are.

The words are Jim's. They are from the speech he has delivered at college campuses across the United States. Jim waits anxiously for the day when he won't have to make that speech. He awaits the day when the military policy banning gays from serving their country is rescinded and the United States joins other civilized countries in treating all of its citizens equally, without prejudice, in all of its employment practices, including the military.

America would not be plunging into the unknown by allowing gays in the military. Other countries have tried it, studied the results, and found that there were no negative effects and quite a few positive ones. The Netherlands integrated openly gay soldiers into its military in 1974, Denmark and Sweden in

1979. Other countries allowing gays to serve unconditionally include Australia, Belgium, Canada, Finland, France, Iceland, Italy, Japan, Luxembourg, New Zealand, Norway, Spain, and Switzerland. Canada, New Zealand, and Australia have only recently ended their bans. Australian officials cited the pro-gay position of American President-elect Bill Clinton as being instrumental in their decision to allow gays and lesbians to serve. The new Czech Republic and Slovenia reportedly do not discriminate either. Austria, Brazil, Germany, Ireland, Israel, Portugal, and South Africa allow gays to serve, though with restrictions. Greece seems to ignore its restrictions. The Grecian armed forces include many gay or bisexual young men who are at least open enough to embrace each other lovingly — even sensually — at bars near their bases. They certainly do not live in fear, as do their American counterparts.

In Denmark, the only country in which gays can officially get married, the government permits no discrimination against gays and its military pays no attention to sexual orientation. The Danish military keeps no statistics on homosexual personnel, maintaining that "this is a personal matter that does not concern the military." The national Danish organization for gays and lesbians (LBL/F-48) says neither it nor the Ministry of Defense has received complaints of discrimination from gays serving in the military.

Five years after gays were allowed into the military in Sweden, the supreme commander of the Swedish armed forces told a parliamentary commission that homosexuality was no reason for special treatment, positive or negative, in the Swedish armed forces, as long as the individual was mature and accepting of his or her sexuality. People uncomfortable with being gay could be a problem, he said, in the same way any heterosexual with sexual problems might "create difficulties." He said the armed forces aimed to get "the right man or woman in the right place" without regard to sexual orientation, and that all sexually troubled personnel, straight or gay, were treated the same. It seems a rational policy, and one befitting a civilized nation.

DNF 48, the national gay and lesbian rights organization of Norway, reports that "gays and lesbians in Norway are not exposed to discrimination in the military ... We have had a case where a gay man was denied the same economic conditions for him and his lover as heterosexuals have, living together without being married, but after DNF-48 took up this case with the military service, this has been changed."

The Dutch policy is that "homosexuals who do not hide their disposition shall be dealt with in the same ways as heterosexuals." According to the Ministry of Defense, "Sexual preference is in no way of any importance for the Armed Forces." Members of the armed forces are allowed to engage in consensual homosexual relationships with civilians or other soldiers (regardless of rank) when off duty and away from military premises. The government has commissioned several studies on gays and lesbians in the military. After concluding that there were no negative results of integrating gays into the military, the government commissioned a study by the University of Utrecht's Interfaculty Homostudies Workgroup to trace prejudice in the armed forces and how gay and lesbian soldiers cope with it.

Several organizations represent Dutch military gays and lesbians. Stichting Homoseksualiteit en Krijgsmacht is a foundation of gays and lesbians in the armed forces. The Working Group for Homosexuals in the Armed Forces became a Dutch foundation in 1987 and is recognized as a discussion partner by the government. Maatschappelijke Raad voor de Krijgsmacht, an independent advisory board of the Ministry of Defense, released in 1990 a very positive report on gays and lesbians in the Dutch army.

In 1987 the Dutch Customs Office and Military Police were accused of informing United States Army officials that several American soldiers stationed in the Netherlands were gay. This led to one soldier's dismissal. The Dutch official responsible for leaking the information was subsequently dismissed, and the state secretary for defense promised that such a breach of Dutch policy would not happen again.

The Military Justice Code of France contains no mention of homosexuality. Gays are allowed to serve and, in fact, are legally protected from discrimination. In addition, according to a French military official, *"l'homosexualite entre militaires dans un lieu privé n'est pas reprehensible au regard des reglements et de la loi"* ("homosexuality between military persons in a private place is not reprehensible in regard to regulations and the law").

In Spain, gays actually have the best of both worlds. They are not disqualified from serving, but can, if they wish, use homosexuality as a reason not to serve.

When Canada changed its regulations, allowing gays and lesbians to serve, former Naval Academy cadet Joe Steffan, recalling the days of Vietnam War draft dodgers, noted that because he was gay he was in the strange position of having to go to Canada if he *wanted* to be in the military.

The United Nations cited discrimination against gays as one of the main reasons the United States ranked only thirteenth in its 1991 Human Development Report, a ranking of countries by human rights standards. Sweden and Denmark were ranked at the top.

The United States does, officially, for all the world to see, discriminate against its gay citizens. Because the policy prohibiting gays from military service is set forth in writing, it is worth looking at to see what it says and how it dares to say those things.

The Pentagon policy that denies gays and lesbians the right to serve their country is contained in Department of Defense Directive 1332.14, issued from the office of Secretary of Defense Caspar Weinberger in 1982. It reads:

> Homosexuality is incompatible with military service. The presence in the military environment of persons who engage in homosexual conduct or who, by their statements, demonstrate a propensity to engage in homosexual conduct seriously impairs the accomplishment of the military mission. The presence of such members adversely affects the ability of the Military Services to maintain discipline, good order and morale; to foster mutual trust and confidence among service members, to ensure the integrity of rank and command; to facilitate assignment and worldwide deployment of service members who frequently must live and work under close conditions affording minimal privacy, to recruit and retain members of the

[194]

Military Services; to maintain the public acceptability of military service; and to prevent breaches of security. As used in this action: *Homosexual* means a person, regardless of sex, who engages in, desires to engage in, or intends to engage in homosexual acts.

That "intends to engage in" could be trouble for military officials if they ever try to reinstitute the draft. Persons not wanting to be drafted need merely claim that at some point in the unspecified future they intend to engage in a homosexual act. How could the military prove that someone actually hasn't the slightest intention to engage in a homosexual act?

Also, the assertion that the presence of openly gay individuals adversely affects this multitude of things is baseless. The Pentagon has never allowed openly gay individuals to serve and can hardly speak from experience. Countries that allow gays in their armed forces have found none of these claims to be true. So just where does the Pentagon get off making policy based on such appallingly erroneous beliefs? In a word, prejudice. Although Pentagon officials have insisted there is no basis for comparison between their excuses for banning gays and their previous excuses for banning blacks, in fact the excuses are exactly the same. Compare, for example, the above policy with a declassified Navy memorandum dated December 24, 1941:

> The close and intimate conditions of life aboard ship, the necessity for the highest possible degree of unity and esprit-de-corps; the requirement of morale — all these demand that nothing be done which may adversely affect the situation. Past experience has shown irrefutably that the enlistment of Negroes (other than for mess attendants) leads to disruptive and undermining conditions. Men live in particularly close association. In their messes, one man sits beside another. Their hammocks or bunks are close together. In their common tasks they work side by side, and in particular tasks such as those of a guns crew, they form a closely knit, highly coordinated team. How many white men would choose of their own accord that their closest associates in their sleeping quarters, at mess, and in a guns crew should be of another race? How many would

[195]

accept such conditions if required to do so without resentment and just as a matter of course? The General Board believes the answer is "few, if any" and further believes that if the issue was forced, there would be a lowering of contentment, teamwork, and discipline in the services.

Clearly, the same reasons once used to exclude blacks from serving their country are now being used to exclude gays. The reasons once used to deny women this opportunity were much the same.

Gay men and women are dismissed from the military for one of three reasons given in section 1.c. of Directive 1332.14. "The basis for separation," it says, "may include preservice, prior service, or current service conduct or statements." A member shall be separated if the member "has engaged in, attempted to engage in, or solicited another to engage in a homosexual act or acts," if "the member has stated that he or she is a homosexual or bisexual unless there is further finding that the member is not a homosexual or bisexual," or if "the member has married or attempted to marry a person known to be of the same biological sex" unless it is found that the purpose of the marriage was to avoid military service.

The third reason listed, marriage, is preposterous, since gay marriages are not recognized as legal anywhere in the United States, nor in Puerto Rico, Guam, the United States Virgin Islands, or American Samoa — the only spots on the globe likely to produce an American soldier. Even so, in April 1991 a military reservist who told her commanding officers she was a lesbian was instructed to produce "a marriage license listing you and your spouse indicating both partners are female" — something they were not likely to obtain legally for any amount of love or money. This bizarre request seemed to say that all three reasons in the "basis for separation" must apply to a person in order for them to be dismissed, in which case no one would ever get kicked out for homosexuality. The incident took place during Operation Desert Storm, when the military needed all of its able-bodied personnel. Apparently, when a war's on the Pentagon is perfectly willing for gays and lesbians to fight. Gays are only unsuitable for peacetime service.

The ROTC "Worksheet for Admission and Retention in the ROTC Program" asks the question, "Have you ever engaged in, desired or intend to engage in bodily conduct with a person of the same sex for the purpose of sexual satisfaction?" For a cadet to say yes is to be booted forthwith.

The Uniform Code of Military Justice, part of the "Manual for Courts Martial," defines sodomy in Article 125. It makes no distinction between homosexual or heterosexual acts, prohibiting all forms of oral and anal sex. It concludes: "Any person ... who engages in unnatural carnal copulation with another person of same or opposite sex or with an animal is guilty of sodomy. Penetration, however slight, is sufficient to complete the offense." Article 125 has historically been used against heterosexuals more often than homosexuals. During fiscal year 1987–88, the Army made 178 charges of sodomy, of which 127 involved heterosexual sodomy. Fifty-four cases were consensual.

From the American Revolution until World War II, separations from the military for homosexuality were made only when "indecent acts" (usually sodomy) could be proven. However, on at least one occasion in Rhode Island, 1919, the Navy set up a sting operation to entrap homosexual sailors.

In 1940, sixteen million men registered with the Selective Service, allowing the service to indeed be selective. It soon followed the advice of psychiatrists and listed homosexuality among reasons for exclusion from service. Potential enlistees and officer candidates were asked questions about their sex habits. If a soldier joined and was later discovered to be homosexual, he could be dishonorably discharged or even imprisoned.

During the 1960s and 1970s several discharged gays sought reinstatement on the grounds that although they were gay, they had never committed acts of sodomy. The Reagan administration closed the loophole in January 1982, when Caspar Weinberger's office reworded the policy to include homosexual orientation as grounds for dismissal. It wasn't necessary to have sex; just being gay was enough.

Oddly, under certain conditions Department of Defense policy allows a soldier to be retained after committing a homosexual act. The "Note" to the policy — as it's printed in Army regulations AR 635-200 UPDATE, page 58, item 15-3 — reads: "To warrant retention of a soldier after finding that he or she engaged in attempted [sic] to engage in, or solicited another to engage in a homosexual act, the board's findings must specifically include all five findings listed in a(1) through (5) above." The five conditions are that the conduct was a departure from usual behavior; the conduct is unlikely to recur; the conduct did not involve force; the soldier's "continued presence in the Army is consistent with the interest of the Army in proper discipline, good order, and morale"; and the soldier "does not desire to engage in or intend to engage in homosexual acts." The note goes on to say, "The intent of this policy is to permit retention only of nonhomosexual soldiers who, because of extenuating circumstances ... engaged in, attempted to engage in, or solicited a homosexual act" (emphasis theirs). Extenuating circumstances include "immaturity, intoxication, coercion, or a desire to avoid military service."

Says Bill Rubenstein of the ACLU, "They'll give you one free bite. They're obviously more interested in policing thoughts than actions."

Pentagon officials have been reluctant to discuss the policy prohibiting gays from serving. The newspaper clippings from Jim's case are replete with "military officials refused comment," or "repeated phone calls to Colonel Bates's office were not returned." A *New York Times* article, "R.O.T.C. Under Siege for Ousting Homosexuals," which appeared May 6, 1990, with Jim's photo, says Pentagon spokesmen "said they could distribute the 130-word directive but are not permitted to discuss it."

Occasionally someone at the Pentagon does say something, but it's usually inane. Pentagon spokesman Doug Hart recently said the usual: "Homosexuality is incompatible with military service and the Department of Defense has no plans to change that policy." Then, asked about the claim that there were tens or hundreds of thousands of gay men in the military, Hart said, "There probably aren't very many at all."

Retired military personnel, however, can discuss the policy — and often come across as idiots trying to defend it. Retired captain "Red" McDaniel, president of the American Defense Foundation, appearing on Cable News Network's "Crossfire" June 25, 1991, went in delirious circles with his argument. He said homosexuals should not be allowed in the service because there is a policy against it, and to join would leave them open to blackmail. That's correct — McDaniel said they should not be allowed because they're not allowed. Mike Kinsley, "Crossfire" co-host, asked how gays could be blackmailed if the policy did not exist and they were openly gay. McDaniel replied, "Well, it could be used against you." Kinsley, for the second time, demanded, "How? When it's out in the open?" McDaniel stared blankly for a couple of seconds, then said, "Well, you can't be out in the open because it's forbidden."

To prove his point, McDaniel offered the example of a minister he knew who had been falsely accused of being homosexual. "They used that, and drove him from the pulpit," said McDaniel. An exasperated Kinsley exclaimed, "But, Captain! That's an argument for the other side!" and pointed out that it was the policy that made such victimization possible. McDaniel, undeterred, responded, "If you remove homosexuals from the service, you eliminate the problem." Kinsley's rejoinder was that you could never eliminate homosexuals from the service, you could only eliminate the stigma.

McDaniel eventually admitted that homosexuals could be good soldiers. But, he said, they are prohibited from joining, so for them to come in is dishonest. It's a good thing gays are prohibited from serving in the military; otherwise, McDaniel could not have given a single reason why they shouldn't be there. To be fair, he did say he wasn't sure homosexuals could exhibit leadership — an argument based on apparent ignorance, not policy.

The other host of "Crossfire," Robert Novak, didn't make much sense either. While acknowledging that there had always been homosexuals in the military, Novak insisted that they should stay in the closet. Kinsley pointed out the obvious Catch-22: If gays are in the closet, they're an espionage risk; if they come out, they get kicked out. Novak's disingenuous response: "Ah, come on! You mean a grunt is going to be accused of espionage!?"

The other guest on that episode of "Crossfire," Air Force Captain Greg Greeley, had just carried the lead banner in Washington's Gay Pride Parade and then been grilled for hours by military officials. Novak asked Greeley if he didn't think his being gay made him a security risk. Greeley responded: "The only people who ever tried to blackmail me was the Air Force. They wanted me to give names of other people in the military. They tried to extort me. They threatened to investigate me all the way back to high school, and I said 'No!' because I'm not blackmailable." Secretary of Defense Dick Cheney later criticized the Air Force for its handling of the Greeley case.

McDaniel is far from alone in asserting that policy is based on policy. Former Pentagon spokesman Major David Super, in an article in the *Village Voice*, March 13, 1990, said: "Our policy is based on many years of experience and, well, on defense policy. That's the way it is."

Remarkably, in the only known confidential survey of military officers' opinions on the matter, a 1980 thesis by Michael McIntyre at the Naval Postgraduate School in Monterey, California, found that 92 percent believed homosexuality should not be grounds for dismissal when it did not interfere with job performance. The percentage is remarkable because it is even higher than that found among the general public. Public opinion polls for more than a decade have shown that the majority of Americans believe gays have a right to serve their country. A 1991 poll by New York's Penn & Schoen Associates found that 81 percent of Americans oppose the policy of discharging gay soldiers, and 65 percent oppose the ban on gays in the first place. The percentage who believe gays should be allowed to serve had increased steadily from 51 percent in 1977. In 1992, however, after President-elect Clinton proposed lifting the ban, a *Newsweek* poll showed a decrease in public support for allowing gays to serve in the military.

The reluctance of military officials to discuss the policy is partly because they've been told not to discuss it, and partly because no one wants to get trapped trying to defend an indefensible policy. One Army officer, a married man with several children who is nearing retirement (and must remain anonymous to keep from jeopardizing his retirement benefits) did agree to discuss the policy but did not defend it at all. This officer is thoughtful and intelligent, what every Army officer should be. He has been decorated with some of the highest awards a soldier in his position can receive. Although he seems tired of Army life after almost twenty years, he is quick to defend it and point out its virtues.

"The Army is very specific on the lifestyle we lead," he says. "You will not use drugs, you will not abuse alcohol, you will not abuse your wife or children. You will support equal opportunity, you will remain within the body fat standards for your age. You will not bring discredit to the U.S. Army. You will not pass bad checks or fail to pay your debts. And you cannot serve in the armed forces as a homosexual."

Does the Army enforce those regulations?

"The Army does a good job of being fair according to their rules. It is not perfect, but abuses are unusual. On something like alcohol abuse or spouse abuse the Army will give a soldier counseling and a second chance. But the fuck-ups don't last long anymore, because now the Army can afford to be choosy."

How are the equal opportunity provisions enforced?

"There is mandatory training in equal opportunity, and this includes women. It's a career-ender if you have on your evaluation that you do not support equal opportunity. Sexual harassment is a big problem, but the cure is there — education and affirmative action — and it's starting to work. Let me throw this at you: The Army as an organization is light years ahead of most. Minorities are accepted and meet no barriers. The health of all soldiers is a number-one priority. For example, the Army bans smoking everywhere a nonsmoker would go. Women are doing more and being accepted more. I have watched this evolve, and I'd say that today most of the women look and act like professionals. It's the men who have the problems. If you look at the statistics, they'll show that everything I've said is true.

"All of our rules are sensible and necessary except one. So why does the Army not accept gays? There is no justifiable reason, just ignorance and prejudice. Gays should be allowed in the Army to help them gain acceptance and their rightful place in America. If gays win this fight with the military, it

[201]

will change how America thinks about gays — not overnight, but eventually. Because of its size, the Army is copied by large corporations. They see what works in the Army and what doesn't. The Army had affirmative action in the fifties. The smoking policy began in 1982 and now everyone is copying it."

What experiences have you had with gays in the Army?

"I've known no open gays since I've been in. I have heard of three cases of gay males who were caught in the act and kicked out within a week. My wife tells me two soldiers filmed themselves out where she works and left the tape in the VCR. The first sergeant found the tape and they were gone in two days. I don't believe the stories I hear about lesbians. Every time we go to the field I hear stories of dozens of women committing cunnilingus in the showers and being caught and thrown out. I think those stories are just jealousy on the part of the story-tellers because they ain't gettin' any."

How much harassment of women goes on?

"A lot. But I honestly think it's the least in our society."

What sort of sexual activity goes on?

"A lot of adultery and visiting prostitutes. I'd say about a quarter of the soldiers under my command are regulars at the whorehouses, and about 5 percent are divorced each year because of adultery."

What would you do if you caught two of your soldiers in the act?

"If I were to catch two soldiers in the act I would hope to get out the door before they saw me. But most of the leaders we have would love to catch two soldiers in the act, just so they could tell the story."

"Bingo!" says Jim. "I think that's a key to a lot of the 'gotcha' stuff against gays in the military. Officers like to tell stories. Sometimes life can be boring, and this gives them something to talk about. In a lot of cases the officers don't really have a problem with it, but it makes a good story."

A final question for our officer: If you caught two soldiers in the act and didn't report it, would you be risking much?

"Yes, I would be risking a lot. But I've always gone with my heart and it hasn't failed me yet."

[202]

The Pentagon's difficulty in defending its policy probably explains why at least three studies of the subject have been commissioned and then suppressed.

The Crittenden report, conducted in 1957 and chaired by Navy Captain S.H. Crittenden, Jr., examined the question of whether homosexuals were a security risk. It found that "the number of cases of blackmail as a result of past investigations of homosexuals is negligible. No factual data exist to support the contention that homosexuals are a greater risk than heterosexuals."

The November 20, 1989, issue of *U.S. News and World Report* cited a congressional source when reporting that of 130 military spy cases, only six involved gays, and of those six only one involved any possibility of blackmail. While the Crittenden report recognized that gays are no greater security risk than heterosexuals, it nevertheless recommended that the policy barring gays be continued. The Navy, however, refused to release the report because of its potentially embarrassing findings. Indeed, they succeeded in suppressing the report until 1977, when a court order finally made it available to the public. It is published as an appendix to E.L. Gibson's *Get Off My Ship* (Avon, 1978).

In 1987, following the Johnny Walker and Moscow Marine Guards heterosexual spy scandals, the Department of Defense established the Personnel Security Research and Education Center (PERSEREC) in Monterey, California, to study personnel security issues. One of the studies the Pentagon commissioned was essentially the same as the Crittenden commission's. It tried to determine whether homosexuality is related to "trust violation."

Although the Department of Defense commissioned the studies, it again tried to suppress them when the conclusions did not jibe with military policy. The first study, prepared by Dr. Theodore R. Sarbin and Captain Kenneth E. Karols, was completed in December 1988; the second, prepared by Michael A. McDaniel, was finished in January 1989.

Acting on an anonymous tip, Representative Gerry Studds of Massachusetts began trying to get a copy of the report in early 1989. He worked six months to get it. During this period his office was told on different occasions that the report didn't exist, wasn't ready, or was unavailable. At one point the Department of Defense even insisted it had no connection with PERSEREC. In fact, PERSEREC is the brainchild and property of the Pentagon, and has "Department of Defense" displayed prominently on its letterhead. In no way is it an independent agency. Studds enlisted the help of Representative Patricia Schroeder of Colorado, chair of the House Armed Services Subcommittee. On October 17, 1989, they were able to obtain the Sarbin-Karols document, "Nonconforming Sexual Orientations and Military Suitability."

Studds's former assistant, Kate Dyer, remembers the meeting between Studds and Maynard Anderson, the Department of Defense official in charge of PERSEREC:

"When Gerry said he'd read it, Anderson went pale. Then Gerry said, 'I have a copy,' and Anderson went paler. Then Gerry said he was going to release it to the press and Anderson went white."

Pentagon officials told Schroeder the report's mandate was to assess the reliability of homosexuals for security reasons, but that the report exceeded its mandate by assessing the suitability of homosexuals for military service. Says Schroeder, "That's a distinction without a difference. In fact, the report shows that gay men and lesbians are both suitable and reliable for military service."

Schroeder asked if other studies had been conducted on this issue and was told none had. After Studds released the report, however, a copy of the McDaniel study arrived in his office in an unmarked envelope.

The following are excerpts from the Sarbin-Karols report:

On the reasonable assumption that the number of military personnel who are homosexual may be as high as 10 percent, only a minute percentage are separated from the service. This discrepancy calls into question the usefulness of Article 125. It may be that the article is simply unenforceable...

The order to integrate blacks was first met with stout resistance by traditionalists in the military establishment. Dire consequences were predicted for maintaining discipline, building group morale, and achieving military organizational goals. None of these predictions of doom has come true. Social science specialists helped develop programs for combating racial discrimination, so that now the military services are leaders in providing equal opportunity for black men and women. It would be wise to consider applying the experience of the past 40 years to the integration of homosexuals...

It is unlikely that the caricature of the male homosexual, the feminized male, would volunteer for military service, or be accepted. It is, however, estimated that such feminized males make up only a small proportion of homosexuals, perhaps 10 percent.

Thus, 90 percent of male homosexuals display no overt behavioral stigmata ... The median age of "coming out" ... is approximately 19 or 20 ... Thus, some persons do not know of or act out their homosexual urges until after induction. Such people are most unlikely to be screened out at the time of entry into military service...

The military cannot indefinitely isolate itself from the changes occurring in the wider society, of which it is an integral part.

Inevitably, the report was not well received at the Pentagon. A memorandum to PERSEREC from Craig Alderman, Jr., under secretary of defense, about the report, dated January 18, 1989, reads:

We, together with other DoD staff elements, have reviewed subject draft study and believe you missed the target. Moreover, you exceeded your authority by extending the research effort beyond the personnel security arena, and into another area entirely, namely suitability for military service.

Wholly aside from PERSEREC's lack of authority to conduct research into the military suitability area, we found PERS-TR-89-002 to be technically flawed, to contain subject matter (Judeo-Christian precepts) which has no place in a Department of Defense publication ... and to suggest a bias which does justice neither to PERSEREC nor the Department...

You will find that your authority to conduct initial research in the sexual misconduct area is rather narrowly set forth in TAB 2-1, item 19, of the Initial Research Plan ... I want you to renew your effort to develop a positive response to this latter memorandum ... Lastly, I must ask that you coordinate in advance, as well as seek appropriate guidance, prior to initiating any PERSEREC research in areas which are questionable or have not been approved by my office.

PERSEREC Director Carson K. Eoyang responded, accepting responsibility "for not meeting your expectations in the conduct of this research." He enclosed with his letter a "Review of Guidance on Homosexuality Research," which contained this entry:

11 Dec 1987 Mr. William Fedor and Mr. Peter Nelson met with Dr. McDaniel and CAPT Kenneth Karols to review homosexual research under development. Preliminary data regarding homosexuals and pre-service suitability were discussed. Mr. Fedor discouraged the pursuit of this particular line of analysis and redirected Mr. McDaniel to consult the collection of homosexual espionage anecdotes in support of DoD policy.

In his response, Mr. Eoyang wrote:

It is our contention that if the study had concluded that there was unequivocal scientific evidence that homosexuals were demonstrably unsuitable and unreliable, then by logical inference such individuals would per force be inappropriate candidates for critical and sensitive positions requiring security clearances. Indeed, had the study results turned out affirmatively, it is likely that these efforts would have been quite instrumental in defending and strengthening current policy. Although the Sarbin/Karols draft did not corroborate this particular conclusion, this was not known until the completion of the study. The nature of research is such that the answers to the focal question are not known in advance. The underlying purpose for asking the question should not be invalidated because the results turn out to be problematic from a policy perspective.

Eoyang's memo was followed by one from Craig Alderman, Jr., to Mr. Peter Nelson, with a copy going to Mr. Eoyang, dated February 10, 1989:

This entire effort, at least to date, is unfortunate. It has expended considerable government resources, and has not assisted us one whit in our personnel security program ... It is as if *Consumers' Reports* [sic] commissioned research on the handling characteristics of the Suzuki Sammurai [sic], and received instead a report arguing that informal import quotas for Japanese automobiles were not justified.

Pentagon officials demanded a second report with no mention of the suitability of homosexuals to serve. The second report was already under way. M.A. McDaniel's "Preservice Adjustment of Homosexual and Heterosexual Military Accessions: Implications for Security Clearance Suitability" was not likely to meet the demand either, even though McDaniel apparently revised his initial report following the December 1987 meeting with Fedor and Nelson. The preface of the McDaniel report says it is "a revision of an earlier draft report entitled 'The Suitability of Homosexuals for Positions of Trust' (November, 1987)."

The following excerpt is from the McDaniel report's "Discussion" section:

While male homosexuals appeared to have better or equal preservice adjustment patterns than male heterosexuals, female homosexuals tended to have somewhat poorer preservice adjustment patterns than female heterosexuals. However, females as a whole tended to show higher levels of preservice adjustment than males, and female homosexuals tended to have higher levels of preservice adjustment than most heterosexual male accessions.

In other words, the rankings for preservice adjustment are: straight women, lesbians, gay men, and straight men, in that order. The "Conclusion" of the McDaniel report states:

the preponderance of the evidence presented indicates that homosexuals show preservice suitability-related adjustment that is as good or better than the average heterosexual. Thus,

[207]

these results appear to be in conflict with conceptions of homosexuals as unstable, maladjusted persons.

A private study of the issue has also been done. C.I. Williams and M.S. Weinberg's book, *Homosexuals and the Military* (Harper and Row, 1971), presents the results of their study of homosexual veterans. The authors concluded that sexual orientation and job performance are unrelated, and that "the vast majority of homosexuals in the Armed Forces remain undiscovered by military authorities, and complete their service with honor."

Even Magnus Hirschfeld's *Sexual History of the World War*, published in 1946, noted that gays (he called them "Urnings") were remarkably courageous on the battlefield — although he thought maybe a death wish explained why "many an Urning officer exposed himself to the thickest rain of bombs and the most deadly attacks."

The arguments against allowing gays in the military are not difficult to refute. In his speeches, Jim often provides rebuttals for a number of them. Beginning with reasons given in Directive 1332.14, the following is a list of arguments against allowing gays in the service, followed by refutations by Jim and, occasionally, others:

*The presence of gays "adversely affects the ability of the Military Service to maintain discipline, good order and morale ... [and] to ensure the integrity of rank and command."*

Jim: "They had the same kind of fears regarding blacks. In fact, several white Southerners did refuse to follow the orders of black officers after forced integration in 1948. Those soldiers were quickly court-martialed and booted out. But most white soldiers realized that even if they didn't like taking orders from blacks, they no longer had a choice in the matter. The same would apply to gays."

*The presence of gays adversely affects the ability of the Military Services "to foster mutual trust and confidence among servicemembers."*

Jim: "I think that refers to the cohesiveness of the unit — that morale will be reduced because the unit won't hold together with the same glue that heterosexual male bonding produces. I think that's wrong. A straight male and a gay male can have male bonding, and can rely on each other, and trust each other, and love each other in a nonsexual way. Once people find out you're gay and spend a lot of time around you, they soon realize it doesn't make any difference in the kind of friend you are, or what kind of fellow soldier you are, or what kind of person you are. Soon they forget about it. It's just not an issue after you spend time around them."

Second Lieutenant Daniel Berger, speaking as an individual, not as a representative of the Army, calls this argument "a questionable assumption. But even if that were true, the problem lies with the prejudices against homosexuals, not with homosexuals themselves."

*New Republic* had this to say: "Common sense and the example of ancient Greece suggest that male affection doesn't have to be platonic to impel heroic deeds. Nor do mutual trust and confidence appear to have been shaken in West Germany, Italy, Sweden, Norway, Denmark or the Netherlands, countries that allow gays to serve in their armies."

*The presence of gays hurts the military's ability "to facilitate assignment and worldwide deployment of servicemembers who frequently must live and work under close conditions affording minimal privacy."*

This is the argument that gay men should be kept out of the military because they would be sleeping beside and taking showers with heterosexual soldiers.

Jim: "There are gay people in those showers now, and no one is getting raped. No one's talking about ending rules for sexual harassment or fraternization. Homosexual activity should be held to the same standards as heterosexual activity in the military. If you've showered your whole life with males, as I have, it's no big deal. In high school I didn't get an erection in the shower or the locker room. I was in those showers at Fort Riley and I didn't attack anyone. Even if you looked at someone with a sexual interest, they don't know about it. They look at women all the time with a sexual interest. If it makes them uncomfortable knowing I'm gay and thinking I might be interested, all I can say is, 'Chances are you're not being looked at.'"

The PERSEREC reports had this to say on the matter: "Homosexuals are like heterosexuals in being selective in their choice of partners, in observing rules of privacy, in considering appropriateness of time and place, in connecting sexuality with the tender sentiments and so on."

*The presence of gays hurts the military's ability "to recruit and retain members of the Military Service; [and] to maintain the public acceptability of military service."*

Jim: "That's the idea that people aren't going to join the military because of gays. But 65 percent of the American public supports allowing gays to serve. If someone applies for a job in a factory, they're not going to turn down that job because homosexuals work in the factory. I don't think people would stay away from the armed services because homosexuals happen to work there. They had the same fears about admitting blacks, but those fears proved to be unfounded."

Lieutenant Berger had this to say: "As in every other sector of society, there always have been and always will be homosexuals in the military. Many gay and lesbian soldiers have served their nation with distinction and have been highly decorated. So the real question is whether the government will continue to force otherwise qualified service members to leave the military simply because their lifestyle does not conform with someone else's values. As an experienced Army officer, I state from personal knowledge that I can see no good reason to exclude people from service due to their sexual orientation and I can see many reasons for permitting homosexuals in the armed services."

It's ironic that the Pentagon cites public opinion, since all public opinion polls conducted since 1977 have shown that a majority of Americans believe gays should not be barred from the military. Indeed, it is a strange reversal of roles from the civil rights era, when the federal government was forcing integration on local communities such as Little Rock and universities such as the University of Alabama. Now, we have local communities and universities trying to end a different kind of segregation ordered by federal officials. It would be fun to see the University of Alabama ban ROTC or Little Rock's Central High School ban military recruiters from campus because of the

Pentagon's discriminatory policy — but so far the best response to come from either state has been the refusal of armed forces advertising by the University of Central Arkansas's student newspaper, whose editorial board said the military policy barring gays was "offensive."

*The presence of gays hurts the ability of the military "to prevent breaches of security."*

This, of course, is the blackmail argument — already refuted by the Pentagon's own studies, i.e., the Crittenden and PERSEREC reports, and by the facts. If the aforementioned congressional source is correct, only six of 130 spy cases involved gays, and only one of those six could have involved blackmail.

Jim: "Present policy makes it much more likely that the existing closeted gays in the military will become security risks. Gays will always be in the military whether it's legal or not. If it's illegal and your career can be ruined when someone finds out, then you're a likely target for blackmail. But if you're out of the closet, it's hard to be blackmailed for being gay."

The blackmail argument has been abandoned by Secretary of Defense Cheney, who told Representative Barney Frank in House hearings during the summer of 1991 that the idea of homosexuals posing security risks was "a bit of an old chestnut." Cheney noted that he had inherited the current policy banning gays.

*The ban on allowing gays in the service keeps those gays who are present in the closet and in line, whereas if you didn't have the policy, openly gay soldiers would likely make advances toward other soldiers.*

This argument is usually not stated outright. But it seems to be on a lot of officials' minds. The charge is sometimes heard that officers would coerce those under their command to perform sexual favors. This is ridiculous, since regulations forbidding sexual harassment and fraternization would remain in effect.

Jim: "If present policy changed tomorrow, you wouldn't see any huge difference in the military. You're not going to see a rush of gay people to join. And you're not going to see a rush of gay soldiers coming out of the closet. Homophobia in general and the fear of being ostracized by your fellow soldiers does a hell of a lot more to keep you in the closet. The only thing that would change is that gay men and lesbians would be able to go to work every day without worrying about someone finding out this big secret."

An additional keep-the-ban argument was promoted by former Representative William Dannemeyer, a Republican from California who seemed to have an obsession with gay-bashing while in Congress. In an article for the Scripps Howard News Service, Dannemeyer wrote:

> But if you need a rational basis to discriminate, there is one. Male homosexuals are generally one of the unhealthiest group of people on record [sic]. Long before AIDS, homosexuals routinely suffered from a multitude of venereal diseases with names like gay-bowel syndrome, genital warts and chancroid. Communicable diseases are bound to be present in a community where a long-term relationship is counted as having shared first names.

At least, the Pentagon is not as homophobic as Dannemeyer.

Sometimes it's possible to score points for one's side by arguing tongue-in-cheek for the opposition. In a February 29, 1988, *Navy Times* article, Michelle McCormick wrote: "Homosexuals are likely to bother people who don't want to be bothered. The bothering that goes on now is between men and women. It is the right and natural way of things that men should bother women who would rather be left alone. But men are not accustomed to being bothered; and they shouldn't have to put up with it."

Jim says with current policy the biggest losers are not gays, but "the armed forces and the taxpayers of the United States. The armed forces is denying itself the services of quality men and women who want to serve and who would do a fine job. It's costing the taxpayers a great deal of money. My training, not including my scholarship, cost $40,000. Multiply that by the fourteen hundred men and women who are discharged for being gay each year, and you're talking about a huge amount of cash."

The amount of money wasted on tossing gays out of the armed services is indeed staggering. The General Accounting

Office, an arm of Congress, reported in June 1992 that the Pentagon spent $27 million in 1990 alone to dismiss and replace gay service members. The report says the ban on gays is "unfair and counter-productive; has no validity according to current scientific research and opinions; and appears to be based on the same type of prejudicial suppositions that were used to discriminate against blacks and women before these policies were changed."

According to Allan Bérubé's *Coming Out Under Fire: The History of Gay Men and Women in World War Two*, "the total number of men and women discharged from the military as homosexuals since 1941 approaches a hundred thousand, averaging fifteen hundred to two thousand a year."

The Navy alone employs 1,200 agents in its Naval Investigation Services (NIS) to find homosexuals in the ranks. In a 1988 interrogation, NIS agents extracted the names of seventy alleged lesbians at the Parris Island, South Carolina, boot camp. Fourteen were discharged. Three who refused to name others were sentenced to one year in prison on charges of sodomy and indecent acts. Captain Judy Mead was prosecuted even though she was not charged with being a lesbian. She was merely charged with once sleeping "in the same bed" with a lesbian and on another occasion being "in the presence" of suspected lesbians. When Mead protested that she did not know her friends were gay, an officer told her she should have suspected something because her friends played softball and "looked homosexual." Mead challenged her less-than-honorable discharge. After going through $16,000 in legal fees, she was reinstated but was refused a routine promotion despite an excellent service record.

Then there's the case of former Marine Sergeant Christine Hilinski. She lost her assignment as a drill instructor after testifying that a fellow Marine accused of being a lesbian "did a fine job."

If the charges against Mead seem to make little sense, consider what the Navy did to two enlisted men, James C. Horvath and David M. Huggins, accused of "falsely" claiming to be gay. In its list of charges the Navy first said Horvath "falsely" denied he had sex with Huggins. Then it said — in the same document

— that Horvath acknowledged having sex with Huggins. The Navy called the second statement "totally false." Obviously, both statements cannot be false. These men had outstanding service evaluations and were later granted honorable discharges. Before the charges against them were dismissed, however, their house was pelted with eggs and rolled in toilet paper. The Navy decided not to pursue charges less than a week after the men hired activist Frank Kameny to represent them. Kameny claimed DoD policy, as written, required the military to discharge a gay service member "any time that it might suit him."

The Navy is hardly the only service branch to have pursued gays with a vengeance. Major Hope Gentle, under investigation for homosexuality at Fort Sheridan, Illinois, said Army investigators interviewed Federal Aviation Administration officials and employees of two airlines, a limousine service, and a hotel trying to find out if she was the lesbian interviewed behind a curtain on a TV talk show. Kate Dyer, the former legislative assistant to Congressman Gerry Studds, told ABC's "20/20" that Army officials in Ohio, suspecting the lesbian behind the curtain may have been stationed at their base, flew Army personnel to New York to interview cabdrivers at Kennedy and Laguardia airports. The lesbian behind the curtain, incidentally, was not Major Gentle, and was not stationed in Ohio.

"Shouldn't these people be out trying to find out who's stealing repair parts?" Gentle asked.

The Air Force often goes off on its own witch- and warlock-hunts. A 1989–90 investigation at Carswell Air Force Base in Fort Worth, Texas, resulted in the dismissal of thirteen airmen. All of them had signed discharge papers — under duress and without legal counsel, according to several gay activists — stating that they were gay. The airmen were reportedly harassed and threatened with dishonorable discharges if they did not name other gays. The *New Republic* interviewed one of the men, who said he had been grilled for six hours in a broom closet with a two-way mirror. As his career in the military came to a close, he provided five names.

For a *New York Times* article titled, "For Gay Soldiers, Furtive Lives of Despair" (April 10, 1990), Jane Gross interviewed "more than three dozen homosexuals with experience in the military." She quoted a 31-year-old naval officer, who said life in the military "is not a life you'd choose for your worst enemy." Gross reported that the vast majority of gays and lesbians were not defiant, but cowed. They had entered the military not realizing they were gay. One had attempted suicide while she was being investigated for homosexuality. Another said she "ended up letting guys violate me, use me, to protect my secret." Some had entered into contract marriages, exchanging protection of their secret for the financial benefits afforded military spouses. This did not always work: one had been turned in by his contract wife during divorce proceedings.

Most of these men and women had been interrogated at some point, and their descriptions of the interrogations were remarkably similar. They also sounded like interrogations in countries such as Turkey and Paraguay: bright lights in the eyes, handcuffs, warnings that their parents and/or hometown newspapers would be told they were gay if they didn't confess and/or name others.

Those with children were threatened with loss of custody. Some reported physical abuse. Gross said, "The youngest and meekest seem to fare the worst." She quoted a gay Army major as saying he wondered why the public allowed such things to go on. He was particularly sympathetic concerning enlisted gay men and lesbians who had joined the service to escape poverty and/or hostile family situations. "We treated Noriega better than we treat these kids," he said. "Why aren't parents calling their Congressmen?"

Rick Eli, a former E4 stationed in Germany, says he "went up in the rank pretty fast. All you had to do was play by the rules, and I did that. I was one of the model soldiers. I had a security clearance, with the codes to all the buildings." All of that changed when his roommate turned him in. Rick, twenty-one, was pressured to expose other gays at his base. "They told me, 'We know who they are already. You might as well help us out,'" Rick reports. Although he knew of several, including a supervisor and two officers, he refused to give any information other than his rank. He was then threatened with a prison term in Leavenworth if he did not sign papers relinquishing his right to sue the government. After he signed the papers, the officials "said something about my right to have legal council to defend myself."

Rick's disposition form reads, in part:

Specialist Four Eli's Commander has recommended an Honorable Discharge ... A review of the record indicates that a discharge under Honorable Conditions would be appropriate. The Chain of Command recommends an Honorable Discharge. OPINION: The case file supports an award for an Honorable Discharge. RECOMMENDATION: That the Commander, BC-Z [Bad Cannstatt-Zuffenhausen Military Subcommunity] sign the endorsement at TAB A discharging Specialist Four Eli with an Honorable Discharge.

However, without explanation, Rick was given a *general* discharge.

"The thing I'll never forget," Rick says, "was being back in North Carolina and them giving me a bus ticket home. I was going to Texas, but they only gave me a ticket to my hometown in Indiana; I had to pay the difference. Everybody else was getting on a plane, and I had this bus ticket. I'd never ridden a bus before."

Most armed services members know that the flouting of sexual taboos by service people is rampant and routine. Rick says the gay bars in Stuttgart were full of military men, which is how he found out that two of his officers were gay.

A former naval enlistee reports that his first child was conceived in the barracks, with a female enlistee. The guard on duty sometimes saw his girlfriend's clothes on the floor and knew she was in bed with him, but never said anything. The Navy man also tells of parties for sailors only, given by a wealthy homosexual man who lived near his base. This former sailor has engaged in sex with men — mostly the same man — on hundreds of occasions, some while he was enlisted. He estimates that about 60 percent of the radiomen where he was stationed were gay, and said women soldiers at the base were often propositioned.

A former soldier stationed in Germany tells of a friend claiming to have had sex with a local prostitute whom everyone knew was a transvestite — although this friend insisted she was a woman. His fellow soldiers and his commanders laughed at him, but his officers took no action. Apparently it's okay to say you've had sex with a male prostitute if you thought it was a woman. The soldier telling this story says the only homosexual experience he had in his life was with another soldier in Germany.

A career Army officer says he has continued a homosexual relationship with his civilian best friend from high school through fifteen years of service.

While Jim was attending ROTC Advanced Camp at Fort Riley, two of the other cadets — one male, one female — had an affair. "She sneaked over to his barracks after hours and they had sex in the shower. They did that all summer."

Public awareness of gays in the military probably began in 1975 when *Time* magazine featured Leonard Matlovich on its cover. At the time, Matlovich, a Vietnam veteran previously awarded a Bronze Star and Purple Heart, was fighting an Air Force dishonorable discharge for his homosexuality. He was also being thrown out of the Mormon Church for the same reason. A judge ruled in Matlovich's favor, ordering the Air Force to reinstate and promote him. The Air Force instead practically begged Matlovich to accept a $160,000 tax-free settlement, along with an honorable discharge. He did. The court decision, however, applied only to Matlovich's case. It was not a precedent-setting case to overturn military policy.

Nor was the victory by Perry Watkins. Watkins had told the military he was gay — and had been since he was thirteen — when he was drafted in 1967. Harassed and labeled "queer" by his fellow soldiers, Watkins three times requested a discharge, and was three times refused. He even told superior officers he had engaged in sex with two servicemen, but nothing happened.

Watkins finally decided he liked the Army and re-enlisted three times, compiling an outstanding service record. During the Vietnam War, he was even asked to perform in drag. Three times he was given a security clearance and told that as an admitted homosexual he was not a risk. However, the fourth time Watkins tried to re-enlist, in 1981, the Army said no, citing his homosexuality. Watkins took the case to court and eventually won in the U.S. Ninth Circuit Court of Appeals. The Reagan administration did not like the ruling and asked the full court to reconsider. It did, and again ruled in Watkins's favor. On November 5, 1990, the Supreme Court also ruled in Watkins's favor, letting the lower court ruling stand. Watkins eventually accepted a settlement of $135,000 in back pay and full retirement benefits.

"It's funny and sad," says Jim, of Watkins's case. "I think it's great that he won. I have tremendous admiration for all of these people who were fighting for this issue."

Others did not win. Navy Petty Officer Dennis Beller lost his case before the Ninth Circuit Court of Appeals in 1980. Judge Anthony Kennedy, later appointed to the Supreme Court, wrote the opinion stating that the Navy has a right to discharge personnel for homosexual conduct.

Miriam Ben-Shalom joined the Army Reserves in 1974. She was discharged in 1976 for being openly lesbian. The first judge to hear her case ruled in her favor. But the Army, claiming her contract had expired in the meantime, said it had no responsibility to enlist her. Ben-Shalom's lawyer, who had been working *pro bono*, quit the case, and nothing happened until 1983 when she hired a new lawyer and filed a motion of contempt against the Army.

The same judge who heard the initial case this time ordered the Army to give her back pay — nothing more. Ben-Shalom appealed and won. The Seventh Circuit Court of Appeals ruled that she must be reinstated effective September 1, 1987. Alas, the Army again refused to enlist her because she was gay, claiming the court order gave her the right to say she was gay, but not to be gay.

In September 1988, the Army was found to be in contempt and was ordered to re-enlist her without delay while a final determination was made. This time they had no choice but to comply. Ben-Shalom served out her enlistment and was promoted to staff sergeant after receiving a high recommendation from her unit commander. Nevertheless, the Seventh Circuit Court eventually ruled in the Army's favor. The Supreme Court rejected Ben-Shalom's appeal February 26, 1990, the same day it rejected the appeal of Navy Ensign James M. Woodward.

Woodward had been allowed to enlist in 1972 even though he admitted he had homosexual tendencies. In 1974 he was seen sitting with a sailor who was facing discharge for homosexuality. When Woodward's commanding officer questioned him, he acknowledged his homosexuality but asked that he be allowed to continue to serve "as an honest, open, gay officer." Fearing one or more of those adjectives, the Navy released him from active duty.

Captain Greg Greeley found out how effective the support of a member of Congress and of gay veterans can be. Greeley was an Air Force communications and computer specialist at the Pentagon. In June 1991, he carried the lead banner in Washington's gay pride parade a day before he was to be discharged. The military held up his discharge and questioned him the next day, but went ahead with his honorable discharge the day after. In the meantime Ben-Shalom had activated gay veterans in Greeley's behalf, and Congressman Joseph P. Kennedy II of Massachusetts, in a House of Representatives floor speech, had accused the Pentagon of using "Stone Age thinking" in the case.

A notable sidelight to the situation with Greeley occurred when Pentagon spokesman Jim Turner, questioned by reporters, admitted that there is "no empirical data" to suggest that gays present a greater risk to national security than heterosexuals.

When Greeley phoned Ben-Shalom to discuss his situation, she activated all East Coast chapters of the Gay, Lesbian and Bisexual Veterans of America (GLBVA). She credits the quick and effective response of chapters in Baltimore and Hampton Roads for helping Greeley win a quick honorable discharge.

In 1991, Ben-Shalom traveled the country establishing more chapters, aiming to open chapters in all fifty states by the end of the year. By late 1992, the GLBVA had established thirty-five chapters representing more than eight thousand veterans. In San Diego, the gay vets group operates a 24-hour Military Freedom Line and provides counseling to an average of thirty-five gay and lesbian service members each month. It also enters floats in local parades.

Ben-Shalom fought the military at her own expense. "When I came out and challenged them, there was but me. The national organizations were not interested in this issue at that point. I think it's great that they are now. My battle cost me $31,000. I'll be paying that off for a while." Miriam later filed a second lawsuit against the Wisconsin National Guard claiming it had violated the state's antidiscrimination law. It is illegal to discriminate on the basis of sexual orientation in Wisconsin, Massachusetts, Hawaii, Vermont, New Jersey, and Connecticut. The court ruled that the national policy superseded state law.

One of the most bizarre cases so far involves Michael Dull, who entered the Army National Guard in 1986, not considering himself gay. In 1988 he realized he was. Michael says he became violently ill from suppressing his sexuality. It's not an uncommon phenomenon. Former MIT ROTC student Robert Bettiker reported the same thing, as did a former ROTC cadet at the University of Oklahoma.

Dull told his commanding officers he was gay in October 1989, and immediately felt better. His commanders asked him under oath if his homosexuality would continue or was based on "immaturity, intoxication, or a desire to avoid military service." Dull assured them it would continue and had nothing to do with the items on their list. Had he been able to get away with it, Michael might have asked them if their *question* was based on immaturity, intoxication, or sheer stupidity. It was certainly irrelevant, since the "exceptions" made for immaturity and intoxication refer only to an isolated homosexual act, not to one's orientation.

Michael waited a year and a half. Nothing happened. Finally, in February 1991, he was summoned for psychological testing by National Guard doctors. Later the same month he was mysteriously told to report for duty.

According to the *Advocate*, Bill Marsicano, public affairs representative for the 40th Infantry Division, said, "The only explanation I can give is that the doctors believe Dull was fit to serve. It sounds like he's a good soldier."

Dull is tall, blond, strikingly handsome. A lot of the present crop of openly gay soldiers and cadets — Dull, Holobaugh, Bettiker, Greeley, Joseph Steffan, Peter Laska, Robert Schwitz,

Tracey Thorne — share certain features. They're not all tall or blond, but they are all attractive, thoughtful, articulate, and they all have a strong sense of conviction. They seem to embody determination. They're all adamant about not "taking it" anymore — at least not without a fight. Ironically, these personal qualities are exactly what would have made them exemplary officers. Instead, these qualities are being well employed in their battles with Goliath.

Joseph Steffan was born in Warren, Minnesota. He was president of his senior class and student council, captain of the wrestling team, and voted "most likely to succeed." He was admitted to the Naval Academy in a year when its acceptance rate was lower than Harvard's. He became one of the top ten students in his class, a battalion commander in charge of eight hundred midshipmen, and twice sang "The Star-Spangled Banner" on national television at the start of Army-Navy games. He was also accepted into the highly competitive Nuclear Power Program. Then, the NIS began to investigate Steffan based on a rumor he was gay. Joe had told two friends, one of whom obviously hadn't kept the secret. When asked if he was willing to "admit" that he was a homosexual, Joe replied, "Yes, sir." Says Steffan: "The Naval Academy's Honor Code is clear: A midshipman does not lie, cheat, or steal. But he was challenging far more than my honor, he was challenging my identity." Joe says that while he has kept his honor, "in many ways, I think the honor of those people involved in my discharge was diminished."

In a beautifully composed piece appearing in the *Village Voice*, March 13, 1990, Francis Wilkinson wrote: "According to Defense Department regulations Joe should have been either a brilliantly successful midshipman or a homosexual. The fact that he was both left the military mindset with an impenetrable conundrum." Wilkinson goes on to express doubts that the Navy will easily give up: "It is its own Mississippi, holding steadfast, vowing before God and man that integration is blasphemy."

Steffan was dismissed six weeks before graduation. He filed suit, asking that his diploma from Annapolis be granted him, that the military's ban on gays be declared unconstitutional and that he be reinstated in the Navy.

At the first hearing on the suit, Judge Oliver Gath of the U.S. District Court for the District of Columbia ordered Steffan to answer questions on any homosexual acts he may have committed. When Steffan refused, his failure to comply led Judge Gash to dismiss the suit. A U.S. appeals court, however, ruled that questions of conduct would have been relevant only if acts had led to Steffan's dismissal, which they had not. Steffan had been ousted just for being gay.

The suit was reinstated and sent back to district court. This time Judge Gash was simply outrageous. Three times during the hearing he referred to Steffan as a "homo." He again ruled against Steffan, this time saying the military's ban on homosexuals was justified by the threat of AIDS. The decision raised eyebrows since the AIDS argument had never been raised by the Pentagon (and rightly so, since all military personnel are tested for HIV).

With Judge Gash presiding in Washington, it is no wonder that the Navy later withdrew a suit it had filed in another district court and refiled it in Washington. That suit concerned sailor Keith Meinhold, who had announced he was gay on ABC news and been subsequently discharged. Meinhold sued to be reinstated and District Judge Terry J. Hatter, Jr., in Los Angeles ordered that he be temporarily reinstated pending trial. The Navy at first refused, then backed down.

Tracey Thorne's case is unique in that he was not dismissed from the military after appearing on ABC's "Nightline" and acknowledging he was gay. Thorne, a skilled fighter pilot, was instead reassigned to a desk job. In his TV appearances Thorne has been one of the most forcefully articulate gay soldiers, winning respect for his breadth of knowledge on the subject and for his courageous matter-of-fact honesty.

Joe Steffan's attorneys came up with an interesting internal memo when they subpoenaed documents from the Justice Department, which tried to suppress the memo as "privileged information." Drafted by an Army personnel action officer, the memo proposes changing current policy to read: "The Army shall not discriminate in recruitment, promotion or retention practices against persons of homosexual orientation" provided they "exercise appropriate restraint and discretion with regard to their sexual behavior." The memo further suggests that commanders be forced to prove that homosexual conduct in their units is harmful to discipline and good order — and not merely make moral judgments about homosexuality. The memo also points out that no current research supports the idea that gays are a greater security risk than heterosexuals. Nevertheless, Army spokeswoman Captain Barbara Goodno was quoted in the June 28, 1991, edition of *Stars and Stripes* as saying, "There is no intent, no plan to change our current policy." She noted that courts have generally upheld the military's ban on gays.

There have been other cases of gays and lesbians challenging their discharges or, in the case of ROTC cadets, "disenrollments." And then there was the case of the gun turret exploding aboard the USS *Iowa* in 1989. The NIS tried to blame the explosion on a sexual relationship between Clayton Hartwig, killed in the explosion, and Kendall Truitt, the beneficiary of Hartwig's life insurance policy. The NIS had no justification for such a charge, and a congressional investigation later discovered that the explosion was probably caused by destabilized gunpowder, the result of improper storage. Jim thinks the Navy tried to kill two birds with one stone:

"One, they tried to take the blame off themselves for those people dying. Two, they tried to make their policy against homosexuals look legitimate — 'See what happens when you have homosexual lovers in an organization?' It sucks. It's hard for me to feel anything but disgust. And that's on top of all the other disgust I have for what they've done to gays. I know someone on the *Iowa* who has had sex with a zillion different people on the *Iowa*, and he thinks the Navy's position was totally false."

Little Rock's *Spectrum* called the Navy's actions "nothing less than bureaucratic gay bashing."

The Navy officially apologized to Hartwig's family October 18, 1991, admitting that the explosion might have been an accident after all.

Lesbian servicewomen have gotten a particularly bad deal. Vice Admiral Joseph S. Donnell, former commander of the Navy's Atlantic Fleet, sent a memo to officers of almost two hundred ships and forty bases on July 24, 1990, instructing them to make more of an effort to find lesbians in their midst and discharge them. How does one hunt for lesbians? What does one look for? "The stereotypical female homosexual is hard-working, career-oriented, willing to put in long hours on the job, and among the command's top professionals," Donnell wrote.

Clearly, such dangerous characters have no business in the military. If you're a female in the Navy, the best way not to be suspected of being a lesbian, obviously, is to be lazy and unprofessional, with no ambition. And you must not play softball. Are these the people Uncle Sam wants defending this country? Sloppy layabouts who don't know how to field a pop fly? Apparently.

Although studies seem to indicate that lesbians outperform most other service personnel, they are discharged at a rate almost four times that of gay men (eight times in the Marines).

"It's a double whammy," said one servicewoman stationed in San Diego. "They don't like women in the military, and targeting lesbians is an easy way for them to get rid of quite a few."

Nor have lesbians received as much moral support as their gay male counterparts. A part of the national lesbian community views the military as a patriarchal system that lesbians should avoid in the first place. According to Ben-Shalom, at the 1991 National Lesbian Conference in Atlanta a lesbian veteran was physically assaulted.

"Frankly, you don't have to approve of the military to support us," says Ben-Shalom. "But you should realize it's a matter of freedom and choice. I think the lesbian community should get its head out of its collective ass, wake up, look around, and realize what this fight is all about. While we're trying to make a difference in this country, they're playing word games. The lesbian community has been mean, vile, and vicious to veterans, and I've got no patience for it."

During the Iraq conflict, Ben-Shalom sent a letter to President Bush. She offered the services of a unit of 230 gay, lesbian, and bisexual veterans with honorable discharges, "all of whom have military training which can be utilized in support or combat services for Operation Desert Storm, all of whom could

[224]

be re-enlisted easily enough, if only their country will have them!" The list of volunteers grew to more than a thousand after Ben-Shalom's letter was printed in newspapers across the country.

As Operation Desert Storm got under way, reports started surfacing of gay and lesbian military personnel coming out to their commanding officers and saying they wanted to fight as openly gay soldiers. Many were told they could fight but might face discharges when the war was over. The *Wall Street Journal* reported on January 24, 1991, that at least fourteen gay and lesbian reservists "were cleared by their unit commanders to serve in the Persian Gulf after stating their sexual orientation." The article reported that reservist Donna Lynn Jackson and at least thirteen others had been told that the military's "stop-loss" policy meant that discharges for homosexuality were not being processed during the Gulf crisis. Jackson was subsequently discharged, but at least half the others were sent to fight. The *San Francisco Chronicle* quoted Pentagon spokesman Ken Satterfield as saying, "Just because a person says they're gay, that doesn't mean they can stop packing their bags."

Some have questioned the soldiers' motivations for coming out just as they were about to be sent to combat. While it's probably true that some were trying to avoid being sent to the Gulf, it's also likely that many, if not most, meant exactly what they were saying — that they wished to serve as openly gay soldiers. Coming face-to-face with a possible early death calls for a certain honesty. If you get killed in action, you don't want to be remembered as just another dead vet. You also want to be remembered, as Leonard Matlovich said, for your "sense of self-worth" as a gay person.

Many gay activists were outraged at the military's double standard. Mary Newcombe of Lambda Legal Defense and Education Fund said, however, "I'm ecstatic. This shows that the military knows that gay and lesbian soldiers are extremely well qualified to serve in the armed forces." Some reservists reportedly received no response at all to their coming-out letters to commanders.

Columnist Clarence Page wrote in February 1991:

"With the nation at war, the Pentagon's hostility toward homosexuals has escalated into practices that, in effect, border on exploitation ... openly homosexual military men and women are being put on hold long enough for them to serve in the Persian Gulf, even though they still face possible discharge after they return home. If so, it revives an age-old question in a new way: Why does the military bother to ban homosexuals at all? ... Prejudice is what this controversy is about, at bottom."

And there can be other reasons for not being booted. Jim recalls meeting a Navy physician in San Francisco who had come out to his commander.

"His commander basically said, 'I don't care.' He came out to a couple of different people, and they were the same: 'We don't care. You're a physician. We need you.' Because he's a physician and they need physicians, they're willing to overlook it. It just shows their hypocrisy."

The Gulf conflict produced some other interesting stories:

The San Francisco Board of Supervisors passed a resolution in March 1991 instructing the city attorney to file friend-of-the-court briefs on behalf of any local gay or lesbian soldiers who served in the Gulf and then were forcibly discharged.

Sergeant Sam Gallegos of the Colorado National Guard was given a general discharge — less than honorable — en route to the Gulf — but nevertheless received a National Defense medal and ribbon for his service during the war. Gallegos told two members of his unit that he is gay and was subsequently confronted by his commanding officer. Gallegos says he never had sex with anyone in the military, but he knows four other gays who fought in the Gulf conflict.

*Publishers Weekly* reported May 17, 1991, that Randy Shilts, author of *And the Band Played On*, had uncovered a gay newsletter circulating among gay troops in Saudi Arabia. The newsletter was prepared in Saudi Arabia using code words and gay slang, mailed to the States for production, then distributed to a network of friends in the Gulf.

*Our Own Community Press* of Hampton Roads, Virginia, interviewed five returning Operation Desert Storm veterans — an officer in the Army National Guard and four sailors. Asked

[226]

if they knew other gays who served in the Gulf, two — including the officer — said they knew of at least thirty. One said, "No, because I was in a new squadron. I was all alone and had no one to express myself to. You can't trust anybody."

A demonstration against the military's policy at Norfolk Naval Base was attended by two marines on active duty.

One Sunday during the Gulf crisis, Reverend Donna Eubanks, minister of San Diego's Metropolitan Community Church (a national nondenominational church for gays and lesbians) asked those attending church how many had a loved one in the Gulf. Virtually everyone raised a hand. The church then formed a support group, giving parishioners the same opportunity for stress relief available to most military spouses. One of the parishioners said he and his lover had exchanged 155 letters. They numbered each letter so they would know if all were received or if any were intercepted by naval authorities.

Then there was the Indiana woman who wrote to her home-state gay and lesbian organization, Justice, Inc.: "Please remove my name from your mailing list — at least for a while. I just received my orders to go into active duty, and I must maintain confidentiality. *You know how they treat us in the military.*"

The National Gay and Lesbian Task Force reported that by May 9, 1991, at least five Persian Gulf veterans had been forcibly discharged for being gay. All five had served honorably during the conflict. Ben-Shalom heard that the military had nine hundred discharges of gays and lesbians waiting to be processed.

"Given the amount of phone calls we've taken at GLBVA and the amount Lambda and some of the other organizations have taken, I can say for certain that there are at least three hundred discharges pending," she said.

Meanwhile, General Norman Schwarzkopf, commander of the Desert Storm operation, repeated his opposition to gays serving in the military. He told Barbara Walters on ABC's "20/20" that he was once "the army's expert witness on the subject of gays in the military" and that he believed having openly gay soldiers serve would "break down the cohesion" of military units.

[227]

When the Gay and Lesbian Military Freedom Project — a civil liberties coalition led by the ACLU — sought to honor gay and lesbian Gulf vets by placing advertisements praising them in the *Army Times, Navy Times,* and *Air Force Times,* the ads were refused. The ACLU's Bill Rubenstein said, "We were told they would not run an ad that suggested there were gay people in the military." An advertising representative for the publisher told Rubenstein's assistant that "there aren't any gays in the military." This came three weeks after Secretary of Defense Richard Cheney acknowledged in an interview with *USA Today,* "No question in my mind, we've got a large number of gays in military service."

Obviously, it is in times of war, and in the aftermath of war, that the hypocrisy of military policy is most evident. On June 10, 1991, the city of New York gave the largest ticker-tape parade in history to the returning Persian Gulf troops. On the weekend leading up to the event, sailors — in uniform, as required by shore leave regulations — were all over Greenwich Village, on the streets and in the gay bars. Some looked uncomfortable, as if they had made a wrong turn and found themselves on Neptune. Others looked at home. Two weeks later, during New York's gay and lesbian pride week, the Empire State Building was illuminated with lavender floodlights. The building's management issued a statement saying, "We are in total agreement with ... leaders who seek to end the bigotry and discrimination directed against gay and lesbian New Yorkers."

When the hot debate over gays and the ROTC erupted on college campuses, it surprised a lot of people. Congressman Studds, quoted in a *New York Times* article, May 6, 1990, which ran with a photo of Jim, said: "I am as astonished as I am delighted by what appears to be happening. A ground swell of outrage like this is not something I expected to see in my lifetime. There is no question which way the tide is running. We just don't know when high tide will be."

On May 14, 1990, a letter was sent to Secretary Cheney by the presidents of the American Council on Education, the Association of American Universities, the American Association of State Colleges and Universities, and the National Association of State Universities and Land-Grant Colleges, representing most colleges and universities in the United States. The letter asserted that arguments against Pentagon policy were "compelling."

In October 1990, the Association of American Law Schools began requiring its 158 member schools to end assistance to all potential employers who do not comply with the association's policy banning discrimination against gays. Most of the 158 law schools seem to be ignoring the directive, however. On March 10, 1991, the National Association of Graduate-Professional Students condemned the Pentagon policy and joined the nationwide campaign to remove ROTC from campuses. Pentagon spokesman Major Douglas Hart, the one who thinks there aren't many gays in the military, admitted to the *New York Times* that if universities began booting ROTC, the Department of Defense could suffer.

By 1992 two colleges had withdrawn from ROTC over the gay issue — Pitzer College of California and Amherst College. Rutgers University had removed four-year ROTC scholarships in protest. Four others had voted to boot ROTC if the policy wasn't changed –– Cincinnati, MIT, Oswego (SUCO, New York), and Connecticut. Rhode Island should soon be joining them, as the faculty senate has voted to eliminate ROTC by 1998 and the university's president supports the measure.

In the case of the University of Cincinnati, the faculty senate voted unanimously to remove ROTC by January 1992 if the policy is not changed. The Pentagon threatened the school with the removal of $64 million in research grants, but the university's board of trustees did not yield to financial blackmail and upheld the faculty senate vote. Reacting to votes at Cincinnati and Northern Illinois, the state legislatures of Ohio and Illinois voted in the summer of 1991 to prohibit the removal of ROTC programs from public colleges and universities. Governor Jim Edgar vetoed the Illinois bill, but the state legislature overrode the veto.

The debate at Northern Illinois University was raucous. The university's faculty council voted February 24, 1990, to boot ROTC, and the University Council voted twenty-nine to sixteen March 7, 1990, to ask the board of regents to eject ROTC by 1992 if Pentagon policy didn't change. Two student protestors were arrested April 4, 1990, and seventeen protestors interrupted board of regents meeting several days later. Students in the Philosophy Forum, intent on exposing university hypocrisy, voted to bar gays and lesbians. Taking the bait, the university withdrew the Forum's official recognition. The Forum then said it would end its ban only when the university banned all organizations that discriminate against gays, including the ROTC. The campus chapter of Amnesty International followed the Forum's example but was ordered by the national body to rescind its antigay measure.

In other actions, Colby College, Harvard, and Yale decided not to reinstate ROTC and Wisconsin–River Falls decided not to establish ROTC. Student and/or faculty groups at the following schools voted to remove ROTC: the 34-university State University of New York System, Alfred (New York), the California State University System (the academic senate voted unanimously to urge all campuses to stop enrolling additional ROTC students and to terminate existing contracts or allow them to expire), Cal State–Northridge, UCLA, Indiana, John Jay College (CUNY), Minnesota, Northwestern, Pennsylvania (the university council's unanimous vote at Peter Laska's school is significant because at least one ROTC delegate was present for the vote), Syracuse, Wisconsin-Madison, Carnegie-Mellon, and Wisconsin-Milwaukee (where a vote by the faculty senate was overturned by a vote of the full faculty).

In a related development, on September 20, 1991, the New York State Division of Human Rights ordered the state university center at Buffalo to ban military recruiters from campus because of the antigay policy. New York governor Mario Cuomo then reversed the ruling of his own agency, calling it "unenforceable."

Additionally, ROTC policy was "condemned" by students and/or faculty at ten schools, including Dan Quayle's alma mater, DePauw. The SUNY-Buffalo Law School and the University of Iowa Law School refused ROTC the use of their buildings until the policy is changed. Officials from Minnesota, Rhode Island, and the University of Washington had met with their states' congressional delegations urging them to do what they could to get the policy changed. And the presidents or ther head officials of California-Berkeley, UCLA, Carnegie

[230]

Mellon, Dartmouth, Harvard, Jamestown Community College (New York), MIT, North Carolina, Washington University, and Princeton sent letters to Pentagon officials and/or President Bush urging that the policy be changed. Major Doug Hart — our favorite Pentagon spokesman — said Cheney, as usual, had no comment.

In addition, the University of Arkansas and forty-seven other schools participated in the ACLU's National Press Conference, May 1, 1990, condemning the policy and urging that it be changed.

On the other hand, the University of North Carolina exempted ROTC from its nondiscrimination policy. The faculty council not only rejected an English department request that ROTC be banned, it agreed to give ROTC representation on the council if the chancellor grants ROTC departmental status.

The president of Saint John's University in Collegeville, Minnesota, said ROTC policy is not illegal since it is sanctioned by the federal government, even though it conflicts with university policy. The regents of the University of Central Arkansas simply refused to consider whether ROTC policy conflicted with university policy, although — as noted — the staff of the student newspaper did what it could, refusing to accept ads from the armed forces.

The most homophobic reaction from a university official came from Tufts University President Jean Mayer, who told the student senate on October 14, 1990, that he supported ROTC policy because gays would ruin morale in the program. While he was on the subject, he said he would support banning women from the Army, as well.

Two Midwest schools, the University of Kansas and Drake University, recently let military recruiters back on campus after Marine Corps officials reminded the schools of a 1972 law denying colleges that bar recruiters from receiving military research grants or financial aid. In the case of Drake, only the law school had a recruiting ban. The ban at Kansas affected the College of Arts and Sciences, the School of Education, and the School of Fine Arts. Kansas officials said they disagreed with military policy, but didn't think they could change national policy by themselves.

One pro-ROTC argument goes like this: The schools consider-ing removing ROTC are among the nation's most progressive universities. Ending ROTC at these schools, therefore, would eliminate the opportunity for more progressive officers to be commissioned in the military. MIT's DDaMIT disagrees:

> Insofar as we are trying to effect national change, we would much rather try to put pressure on the DoD in this direct manner than to take the small chance that some open-minded MIT cadet will decide to make the military his career, progress through the ranks, retain his tolerant views in the midst of exposure to a very intolerant military, and in forty or fifty years become a general or an admiral in a position to effectuate change. This "trickle-up" theory of constructive engagement is most unrealistic.

Some land-grant universities argue that the Morrill Land Grant Act of 1862, which provided the land for these schools, requires the schools to offer "military instruction." It does not, however, say they must offer ROTC, which wasn't even estab-lished until the National Defense Act of 1916. In fact, some land-grant schools, such as the University of California at Santa Cruz, do not offer ROTC now. Cornell and a handful of other land-grant schools, nonetheless, have refused to add "sexual orientation" to their antidiscrimination policies because they feel they are bound to offer ROTC and can't have both ROTC and the clause. Other land-grant schools do have both.

And then there's House of Representatives Resolution 1651, introduced in April 1991 by Representative Gerald Solomon, a New York Republican. It would "deny funds to programs that do not allow the Secretary of Defense access to students on campuses or to certain student information for recruiting pur-poses." Tim Drake of the National Gay and Lesbian Task Force says, "As written, this legislation goes way beyond a mere interest in the mechanics of selective service. It could easily be used to punish colleges that boot ROTC units off campus."

Even if HR 1651 does not pass, the military's recent scaling down of operations could diminish the impact of the campus movement to oust ROTC. The military has phased out ROTC units at fifty campuses. General Colin Powell has complained that "young people are graduating, but we can't bring them on active duty because [the force] is getting smaller. I'm getting lots of letters from parents who are disturbed by that."

According to the *Wall Street Journal*, the Army recently forced out more than nine hundred active-duty colonels and lieutenants within a matter of months. The number of ROTC graduates assigned to active duty has dropped 25 percent in recent years, causing thousands of ROTC would-be officers to quit the program rather than accept part-time reserve assignments. Even as the need for ROTC cadets has fallen, the wasteful military bureaucracy keeps recruiting at full tilt. The advertising budget for the Pentagon remains enormous. And, while cadets are being pressured out of the program because no assignments await them, ROTC instructors are still evaluated on how many new cadets they enlist.

In late 1990 Jim received a call from Robert Schwitz, the ROTC cadet at Washington University who had been so outraged by Jim's case that he sent letters to President Bush and his congressional representatives. Schwitz had been given Jim's number by author Randy Shilts. Rob had called Shilts after Rob realized that he, too, was a gay in the military.

Like most of the other gay ROTC cadets who have come out, Schwitz is a good-looking young man. His bearing reflects his military training — upright, straightforward. Interviewed near his Washington University dormitory within weeks of his coming out in the Saint Louis press, Schwitz displays the determination typical of these young gay warriors. If the pressure is getting to him, it's visible only in an occasional popping of the jaw — teeth may be grinding. His brown-blond hair is, of course, cut short. He's wearing blue jeans and a t-shirt with the Washington University emblem, and a class ring.

Schwitz was a sophomore when Jim's case hit the press. Did he know then that he was gay?

"I guess I did. In November of '89 I briefly dated a girl. That just didn't work, and ended pretty quickly. Looking back, I can say that was me trying hard not to be gay. But even when I was going with her I signed up to take a class called 'The Sociology of Homosexuality' in the spring. So I was in that course when

Jim Holobaugh's story broke. I guess it was good because it gave me a chance to hear a lot of people's thoughts on being gay without me saying anything.

"I had just been to my first Growing American Youth meeting. That's a Saint Louis organization for gay youth. I was nervous and didn't know if I should be there or not. I went under the guise that it was for the class I was taking. When I walked in the door, the first person I saw was the guy who had sublet from me all summer. Afterwards, he asked me if I was there because I was gay or because I was in that class, and I said, 'Well, I don't know.' A couple of days later Jim's thing came out, so this was really starting to eat on me.

"When I went to field training, there were people talking about Jim. They said, 'Yeah, well if it was me, I'd turn him in.' Then they said, 'We know there's a homosexual in our camp, and we're going to give that person an opportunity to come forward.' I didn't know this was a tactic they often use to flush people out. They had no clue that there really was. Somebody said, 'We'll flush him out. We'll watch everybody's eyes in the shower and we'll know who it is.' That was before I made up my mind to go through with this. You can't really take it back once you tell the military. I remember thinking at the end of camp, 'I like the military. This is really nice and I want this, so if I do have those feelings I'm just gonna shelve them.

"I've had people ask me why they should care about gays' problems in the military when they don't even believe in the military. But the military is the country's largest employer, so if we're talking about employment opportunities for gays, this issue needs to be addressed."

Rob Schwitz's credentials are typical for a booted gay cadet. He was valedictorian of his Mount Vernon, Illinois, Township High School class, in the top 15 percent of his Washington University business school class, and made the dean's list. His ROTC evaluations said things such as, "doing an outstanding job," and "It is always a pleasure to have this type of talent in the corps."

Schwitz, only twenty at the time, sent a letter to his commanders March 4, 1991. It said, "I wish to advise you that I have recognized that I'm gay. I do, however, wish to continue in the

[234]

ROTC program, and upon completion of the program to be commissioned as a United States officer and to serve as an openly gay man in the United States Air Force."

"My attorney was Arlene Zarembka, who was suggested to me by Randy Shilts and by Mary Newcombe of Lambda in California," says Schwitz. "I talked to Arlene in late 1990 and we set a strategy. I first talked to Jim around this time, too. I told my parents the day after Christmas of 1990. I made a special trip to Mount Vernon to tell my grandparents. I gave them the background on Jim, and then just tagged my name on at the end. My granddad says, 'You mean you're a homosexual!?'

"I sent my letter March 4, and March 6 they wrote back saying they were 'disenrolling' me. They said I had twenty-four hours to answer their questions. Well, Arlene was out of town. I completely flipped out, so I called up Jim. He told me to relax and just call them up and say I couldn't do anything until my attorney returned. My story hit the papers April 4, the result of a Lambda news release. That was partially to expose the injustice. Also, the military is less likely to mess with people if their case is made public.

"I got calls starting at seven o'clock in the morning April 4. Some were really weird calls. Some were from gays searching for help and some were from crackpots. I only had one or two negative calls. I got letters, one from a gay marine. I get really sick of people calling me. Lots and lots of people called me for dates. I guess I should be flattered, but I got sick of it real quick. It wasn't all that flattering because they don't know anything about me except this picture and this article."

The Okaw Valley Council Boy Scouts read about Rob in his hometown newspaper and kicked him out, as well. They said he wasn't "morally straight," and that he must "sever any relations that you may have with the Boy Scouts of America" — including, presumably, sexual relations. When the Washington University campus newspaper reported that Rob had been booted from the Boy Scouts, an irate freshman wrote a letter to the editor wondering, "What will they do next, kick him out of the CD club and demand the return of all his CDs?"

"I thought using Jim's former attorney was only to my advantage," says Rob. "She already had knowledge that I

[235]

wouldn't have to be charged for. And she had been recommended by people all over the country. Jim said she was good, and I'm very pleased with her. She's been good to me, a big help. She let me do some things on my own — get regulations, research — to save me money. But if it drags on and this could make a good test case, Lambda may take my case."

Rob describes the time between Jim's coming out and his own decision to tell ROTC as "a year of complete paranoia":

"I was constantly looking over my shoulder. I had to watch what I said and be careful which pronoun I used. My roommates tell me now they wondered if I was gay. And the girl I went out with told her cousin that I had to be gay because I didn't kiss her. So, people knew before I did. I guess the easiest person to deceive is yourself."

Rob needed the ROTC scholarship to attend Washington University.

"My parents are not wealthy and do not have the means to send me here. My financial aid package without the scholarship didn't cut the mustard. So, the scholarship enabled me to be here. I was indifferent about ROTC the first couple of years, and then I started getting into it. Then I thought, now that I like it, I have to tell them I'm gay."

Rob says he owes a lot to Jim:

"I don't know how I could thank him enough. He tested the water and shined a light in front of me. He told me Washington University had offered to repay his ROTC scholarship. That was a relief, because outwardly the university didn't look sympathetic. But they've given me a tuition grant. It's a very special deal. I had to talk to I don't know how many people in the administration, all the way up to the chancellor of the university."

It is a scholarship-for-Robert-Schwitz-because-the-ROTC-kicked-him-out-for-being-gay. It's probably the first such scholarship ever given in this country. Rob says, "My understanding is they would have done it for Jim had he been here another year."

Rob says he talks to Jim often, as well as some of the other gay cadets:

"Recently, Robb Bettiker called. It's almost like a private club. It's really neat. Jim and I were joking and we said, 'Membership has its privileges and its costs.' It's a little bit of empathy, a little bit of one-upmanship — but it's comforting. Jim gave me a lot of good advice. He told me questions they might ask during my disenrollment hearings. Like, 'Why do you want to be an officer?' There are a lot of reasons, but I hadn't thought about that question. He took me through his hearing so I'd know what to expect. His was much different from mine. Mine was less intense. His had a transcriber; in mine they wouldn't even let *us* tape it. In our initial meeting, they kept asking these questions and Arlene would say, 'I advise him not to answer.' I felt really stupid paying her eighty dollars an hour to sit there and say, 'No, no, no, no, no.' But if it had been just me and the officers, I would have found it difficult not answering those questions. So, I think it was probably money well spent.

"I guess I'd do it over again. I think if Jim hadn't gone before me, I couldn't have done it. I would have felt like a piranha was eating at me. I really respect him. I always thought he had so much courage. Now that it's my turn, people tell me, 'You've got so much courage,' and I feel like saying, 'It wasn't courage. I was scared to death.' The way I saw it, I was cutting my losses. If you get commissioned and then something happens, it's really bad. I was slotted to be a missile launch officer with top-secret security clearance. I knew they'd hook me up to a lie detector, and I was absolutely panicked. I knew how bad it might be, but I felt that waiting longer would only compound the problem. When I talked to Jim, he kept saying, 'It'll be okay. You won't have to pay back the money.'"

"When I talked to Rob," says Jim, "I tried to impress on him that your worst fears are never realized. That's why I wish I'd kept a journal. It would be interesting to go back and read about all my fears and how I built them up in my mind and then they were never played out. I could use that today, with things I worry about now."

Along with Jim and Arlene, the people in the youth group helped Rob a lot — especially the leader, who owns Our World Too, the gay and lesbian bookstore in Saint Louis. Even Rob's commanders were sympathetic.

"I've talked to the officers. They've all been wonderful to me through this. It's odd. We'll sit down and talk about when and how we think this policy will change. I even had one of my captains tell me, 'If I had been in your position, I don't know if I could have done that. That really took guts.' I mean, they're almost commending me for it. But I understand that they're not going to throw away their career, so they'll do what they have to do according to regulations. I know Jim didn't get any support from his commanders. But he was in the Army ROTC, and I was in Air Force ROTC, which is different."

Rob says support from fellow cadets has been "tremendous":

"If every person who has expressed support for me wrote to the president and their congressional representatives, the policy would change next week."

Rob sent letters to his congressmen and to President Bush, just as he had on Jim's behalf. His letter to Bush ends: "I can only hope and pray that I am not discriminated against for the rest of my life because the Department of Defense says it's right."

"I don't wish this on anybody," says Rob. "But I hope somebody else does it next year. I know there's another gay person in my unit. I've sent word to him not to worry, that I'm not into outing, but if he wants to talk to call me up."

"I was excited when I talked to Rob, knowing it was going to happen again," Jim admits. "I wanted more than anything for him to come out. I think it's great. One person may be a fluke, but now that a second has come along, they have to deal with it. I think Washington University has treated Rob so well that it's likely to happen again. For someone in ROTC, a big incentive to keep quiet is the thought, 'How am I going to finance my education?' Now that Wash. U.'s paying for Rob, I think it's likely others will come out. Everyone should, and I hope they all do."

Rob was told May 24, 1991, that the ROTC had "approved" his disenrollment. "As if I applied for it," he says. Meanwhile, Rob was elected president of the gay organization at Washington University.

When forty members of Congress sent a letter to President Bush March 15, 1991, during Operation Desert Storm, asking him to issue an executive order lifting the military's ban, the response was a virtual rebuff. The congressional letter, from the office of Congressman Studds and signed by Patricia Schroeder, Craig Washington, Barney Frank, and thirty-six others, noted that thousands of gay men and women took part in Operation Desert Storm. It read, in part:

> We support all our military personnel in the Gulf — including some fifty thousand gay and lesbian soldiers who have served and are continuing to serve so valiantly ... We submit that discrimination on the basis of sexual orientation is as wrong as discrimination on the basis of race ... Mr. President, you have praised our service personnel and encouraged us to support each and every one of them fully and proudly. We urge you to afford our gay and lesbian troops [their] well-deserved respect and to end the military's shameful discrimination.

Studds and Frank might have added personal notes pointing out that as congressmen they can vote to declare a war, but as openly gay men they cannot fight in one.

President Bush did not respond to the letter, but on May 8, the Pentagon did. Captain T.D. Keating, Pentagon director of legal policy, restated all the old objections and said the Department of Defense had no plans to reassess its policy. Keating also said that discrimination against gays could not be equated with discrimination against blacks because "societal attitudes about homosexuals ... derive from conduct that defines the class, not from a neutral characteristic such as skin color." It is outrageous for Keating to say that homosexuality is defined by conduct when Pentagon policy bans gays on the basis of *being* gay, regardless of conduct.

Greg King of the Human Rights Campaign Fund said, "I think the [Keating] letter is an insult to the intelligence and intellect of members of Congress. Captain Keating suggests that conduct is what defines homosexuality. If that were truly the case, and if the Pentagon were excluding people solely for conduct, then they should give Joe Steffan his diploma today."

Congressman Studds released this statement: "The Pentagon is essentially saying that it has the obligation to mirror the worst of society's prejudices. That is ignorant and that is wrong."

Gay activists expressed shock that the Pentagon's response to members of Congress was just as arrogant and ignorant as the responses the activists had received over the years.

Legislation to rescind the ban was introduced in Congress by Representatives Ted Weiss of New York and Barbara Boxer of California. Said Weiss: "We have two choices before us: We can act with courage, as President Truman did forty-three years ago when he integrated the armed services, or we can act from fear and cowardice, continuing an injustice to a part of our population that has served our nation with distinction and honor."

Despite more than seventy co-sponsors, the bill never made it out of committee.

Ted Weiss died of heart failure on September 14, 1992. On November 3, Barbara Boxer was elected to the U.S. Senate.

Secretary of Defense Cheney, at least, seemed tired of defending the policy by the summer of 1991. First, Cheney criticized Air Force officials for their handling of Captain Greg Greeley's case after he marched in Washington's gay pride parade. A few weeks later Congressman Barney Frank asked Cheney how openly gay soldiers could be security risks. Cheney dismissed the idea that gays were security risks, calling the idea "a bit of an old chestnut."

The following week, on August 4, Cheney appeared on ABC's "This Week with David Brinkley," where he was ambushed by Sam Donaldson. The reporter produced a copy of the *Advocate* containing an article claiming that Pete Williams, one of Cheney's top aides, was gay.

"I take it, Mr. Secretary, that this individual who must defend department regulations as a spokesman is not going to be asked to resign," said Donaldson.

"Absolutely not," said Cheney. "I have operated on the basis over the years with respect to my personal staff that I don't ask them about their private lives. As long as they perform their professional responsibilities in a responsible manner, their private lives are their business. I would also argue that it's none of *your* business."

Cheney went on to note, for the second time in two weeks, that he had inherited the current policy banning gays. He said the policy applied to the military, not civilians, and that he did not see anything "fundamentally wrong" with it. While the last statement may be discouraging, Cheney's comments as a whole left room for optimism. If nothing else, he was on record as stating that he did not think gays were a security risk.

As Christmas approached, Barney Frank said on C-SPAN that he hoped Cheney would roast that chestnut over an open fire. Frank mentioned a discussion with Arkansas governor and presidential candidate Bill Clinton in which Clinton had assured him he believed gays and lesbians should be allowed to serve. Then Frank said of the Defense Department's exclusion of gays: "Not only do they not have any good reasons, they don't have any *bad* reasons — they won't give *any* reasons, because there aren't any."

The issue became part of the 1992 race for the White House when Clinton announced that if elected president he would sign an executive order banning discrimination against homosexuals in the military. Clinton cited the double standard gay and lesbian soldiers faced during the Persian Gulf war: "During the Gulf war, when we had a manpower shortage, the expulsion of homosexuals from the military basically was slowed to a walk. You had people in combat there who were gay. We have had them in every war we ever fought, which everybody knows, and every other army always has."

To his credit, President Bush did not make an issue of Clinton's pledge. It wasn't until after Clinton won the election that other politicians began to publicly question his decision. Senator Bob Dole predicted that if Clinton issued an executive order it would "blow the top off" Capitol Hill. In news conference after news conference, the president-elect forcefully restated his conviction that the Pentagon's discrimination against gays and lesbians must end.

But even as Clinton underscored his intention to lift the ban, Navy officials released a new policy requiring approximately seven thousand ROTC cadets at sixty-six campuses to sign a form that said they could be discharged and required to repay their scholarships if they were found to be homosexual.

Said Jim: "They had to add one last insult to the injury. But when Clinton changes the policy, the victory will be ours."

# Other books of interest from
# ALYSON PUBLICATIONS

**GAYS IN UNIFORM, edited by Kate Dyer, $7.00.** Why doesn't the Pentagon want you to read this book? When two studies by a research arm of the Pentagon concluded that there was no justification for keeping gay people out of the military, the generals deep-sixed the reports. Those reports are now available, in book form, to the public at large. Find out for yourself what the Pentagon doesn't want you to know about gays in the military.

**REFLECTIONS OF A ROCK LOBSTER, by Aaron Fricke, $7.00.** Guess who's coming to the prom! Aaron Fricke made national news by taking a male date to his high school prom. Yet for the first sixteen years of his life, Fricke had closely guarded the secret of his homosexuality. Here, told with insight and humor, is his story about growing up gay, about realizing that he was different, and about how he ultimately developed a positive gay identity in spite of the prejudice around him.

**THE GAY BOOK OF LISTS, by Leigh Rutledge, $9.00.** Rutledge has compiled a fascinating and informative collection of lists. His subject matter ranges from history (6 gay popes) to politics (9 perfectly disgusting reactions to AIDS) to entertainment (12 examples of gays on network television) to humor (9 Victorian "cures" for masturbation). Learning about gay culture and history has never been so much fun.

**BETTER ANGEL,** by Richard Meeker, $7.00. The touching story of a young man's gay awakening in the years between the World Wars. Kurt Gray is a shy, bookish boy growing up in a small town in Michigan. Even at the age of thirteen he knows that somehow he is different. Gradually he recognizes his desire for a man's companionship and love. As a talented composer, breaking into New York's musical world, he finds the love he's sought.

**QUATREFOIL,** by James Barr, $9.00. Ensign Phillip Froelich is about to be court-martialed for challenging an incompetent captain in the closing days of World War II. But soon that conflict is overshadowed by greater forces that enter the life of the handsome young officer, in this early, classic novel of gay love and intrigue.

**THE SPARTAN,** by Don Harrison, $8.00. Pantarkes' goal is to enter the Olympics and win the laurel crown. But at the age of sixteen, after accidentally killing the son of a high official, Pantarkes is forced to flee from his native Sparta. This novel of classical Greece and the early Olympics provides a vivid portrait of an era when homosexual relationships were a common and valued part of life.

**BROTHER TO BROTHER,** edited by Essex Hemphill, $9.00. Black activist and poet Essex Hemphill has carried on in the footsteps of the late Joseph Beam (editor of *In the Life*) with this new anthology of fiction, essays, and poetry by black gay men. Contributors include Assoto Saint, Craig G. Harris, Melvin Dixon, Marlon Riggs, and many newer writers.

**MATLOVICH,** by Mike Hippler, $9.00. Air Force Sergeant Leonard Matlovich appeared on the cover of *Time* magazine when he was discharged for being gay — and decided to fight back. This courageous activist did not fit the usual gay stereotype, and his outspoken, generally conservative views created controversy over his role as a community leader. Mike Hippler has written, with Matlovich's cooperation, the definitive biography of this gay hero.

**SOCIETY AND THE HEALTHY HOMOSEXUAL,** by George Weinberg, $8.00. Rarely has anyone communicated so much, in a single word, as Dr. George Weinberg did when he coined the term *homophobia*. With a single stroke of the pen, he turned the tables on centuries of prejudice. Homosexuality is healthy, said Weinberg: homophobia is a sickness. In this pioneering book, Weinberg examines the causes of homophobia. He shows how gay people can overcome its pervasive influence, to lead happy and fulfilling lives.

**HIV-POSITIVE: WORKING THE SYSTEM,** by Robert A. Rimer and Michael A. Connolly, $13.00. Nobody — including your doctor — cares as much about keeping you alive as you do. That's the fundamental message of this innovative, humorous, and immensely useful guide for anyone who is HIV-positive. Don't leave the decisions up to your doctor, the authors advise. Make sure that *you* understand what your options are, and what the consequences are likely to be. Your life depends on it.

**THE MEN WITH THE PINK TRIANGLE,** by Heinz Heger, $8.00. For decades, history ignored the Nazi persecution of gay people. Only with the rise of the gay movement in the 1970s did historians finally recognize that gay people, like Jews and others deemed "undesirable," suffered enormously at the hands of the Nazi regime. Of the few who survived the concentration camps, only one ever came forward to tell his story. His true account of those nightmarish years provides an important introduction to a long-forgotten chapter of gay history.

**THE TROUBLE WITH HARRY HAY,** by Stuart Timmons, $13.00. This complete biography of Harry Hay, known as the father of gay liberation, sweeps through forty years of the gay movement and nearly eighty years of a colorful and original American life. Hay went from a pampered childhood through a Hollywood acting career and a stint in the Communist Party before starting his life's work in 1950, when he founded the Mattachine Society, the forerunner of today's gay movement.

**GAY MEN AND WOMEN WHO ENRICHED THE WORLD,** by Thomas Cowan, $9.00. Growing up gay in a straight culture, writes Thomas Cowan, challenges the individual in special ways. Here are lively accounts of forty personalities who have offered outstanding contributions in fields ranging from mathematics and military strategy to art, philosophy, and economics. Each chapter is amusingly illustrated with a caricature by Michael Willhoite.

**THE FIRST GAY POPE,** by Lynne Yamaguchi Fletcher, $8.00. Everyone from trivia buffs to news reporters will enjoy this new reference book, which records hundreds of achievements, records, and firsts for the lesbian and gay community. What was the earliest lesbian novel? Where was the first gay civil rights law passed? When was the biggest gay demonstration? For the first time, the answers are all in one entertaining, well-indexed volume.

**THE COLOR OF TREES,** by Canaan Parker, $9.00. Peter, a black scholarship student from Harlem, takes life too seriously at his new, mostly white boarding school. Things change when he meets T.J., a wellborn but hyperactive imp with little use for clothing. Here, in his first novel, Canaan Parker explores the formation of both racial and homosexual identities, and the conflicts created by the narrator's dual allegiance.

## SUPPORT YOUR LOCAL BOOKSTORE

Most of the books described above are available at your nearest gay or feminist bookstore, and many of them will be available at other bookstores. If you can't get these books locally, order by mail using this form.

---

Enclosed is $_____ for the following books. (Add $1.00 postage when ordering just one book. If you order two or more, we'll pay the postage.)

1. _____

2. _____

3. _____

name: _____

address: _____

city: _____ state: _____ zip: _____

## ALYSON PUBLICATIONS
Dept. J-51, 40 Plympton St., Boston, MA 02118

*After December 31, 1994, please write for current catalog.*